DUTY BOUND
Elder Abuse and
Family Care

Volume 166 Sage Library of Social Research

RECENT VOLUMES IN . . .
SAGE LIBRARY OF SOCIAL RESEARCH

13 Gelles **The Violent Home, Updated Edition**
29 Douglas **Investigating Social Research**
40 Morgan **Deterrence**
59 Zurcher **The Mutable Self**
71 McCleary **Dangerous Men**
78 Matthews **The Social World of Older Women**
84 Gelles **Family Violence, 2nd Edition**
89 Altheide **Media Logic**
96 Rutman **Planning Useful Evaluations**
97 Shimanoff **Communication Rules**
100 Bolton **The Pregnant Adolescent**
117 Levi **The Coming End of War**
119 LaRossa/LaRossa **Transition to Parenthood**
126 McPhail **Electronic Colonialism, 2nd Edition**
128 Froland/Pancoast/Chapman/Kimboko **Helping Networks and Human Services**
130 Levine/Rubin/Wolohojian **The Politics of Retrenchment**
132 Phillips/Votey **The Economics of Crime Control**
133 Zelnik/Kantner/Ford **Sex and Pregnancy in Adolescence**
135 House **The Art of Public Policy Analysis**
137 Macarov **Work Productivity**
139 Druckman/Rozelle/Baxter **Nonverbal Communication**
140 Sommerville **The Rise and Fall of Childhood**
141 Quinney **Social Existence**
142 Toch/Grant **Reforming Human Services**
143 Scanzoni **Shaping Tomorrow's Family**
145 Rondinelli **Secondary Cities in Developing Countries**
146 Rothman/Teresa/Kay/Morningstar **Diffusing Human Service Innovations**
148 Schwendinger/Schwendinger **The Political Economy of Rape**
149 Snow **Creating Media Culture**
150 Frey **Survey Research by Telephone**
151 Bolton **When Bonding Fails**
152 Estes/Newcomer/and Assoc. **Fiscal Austerity and Aging**
153 Leary **Understanding Social Anxiety**
154 Hallman **Neighborhoods**
155 Russell **Sexual Exploitation**
156 Catanese **The Politics of Planning and Development**
157 Harrington/Newcomer/Estes/and Assoc. **Long Term Care of the Elderly**
158 Altheide **Media Power**
159 Douglas **Creative Interviewing**
160 Rubin **Behind the Black Robes**
161 Matthews **Friendships Through the Life Course**
162 Gottdiener **The Decline of Urban Politics**
163 Markides/Mindel **Aging and Ethnicity**
164 Zisk **Money, Media, and the Grass Roots**
165 Arterton **Teledemocracy**
166 Steinmetz **Duty Bound: Elder Abuse and Family Care**
167 Teune **Growth**
168 Blakely **Planning Local Economic Development**
169 Mathews **Strategic Intervention in Organizations**
170 Scanzoni **The Sexual Bond**

DUTY BOUND
Elder Abuse and Family Care

Suzanne K. Steinmetz

Volume 166
SAGE LIBRARY OF
SOCIAL RESEARCH

SAGE PUBLICATIONS
Newbury Park Beverly Hills London New Delhi

For information address:

SAGE Publications, Inc.
2111 West Hillcrest Drive
Newbury Park, California 91320

SAGE Publications Inc.   SAGE Publications Ltd.
275 South Beverly Drive   28 Banner Street
Beverly Hills   London EC1Y 8QE
California 90212   England

SAGE PUBLICATIONS India Pvt. Ltd.
M-32 Market
Greater Kailash I
New Delhi 110 048 India

Printed in the United States of America

Library of Congress Cataloging-in-Publication Data

Steinmetz, Suzanne K.
    Duty bound : elder abuse and family care / by Suzanne K.
Steinmetz.
        p. cm. — (Sage library of social research ; v. 166)
    Bibliography: p.
    Includes index.
    ISBN 0-8039-2918-8 :   ISBN 0-8039-2919-6 (pbk.) :
    1. Abused aged—United States—Case studies. 2. Parents, Aged-
Care—United States—Case studies.   I. Title.   II. Series.
HV6626.3.S74 1988
362.6′042—dc19   87-30770
                                                       CIP

FIRST PRINTING 1988

CONTENTS

Acknowledgments   7

1. The Other Side of the Mountain   9
2. Prestige and Power or Pity and Poverty:
   A Historical Overview of the Elderly in America   31
3. Parenting Your Parent: A Contemporary
   Analysis of the Problem   47
4. Elders and Their Caregivers: A Profile   80
5. In Their Best Interest: To Care or Not to Care   100
6. Is It Worth the Effort? The Impact of Stress on
   Caregivers and Their Families   137
7. Elder Abuse: Victims and Perpetrators   178
8. Patterns, Perceptions, and Predictions   202

Appendices

A. Questionnaire on Caring for an Elderly Parent   229
B. Research Issues: Human Subjects,
   Sampling, Reliability, Validity, and Indexes   242
C. Tables   249
D. Findings from the Service Provider Sample   266

References   269

Author Index   279

Subject Index   280

About the Author   288

ACKNOWLEDGMENTS

Any book based on the intimate details of individual's lives owes its first debt of gratitude to those individuals who graciously shared their stories, insights, and concerns. I wish to thank the caregivers who gave of their time and their souls. Three interviewers carried the bulk of the responsibility for collecting the materials: Sally Foulke, Debbie Amsden, and Mary Beth Reese. Their persistence, perseverance, and empathy was a valuable contribution to this study. Eleanor Cain, State Director of the Division of Aging in Delaware, provided a wealth of knowledge and encouragement.

Many individuals have provided assistance over the years. Cathy Sullivan deserves special thanks, not only for typing early drafts but for "creating" the tables from computer printouts as do Nancy Pagan and Sherry Rowland for their many favors (not in any job description) that have enabled me to complete this book.

I have benefited from the advice, and comments of many colleagues. I want to express my appreciation to Joy Pellicciaro, Thomas Pickett, and Karen Stein for valuable suggestions throughout this project. Maximiliane Szinovacz spent considerable time reviewing earlier drafts and providing thoughtful comments and advice. I am glad that she insisted on the need to do an additional statistical test for skewness and stability of the data in the regression analysis, as I now have considerably greater confidence in my findings. I owe a debt of gratitude to Murray Straus, who probably has the unique distinction of having taught path analysis via the telephone. Trying to explain, in the abstract, concrete handling and interpreting of data takes skill and patience. Sarah Tung, Richard Gordon, and the staff at the computing center provided much needed assistance especially during the transition from the Burroughs to the IBM computer—a most trying period. I wish to thank Robert Wilson for help with the interpretation of statistical techniques, and Bruce Robinson for computer-generated figures.

Without the resources of the University of Delaware, it would not have been possible to conduct this research and prepare this monograph. I want to thank Alexander R. Doberenz, Dean of the College of Human Resources, for supporting my attendance at a SAS training workshop; Donald L. Peters, the Chair of Individual and Family Studies, and the University for a generous computer budget; and L. Leon Campbell, Provost, for granting me a sabbatical leave and for his continued support during my tenure at the University of Delaware. Finally, this study was funded by a grant from the State of Delaware, Division of Aging. Partial funding for the preparation of this book was made possible by a grant from the Administration of Aging #90-AM-0204.

—Suzanne K. Steinmetz

1

THE OTHER SIDE OF THE MOUNTAIN

> When you have small children, who also need your time and attention and a home to manage and you are working five days a week and you have an older person whose needs are even in excess of those of the children, it is almost next to impossible to handle it all and do it to any degree of satisfaction. You always feel like you are not cutting the mustard. What you do is just handle the priorities and emergency situations and take just one situation and one day at a time . . . You are constantly pressured . . . you feel like there is someone behind you ramming you with a ramrod. You push as hard and as much as you can but you can't do it . . . It leaves its mark [#43—57-year-old daughter-in-law who had cared for her 81-year-old mother-in-law for 14 years].

The title of this opening chapter, "The Other Side of the Mountain," was selected with care and caution. The socialization process throughout our early and middle years attempts to prepare us for reaching the pinnacle of success. The measure of success may be based on our ability to marry the "appropriate" spouse and raise model children, or to achieve some measure of success in the occupational world as judged by our peers. Throughout this process our eyes and goals are fixed on the mountain top.

As we near the end of our middle age years, somewhere in our mid- to late fifties, most of us will have completed those tasks for which we have devoted a lifetime of learning. Even couples who have delayed parenthood until their thirties will have adult children and possibly some grandchildren by this time. We will be able to measure our achievement in parenting roles by the accomplishments of our progeny— or at least by our perception of their successes and failures.

For most individuals at this stage, careers will have reached their high point. We are no longer eligible for the "fast track," and our achievements as well as our earning power are likely to be reaching a plateau. Our view of our own occupational success will probably reflect this level of achievement. Some of us will continue to maintain a high level of interest in our careers, whereas others will begin to place a higher value on activities that are not work-related.

In 1984, over 91% of all noninstitutionalized males between the ages of 45 and 54 years, and over 62% of women in this age group were in the labor force. For the age group 55-64, nearly 69% of the males and 42% of the females remain in the labor force. For the group 65 and older, just 16% of males and about 7.5% of the females remain in the labor force (U.S. Bureau of the Census, 1986: 392). Thus for an overwhelmingly large segment of the population, a major status-confirming entity—labor force participation—has been obliterated.

The pattern of our social life at this stage is also firmly established. Although many believe that retirement will allow them the opportunity to engage in new activities and hobbies, experience indicates that although retirees may have new options for hobbies and social activities, individuals who have not engaged in leisure-time activities, or who did not enjoy a fast-paced, involved social life are not likely to change their life-styles drastically after retirement.

Thus at this time in our lives—standing at the pinnacle of the mountain—we have two ways to look: backward, down the mountain to where we have been; or forward, to where we are going. This is not to suggest that life is downhill after we reach 60 years of age. Rather, it illustrates that the socialization process, which so carefully prepared us for adulthood and its various roles, has not portrayed the years beyond 60 as a goal-oriented stage characterized by newer and greater achievements. In fact, very little socialization has prepared us for any of the numerous new roles that we will fulfill beyond those of middle-aged adulthood.

Those of us at the pinnacle can judge our success by past performances, but we have had very few experiences that will enable us to judge, or to even set standards of accomplishments, for the remaining decades of our lives. One of the major roles that this group will face is a return to the "parenting" or caregiving role. As we look behind us, down the mountain, we see our adult children looking up at us, still needing our care and support. With the fairly high divorce rate and difficulty maintaining an adequate standard of living, many young adult children are returning home, as "renesters." When we look down the mountain toward the future, we see our elderly parents also looking up to us for assistance in care and support.

As we look down toward our children, we recognize how difficult it was for us at that stage, but we also know that we successfully overcame most of the difficulties. However, when we look down toward our parents, we also have a glimpse of our future roles as elderly parents being cared for by our own adult children. It is, for us, new and untried territory. However, unlike our parents' or grandparents' generation, we do have the opportunity to engage in anticipatory socialization for "role exits" (Blau, 1973: 209-245).

Since marital, parental and occupational roles become the anchoring points for adult identity, the loss of these roles, through death or divorce of a spouse, launching of children, and retirement, requires a redefinition of self. If one has passed active adulthood and no longer has these roles to fulfill, then one must define new bases of status in order to maintain a sense of identity.

Caring for our own elderly kin helps us prepare for our own aging in much the same way as playing house helped us learn partnering and parenting roles, or as Deutscher (1958) notes, sending children to camp helps us prepare for the "empty nest" stage of the life cycle.

Because we have so little formal education or actual experience to help us prepare for this role, those on the top of the mountain struggle valiantly to maintain their footing while being simultaneously pulled by kin on each side. The resulting frustration and stress is inevitable as illustrated by two respondents in this study.

> The combination was a lot of stress. I didn't realize how dependent my children were on me. After my mother-in-law came, all my energy went to her and the children missed my attention [#135—58-year-old daughter-in-law, with one preteen and three teens, who had been caring for her 79-year-old mother-in-law for eight years].

> I feel like I had deprived my children of the time that would have probably been spent with them—had I not been so exhausted [#143—46-year-old daughter who had been caring for her 72 year old mother for about one year].

As a result of the multiple responsibilities, those who endured the responsibility for the care for others often experienced feelings of stress and burden. What is most unique in contemporary society is the increasing numbers of families facing this situation and the relatively long periods of elderly parent dependency on their adult children.

Methodology: Who We Studied and How We Did It

This book will examine the impact that caring for an elderly parent had on the lives of the middle-aged and older caregiving offspring. The daily tasks that were provided for the elderly by these caregivers and the resulting stress, conflict, and abuse is detailed.

The tremendous sacrifices that these 104 caregivers and their families made in order to care for the 119 elderly kin that composed the sample

were remarkable. In most instances, these caregivers probably represented model caregivers, yet the psychological, verbal, and physical
abuse that they perpetrated on the elders was astonishing. In fact,
roughly 23% of them engaged in acts with the potential of severe
physical harm to the elder. One can only wonder about the treatment
being provided by caregivers with less noble intentions.

OBJECTIVES OF THE STUDY

There were several research questions that guided this study. First,
what was the demographic profile of families that were caring for an
elder (or had done so recently)? Second, what was the nature of tasks
that these families were performing for the elderly? Third, was the elder's
dependency, as measured by task performance, perceived as stressful or
burdensome by the caregiver. Fourth, how did these caregivers and
elders resolve conflicts or attempt to gain or maintain control? Sixth,
was there a relationship between the actual level of dependency, the
caregiver's perception of stress resulting from this dependency, and
elder abuse? Finally, was there evidence of intergenerational transmission of patterns of interaction by adult children and elderly parents?

Although analysis of the abuse and neglect in these caregiving
families is one of the primary goals of this study, a symbolic-
interactionist perspective requires one to gather data on the symbolic
embeddedness of the act as well as on the act itself in order to
comprehend the behavior. To understand the abusive or neglectful
behavior, or to even be able to label an act as abusive or neglectful, one
must consider several dimensions of the behavior.

Expressive-Instrumental dimension. One dimension to be considered
is the expressive-instrumental dimension. Is the act an expressive one, in
which the behavior is a means to an end; for example, locking an elder in
a room because you are annoyed or angry? Or, is it an instrumental act,
such as locking an elder in his or her room in order to protect the elder
who must be watched or securely confined at all times, when you must
attend to other tasks?

Deliberate-Accidental dimension. The second dimension is intent.
Was the act deliberate or the unintended result of some act designed to
protect the elder? The resulting bruises and lacerations from restraints
might be viewed by a visiting nurse or social worker as indication of
abuse. However, if the intent was to protect a senile but mobile elder
from getting out of bed and risking injury because it was not possible to
watch this individual constantly, 24 hours a day, can we label this act as
"abusive," even though the outcome was injurious?

Active-Passive dimension. A third dimension is the active-passive continuum. Was the act an active form of abuse such as yelling, hitting, or force feeding an elder, or passive, that is, ignoring them, abuse resulting from a lack of attention?

Offensive-Defensive dimension. A fourth dimension is the offensive-defensive continuum. Was the act initiated by the caregiver or was it the defensive reciprocation of some previous behavior or act by the elder? For example, when the caregiver threatens to: "send the parent to a nursing home if. . .," is the caregiver using that threat to obtain compliance with some demand: the "offensive" role of an initiating behavior. Or, is this in reaction to behavior on the part of the elder, such as repeated refusal to take medicine or food, a "defensive" reaction: a putting into words the realization that the caregiver can no longer provide adequate care?

Success-Failure dimension. A final dimension is the success-failure continuum. As was demonstrated in an earlier study (Steinmetz, 1977a), behaviors that are perceived to be successful are much more likely to be continued than are behaviors that are perceived to be failures.

Theoretical Perspective

The theoretical perspective used by the researcher, whether stated or implied, clearly reflects as well as shapes their view of reality. Each perspective is valuable and can add understanding to human behavior. However, each perspective does uniquely influence the data collected as well as the way the data are analyzed and interpreted. In this research, a somewhat eclectic theoretical approach was used.

The theoretical perspectives guiding this study do, however, share one major similarity—they are all interactive perspectives that are useful for studying processes. Their differences enrich and compliment each other by providing an understanding of these adult child-elder parent interactions, rather than providing competing explanations of the phenomena.

Symbolic interaction theory is the major theoretical perspective used for interpreting this data and for the development of an understanding of the attitudes, behaviors, and interactions between elders and their caregiving kin. Attempting to understand not only the behaviors engaged in by the caregiver and elder, but also the symbolic interpretation of these behaviors by the actors, makes this approach most useful. Earlier work on family violence suggested that the subjective perception of the situations was as important, and perhaps more so, than the actual objective, characteristics measured (Steinmetz, 1977a; Steinmetz, 1987; Steinmetz and Amsden, 1983). In this study, caregivers reported having to provide numerous tasks for the elderly. However not all caregivers found the same tasks to be stressful. In fact, even the level of care needed did not automatically predict stress.

Because of the symbolic meaning attached to the resources one possesses, resource theory, which posits that decisions and behaviors are made possible by virtue of the resources, such as education, money, power, influence, and prestige, that an individual possesses and can use to control others is valuable for understanding the decision-making processes. This theoretical perspective is especially useful for providing a framework from which to understand the decision-making process of bringing an elderly parent into one's home, and the circumstances under which one continues to provide this care. In this study the resources that seem most important were of two distinct types. The first, the material resources of the caregiver or elder, defined the parameters of the living environment. Adequate housing, so that children or adults do not have to give up their bedrooms, the ability to cover sufficiently all family members' needs, and ample money to purchase essentials and luxuries are examples of valuable material resources. The second type of resource, social/emotional resources, consisted of factors such as personality, the elder's ability to "fit in," the caregiver's ability to deal with the additional responsibility and attendant stress, and their mutual "likability" of each other. Social/emotional resources played an important role in regulating stress, feelings of burden, and conflict. Material and social/emotional resources may not be provided by the same caregiver. In fact it is quite common for various offspring to be able or willing to provide various forms of resources. A caregiver in her early forties, quoted next, discussed the help that her sister provided in caring for their mother. She noted that her sister would stay with her,

> And one time she cooked all through one night and made mother something like three weeks' worth of incredible gourmet frozen dinners, then purchased a microwave for her . . . I have seen my sister sit down and write out a $10,000 check for mother to have her house painted with no questions asked . . . my sister has put on a lead apron and stood by mother and held her while they X-rayed her and did barium X-rays . . . She'll do anything for mother *except* have mother live with her [#6—40-year-old daughter who had been caring for her 68-year-old mother for three months].

It is clear from this quote that the sister was extremely willing to provide generous material resources but only limited social/emotional resources. Studies using the resource theory to predict the likelihood of family violence (Gelles and Straus, 1979) found that the greater the resources that are available for the caregiver to use in providing care, the less stress and violence one might expect.

Exchange theory, which shares many similar concepts with resource theory, is also useful. The decision-making process used in arranging care for a dependent elder, is clearly based on an assessment of the rewards and penalties of this caregiving role. Such comments as "It is my duty" or "She is my mother!" indicate that the rewards of fulfilling filial responsibility (often at any cost) outweigh the penalties of financial, social/emotional, and physical burden. Other caregivers, when reevaluating their "exchange," did not consider it to be equitable. When asked if she would advise others to consider caring for an elderly parent in their home, she noted:

> I would discourage it. I would say, if they want to be close, fine. Help them rent a close apartment or some situation like that. I think it's harder on the parent than it is on the child. Now as I look back, these 15 years with my mother were not difficult for me but I think they were for her. I think we made a terrible mistake, not so much for us but for her. I think we gained out of that whole situation, I don't think she gained [#26—50-year-old daughter, who had been caring for for her 87-year-old mother for nearly 15 years].

This daughter noted that the gains that she and her family enjoyed included:

> a built-in babysitter... an interesting person... I gained because I learned a little patience, which I'm rather short on ... my son gained because he loved her and she was always part of the family ... my husband gained because he came from a family where they don't put much emphasis on that. . . .I learned a lot [#26].

Thus, although resource theory examines the resources each person possesses and how these resources allow them to carry out their wishes, exchange theory examines the subtle ways in which one individual exchanges, for example, privacy, leisure time, or the financial "cost" of caring for an elder, for companionship, babysitting, patience, and the feeling that one has done his or her duty.

Role theory is valuable for studying socialization in our "golden years." One learns roles by observing others in these roles and by role playing. Unfortunately, for most caregivers there was no opportunity, until recently, to observe family members fulfilling these roles. This is truly a new role for most families. The doll-playing behavior of young children and babysitting by teens provides role-playing opportunities in preparation for the caring for our own children. For most individuals, interacting with grandparents who were often young, vital, and in good health, does little to prepare them for the eventual care of a frail, elderly parent.

Those caregivers who appear to have made the best adjustment to this new role and the attending responsibilities seem to be able to draw on a vast reservoir of experience. For example, the caregiver quoted above who believed that she and her family gained considerably from the experience of caring for her mother later reported:

> I was always with a grandmother . . . my mother's mother was a true matriarch . . . it was her house until she died at 86 . . . I was always around that grandmother until she died. After she died, my father's mother came to live with us. My mother took care of my father's mother for 20 years . . . my mother did for that woman every day because she was having spells where she didn't know where she was. I was always around a grandmother [#26—50-year-old daughter, who had been caring for her 87-year-old mother for nearly 15 years].

Successful caregiving arrangements were also predicated upon setting clear guidelines. One respondent suggested:

> Don't let the parent take over your life and your home. Remember it is your home and you are the mistress in it and it is your decision and your thoughts and your plans on what is going to take place. Treat them with the greatest of kindness. Treat them like you would want to be treated, but at the same time don't let them rule your life telling you what you should do when this is your home [#134—65-year-old daughter, who had been [caring for her 91-year-old mother for 15 years].

PROCEDURE

This study contained two samples. The first consisted of 104 caregivers who were providing care to 119 elderly kin. The information was obtained through semistructured in-depth interviews, which form the basis of this book.

The second sample, 350 questionnaires mailed to service providers, produced 153 usable questionnaires that enable comparisons of the general characteristics of abused elders in this locale with those of other studies using third-party reports. A description of the sample and results from the service-provider questionnaires is contained in Appendix D.

Sample. At the time this study was designed, 1979-1980, there was very little awareness of the problem of family abuse of elders. There were few, if any, services for these families and no mechanism for systematically identifying them. Even using census data for developing a sampling frame was impractical since it is virtually impossible to ascertain whether the older person was the *head* or the *dependent* individual in these multigenerational families. As evidenced by this sample, a 65-year-old could be an adult caring for his or her own offspring (as well as an elderly parent), or be the elder in need of care. Furthermore, home ownership, which might be an indication of head-of-household status, is not reliable because adult children often leave their own homes to move in with the elders, or put their homes in the elders' names for tax purposes.

Although there are no census statistics available that would enable one to estimate accurately the number of dependent elders residing with adult children (Paul Glick, personal communication, April 1986), the household survey data collected in 1985 by the College of Urban Affairs, University of Delaware does allow rough estimates of this population. In the State of Delaware, approximately 7.2% of those 65-74 years old and 17.2% of persons 75 or older live with a relative other than a spouse. Of the 207,081 households in Delaware, 5,803 were composed of elders living with a relative other than a spouse. These computations might be overestimated, since it is possible that those in the 65-70 age group were widows or widowers responsible, to some degree, for a young adult still living at home. However, these figures could also underestimate the number of elderly being cared for by adult children since an adult child might be providing considerable care without sharing the same household, for example, in an adjoining apartment, living next door or in a house on the same property—situations that were represented in this study. These numbers do enable the rough estimation that about 1 out of 36 households are generationally inverse—households in which adult children are providing some degree of daily care for their dependent elderly parents. Nationwide this represents over 2 million households.

A major goal of this study was to obtain reliable data that would provide not only information on abusive and neglectful interactions between caregivers and their elderly dependent parents, but also to illuminate the relationship between increased levels of dependency, stress, and feelings of burden and elder abuse.

RESPONDENTS

Gathering data from only one side of an interacting "dyad" has been criticized on several levels. First this presents a biased view of the interaction and the bias might be in favor of the respondent. Safilios-Rothschild (1969) has noted this bias in terms of the wife's view of most family sociological data; Steinmetz (1973) addressed this issue in terms of parenting studies and social mobility studies. Szinovacz (1983) has suggested that even when the sample is composed of both males and females, if they are not spouses we are still not accurately perceiving the total "couple" interaction.

The same criticism can be leveled at this study. How can we understand the complete picture when we have obtained data from only one member of the family based on his or her "biased" view?

A second concern is the lack of concurrent validity of data gathered from only one person or one instrument, or one data point. Obviously, not only will the wife's view of the impact of caregiving on the family differ from the husband's view of this situation, but the elder's view is also likely to be quite different. Given these concerns, the decision was made to interview the individuals who defined themselves as primary caregivers.

The use of data collected from the "perpetrator" or caregiver rather than the "victim," or elder, also needs to be addressed. In order to be included in this study, the parent must have a level of dependency that *necessitated* caregiving by the adult child. Because of this factor the elders in our study might best be considered as "frail elderly." With this in mind we did not consider interviewing the elders for several reasons. First, it was felt that even a brief interview might be stressful for a large number of these elders who were experiencing numerous health and physical functioning limitations.

A second point is that existing data on abuse of the elderly clearly indicate that it is the frail elderly, those 75 and older, who are at risk. These elders are considerably more likely to be suffering from Alzheimer's disease or other mentally disabling problems. Thus there are serious concerns about the elder's ability to remember events accurately, even those that occurred the day before. Data collected from these individuals would have to be considered extremely unreliable unless additional sources of information were used for substantiation. Therefore, if one were to attempt to obtain data from the elders, the interviewer would be placed in the position of having to assess the respondent's level of cognitive functioning before even attempting to assess the veracity of the information obtained. This is quite similar to the problems faced by those working with child sexual abuse. Although the 3- or 4-year-old might accurately relate what has occurred, the 2-year-old's ability to do so is seriously questioned. Since it is unlikely in a sample of this size or selection that we would encounter incidents of repeated, severe physical abuse with visible symptoms, ascertaining the accuracy of the reports by the elder in families not identified as having "problems," by nonclinical interviewers, would be problematic. This age group is also in the high risk group for strokes, which can destroy the elder's ability to communicate. As one caregiver related:

> She has a great deal of difficulty in talking and communication is very difficult with her. She has difficulty finding the words to indicate what she is talking about. It is getting so I do too. It's very hard to understand what she is talking about . . . she has difficulty remembering somebody's name . . . she will use the wrong words [to identify something] [#4—60-year-old daughter, who had been caring for her mother for four months].

Obviously elders with these illness-related difficulties would have problems communicating with the interviewer, even if their cognitive functioning were not seriously impaired. Other elders, however, do suffer cognitive impairments and have lost their ability to deal accurately with reality as illustrated by the following statement:

> He started wandering. He got up at 2-3 o'clock in the morning, got dressed thinking he was going to a meeting . . . He'd be sitting in the kitchen and would think that the dishwasher was moving. Or he would see animals. He started referring to my [deceased] mother . . . he had seen her . . . he could remember things 50-60 years ago, but he couldn't remember what happened the day before [#16—52-year-old daughter, who had been caring for her 89-year-old father for 14 years].

Finally, with the onset of senility, or in some cases just advancing age, many elders become paranoid and fear that someone is out to get them or steal their possessions. Without corroboration from others, it would be difficult for the interviewer to assess financial exploitation or neglect. Similar to many of the stories told by caregivers is the quote describing the behavior of a relatively young elder:

> She is very suspicious and paranoid. She always feels people are coming to get you. They are stealing things. They are walking on your property . . . [#7—36-year-old daughter, who had been caring for her 65-year-old mother for two years].

The decision to obtain data from the caregiver rather than the elder is further supported by the almost impossible task of finding reliable witnesses for the Congressional hearings on elder abuse. Almost all witnesses were in their early sixties; ages that were more similar to the ages of the caregivers in this study of elder abuse than to the age of the elders. Further, few of the witnesses had suffered physical abuse, which tends to predominate among the vulnerable or frail elderly (over 75); most had suffered financial or resource abuse, such as having their homes taken over or having their checking accounts pilfered.

Finally, the process of eliminating "unreliable" respondents would require specially trained personnel to conduct the interviews, would be time consuming, and would considerably deplete the sample, thus defeating the major goal of this study: an examination of the interactions between "dependent," that is, vulnerable, elderly and their caregiving kin.

The description of events provided by the caregiving kin supported this decision. One respondent explaining the difficulty she and others had caring for her mother noted:

> You don't know what I went through! She got on my nerves so bad that my niece came and got her . . . she kept her for a while and got on her nerves so bad that I had to go down south and get Mamma and bring her back . . . I put her in a foster home and had to go and get her . . . she didn't fit in. If I said "Mamma, here's your dinner," she'd say "I don't want it." She broke her hip and told the doctor that I threw her down and broke her hip—Lord, have mercy! [#98—58-year-old daughter, who had been caring for her 93-year-old mother for eight years].

Had we interviewed this elder, could we report, with confidence, that the adult child had thrown her mother down the stairs? Another caregiver describing her mother's inability to deal with reality reported:

> One day she called us up and said that she had been shot. Several times in the middle of the night she would come to our bedroom door and she would want to know where her [dead] sister Helen was now [#127—47-year-old daughter, who had been caring for her 84-year-old mother for five months].

The interviewer could only wonder, in the above situation, who "shot" the mother and why mother was not allowed to visit with her sister Helen. The decision to rely on the caregivers' reports of caregiving interaction should not be interpreted as a lack of sensitivity to the elders' perception of the situation. Caregivers made it quite clear that their perceptions of events probably differed from their parents' perceptions of the same events. Family therapists have long recognized that there is the wife's marriage, the husband's marriage, and the couple's marriage. Similarly, there is the caregiver's view of parent-child interaction as well as the elder's view. This recognition of differing perspectives is illustrated by the following quote from a divorcee with multiple responsibilities: two elders, an unmarried daughter and an infant grandchild:

> My mother intimidates me. She makes remarks to me about how she took care of so and so. "I took care of your father when he was ill." Of course she doesn't realize that when my father was ill there were 11 people. I was here, my husband was here, my children were here, and it sure did make a difference [#110/111—55-year-old daughter who had been living with and later caring for her 74-year-old mother for 55 years and an 89-year-old great aunt for 5 years].

Other respondents, describing their provision of a clean, warm, safe environment, noted that the elder, because of the limitations resulting from physical or mental conditions was most likely to see this environment as a virtual prison.

Gathering data from the caregivers is not without problems. One must be concerned about the possibility that respondents might provide socially desirable responses. As one respondent noted when asked if she ever hit or slapped her parent to get her to mind, replied:

> No I never did that, but I would be ashamed to say yes even if it were true, you do need to be patient. I saw the attitudes of sons and daughters when I worked in the nursing home [#151—46-year-old daughter-in-law, who had been caring for her 75-year-old mother-in-law for 20 years].

The caregivers' emotions, as evidenced by the tape recording and the interviewer notes, provide considerable support for the veracity of the caregivers' responses. The most sensitive questions, those dealing with the control maintenance techniques (CMT), such as talking, hitting, yelling, forcing food or medication used by the caregiver, were near the end of the interview (see Appendix A for the interview schedule). By this point the caregivers had discussed the tasks they perform for this person, the stresses resulting from performing these tasks, family problems, feelings of guilt and burden, and the effect that caring for the elder has had on the entire family. Many of the respondents were in tears, or on the verge of tears at this point in the interview. It is unlikely that they would deliberately change their answers to make them appear more socially acceptable since they had already discussed, with considerable candor, intimate family interactions. In fact, one respondent apologized for not having been able to offer information on how she coped, because she hadn't had a problem:

> I wish I could have said that I had some of those other problems in there so I could tell you how we coped with it. We have been so fortunate because

Dad's health and mental stability have been so good. You never know how you may cope with some of those other problems. I hope you are going to be able to interview some people with some of those problems to see how they coped [#12—39-year-old daughter, who had been caring for her 84-year-old father-in-law for 11 years].

Interpreting responses. There is, however, another concern about the use of a questionnaire, especially the fixed-choice responses used by most surveys. In this study, an individual's interpretation of the frequency of task performance and the amount of stress experienced does appear to be redefined according to the respondent's idea of a "normal" or standard amount of task performance and stress. For example, how much is "sometimes"?

Interviewer:	Does your mother ever refuse to eat?
Caregiver:	Yes.
Interviewer:	How often would you say?
Caregiver:	Would once a week be sometimes?
Interviewer:	Yes.
Caregiver:	Okay, sometimes [#4—60-year-old daughter, who had been caring for her 86-year-old mother for four months].

During an interview with another caregiver, "sometimes" was defined in the following way:

Interviewer:	Does she make excessive demands, or complain if you don't do things she wants done?
Caregiver:	I don't take care of the kids the way she thinks they should be taken care of. I'll get mad and scream at the kids and she'll say, "I never did that when you were growing up."
Interviewer:	How much does that bother you?
Caregiver:	Two [sometimes]. It doesn't bother me to any extent [#19/20—27-year-old daughter, who had been caring for her 64-year-old mother and 62-year-old father for six years].

For the above respondent, "sometimes" was a relatively infrequent occurrence of little consequence. However, for the preceding caregiver (#4), "sometimes" meant about once a week. Still other respondents, would go to great lengths to explain the stress they experienced as a result of having to provide some task for the elder. One might expect them to rate their stress level, on this item, as extremely high in light of their verbal description of this experience. However, many caregivers verbally *described* their stress as being overwhelming, but when asked to rate their stress on a scale in which 0 = none and 4 = always rated it as "1" or possibly "2."

The caregiver, quoted next, had answered the 13 stress items for the father-in-law, and 8 of the items for the mother. At this point the terminology becomes a problem when asked about "excessive demands," because the answer is in the affirmative—the first such response for questions about the care of the mother.

Caregiver: No, she doesn't demand. She needs, and consequently, I feel that it's a must, so it is a personal requirement upon myself. But she does not demand.

Interviewer: How would you sum up this feeling of your meeting her needs? Would you say that "sometimes" it bothers you, or "usually" it bothers you?

Caregiver: Three, usually bothers me. Bother is a hard word. You think of bother as being annoying. I wonder if I could use the word concern . . . it doesn't necessarily annoy me, but it does concern me all the time [#12/13—39-year-old daughter, who had been caring for her 60-year-old mother for five months, and 84-year-old father-in-law for 11 years].

This caregiver spent considerable effort redefining the word *bother*. Since this term had been used interchangeably with *stress* for 13 items for the father-in-law and eight items for the mother, it is obvious that there is reluctance to report her feelings about her mother's "excessive demands," in what she perceives as negative terms. First she gives the response, three (almost always), and then after redefining the wording, admits that the true response was actually a four (always). Another daughter who is taking care of her ill mother reported:

I can't say that I was all of her social life. But most of it. A good 95% and the other 5% required my driving her. So I was involved with it.

Interviewer: Did providing the emotional support bother you a lot?

Caregiver: It drained me. It didn't bother me in the sense that I was unwilling to do it, but I had no time for anything else. I was willing to do it for that short period of time, but it was draining [#30—38-year-old daughter, who had been caring for her 64-year-old mother for 6 months].

Since this pattern appeared to occur frequently, there are obviously other factors influencing their definition of the situation. Perhaps caregivers need to redefine their situation as less difficult and stressful than it actually is in order to maintain the emotional and physical strength necessary for continuing to provide care. It is also possible that even in the face of being in these extremely stressful situations, they know of or can imagine other situations in which it would be even more difficult. One woman noted:

> My husband says it could be worse. It could be his mother and he would have a very difficult time living with his mother as I would [#131—53-year-old daughter, who had been caring for her 95-year-old mother for 3 years].

OBTAINING A SAMPLE

A nonrandom sample, obtained through a "snowball technique" was used (Bailey, 1978). An attempt was made to advertise the project through a variety of sources. First, announcements were mailed to all departments of the University of Delaware. Second, notices were placed in the University newspaper, *The Review,* and the faculty newsletter. Third, articles appeared in state and local newspapers explaining the project and inviting individuals to participate. A fourth source of reaching families who were caring for an elder was to place announcements of the project in the various newsletters that were sent to social services agencies and senior centers throughout the state. Requests for volunteers were also made at the annual Division of Aging's director's retreat, and on a local radio talk show.

These announcements requested the names of families in which an elderly parent was being cared for by an adult child. Volunteers were asked to contact the "elder project." There was no mention of gathering data on *elder abuse* in these announcements or during contact with these families. In explaining the project to families we emphasized our desire to gather information that would help us understand how families were providing this care and how they coped with the day-to-day responsibilities.

Upon receiving leads, potential participants were contacted by telephone in order to explain the scope of the project as well as to determine if they met the following criteria for inclusion in the sample:

(1) the family shared a residence and the elder was not a house guest or visitor (or had shared a residence within the past three years)
(2) the adult child was *required* to perform tasks for the elder, which indicated that there was some degree of dependency
(3) the elder was over 55 years of age
(4) the caregiver was the adult responsible for the household

(5) if the elder was deceased, death had occurred within the preceding three years.

At the conclusion of the study, participants were asked if they knew other families who were currently caring for an elder or had done so in the recent past. As respondents provided leads of additional families, the sample increased in a "snowball" fashion.

If the respondent felt uneasy about providing the names and telephone numbers without first consulting the friend or neighbor, we provided the respondent with a card clearly identifying the director of the project as a member of the University of Delaware faculty, and asked if he or she would contact the friend or neighbor for permission and either call us with the information or have the potential respondent call us directly. This snowball technique was extremely successful in providing the names of other families caring for an elderly kin.

When it became obvious that the sample was predominantly a white, middle- class sample, a conscious effort was made to obtain minority and working class representation by identifying senior centers located in areas serving these populations and contacting the directors for leads. We were able to broaden the base of the sample in this manner.

THE SAMPLE PROFILE

Because a nonrepresentative sampling technique was used in this study, it is not possible to generalize the results to the population at large.[1] However, this fairly broad-based, though nonrepresentative, sample does provide insights into the interaction process and resulting stresses, and probably describes fairly accurately the problems faced by most working-/middle-class families who are caring for an elder in their homes.

Overall, 15 of the caregivers had cared for more than one elder, thus 119 dependent elders are represented in this study. Because of different health status and levels of dependency, as well as differences in interactions between the caregiver and each of these dependent elders, caregiver/elder information in families caring for two elders was handled as separate cases.

For example, a caregiver might report little or no stress and no sense of burden as a result of caring for elder "A," yet a lot of stress and burden when caring for elder "B." One woman, who was currently caring for her mother-in-law carefully noted the differences:

It depends on the nature of individual, their past experiences. If I hadn't had to live with my own mother for 20 years and knew what it was like and made all these concessions, I probably would have found it [taking care of mother-in-law] to be very distasteful. I had been conditioned to this because of a previous experience so I was able to take the good out of it and enjoy that as well as the bad. . . . If I had not had the other experience . . . and felt duty bound . . . my report would be all together different . . . I would not be able to compare this experience with anything else.

She told her mother-in-law one day:

"I really didn't want you [to live with us] because I had taken care of my mother for 20 years prior to that and I felt like I had served my sentence as far as catering to people and doing what they wanted rather than what I wanted. But I found that . . . you are a companion" [#43—57-year-old daughter-in-law, who had been caring for her 81-year-old mother-in-law for 14 years].

Another caregiver compared the demands made on her by her mother, who has lived with her for one year, and mother-in-law, who has lived with her for 18 years:

The thing that bothered me the most was the mother-in-law's constant demands—unreasonable demands—toward the end she really got bad. She wouldn't let me sleep; 10-15 minutes then she would call me again. All day and night she would do this all day and night . . . demands don't bother me, but EXCESSIVE demands—she was running me down into the ground. She always was demanding . . . and [I met her demands] that's the kind of person I am. I figured if she wants a drink, she wants a drink. She wanted a drink every 20 minutes. [She was] constantly going to the bathroom and drinking . . . Mother usually gets what she wants for herself—she is spunky—she will do it for herself. She is too independent. There are a lot of things I should be doing for her and she won't let me do them. Mother is a spirited person [#140/141—62-year-old daughter, who had been caring for her 83-year-old mother for one year and her 90-year-old mother-in-law for 18 years].

A caregiver who was currently providing care for her mother noted that she had a relatively easy time but recognized the difficulty that would be encountered if she had to care for the mother-in-law. In the next quote, she empathized with the sister-in-law who had recently taken on that responsibility.

My mother is very easy to get along with . . . My mother-in-law is a woman that is not going to be like my mother . . . When she wants something, she wants it now. When she wants to go somewhere, she wants to go there now. And she has all these people to wait on her and they all drive and she'll be on that phone wanting them to do for her. . . . I've known her for 40 years now, and I know her. If she wants something and you can't do it right away, she will pout . . . not talk to you for a week . . . won't call you up . . . [#22—60-year-old daughter, who had been caring for her 80-year-old mother for 14 years].

Had the data been combined from the two elders by summing or averaging it, the uniqueness of the dyad would be blurred and the impact of providing care for a specific elder on the family relationship would be misrepresented. Likewise, selecting one individual would not allow us to examine the possibility that the specific elder/caregiver interaction, rather than the general caretaking ability of the adult child, defined the quality of care and the perceived success or failure of the experience. Therefore, the best solution was to treat each caregiver/elder dyad as a unique unit.

Since the focus of this study was on the middle-aged "child" caregiver who lives with and cares for an elderly parent, our notices for volunteers specified caring for an elderly *parent*. We discovered that our respondents considered a variety of relationships to represent "parenthood" and these were not limited to biological or legal mothers or fathers. These relationships included three grandmothers, four aunts, one great aunt, and two friends of the family in addition to 74 mothers, 17 mothers-in-law, 13 fathers, and 5 fathers-in-law (see Figure 1.1 for a profile of the sample).

The initial design of the study called for a random half of the interviews to be conducted with the wife and a random half with the husband when the caregiver was married. Although the wife was more likely to be defined as the primary caregiver, we felt that the husband's perspective of the effect on the family's interaction and life-style when the older person moved into the home would provide a valuable source of information. Since the women were likely to be more intimately and intensely involved in the caregiving on a day-to-day basis, this might hinder their ability to assess the situation objectively.

Unfortunately, we were not able to use this plan. First, we quickly discovered that a considerable number of the families were female-headed. Second, when we contacted the husband in an intact marriage, many quickly informed us that they really weren't very involved in the day-to-day care and that they really wouldn't know the answers.

Six males were interviewed. Three of these males were in families that were caring for two elders, and a fourth provided adult foster care for

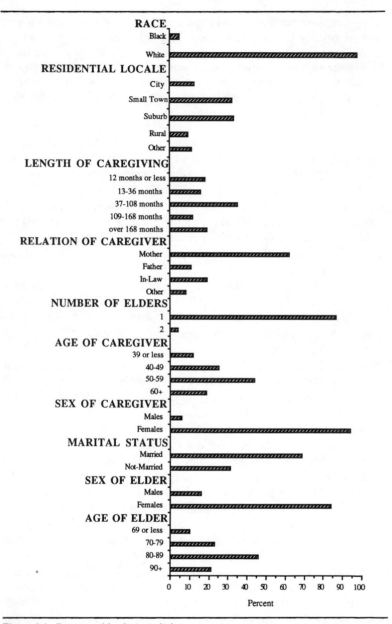

Figure 1.1 Demographic characteristics.

three elderly males. Apparently having additional elders in the household requires that the husband help with caregiving responsibilities. In all, 96 females identified themselves as caregivers; 13 women were caring for two elders. Although 69% of sample (n = 72) was composed of intact marriages, only 8% of the males in these intact families (n = 6) identified themselves as caregivers. There was no single male in the sample who was caring for an elder in his home.

However, one male was living a considerable distance from his family (they remained in Canada) and maintaining a commuter marriage in order to be able to care for his elderly parents.

The sample was predominantly white (N = 99). There were five black families but no Asian or Hispanic families in the sample. The sample was geographically diverse: 12% of the elders lived in the largest city in the state, 30% resided in the suburbs; 30% lived in small towns, and about 17% resided in rural areas. About 10% who were interviewed in locations other than their homes could not accurately be classified.

The average age of the caregivers was 53 with the largest group in the 50-59 age category. However, 19%, nearly one-fifth of the caregivers, were 60 years of age or older—an age defined by the Census Bureau and many social programs as elderly. The average age of the elder was 83, with nearly half (n = 46) in their eighth decade. A total of 21% of the elders were 90 or older.

The relationship of the sample profile to measures of dependency, stress, burden and abuse will be discussed more fully in Chapter 4. A complete description of human subjects' issues, sampling techniques, reliability, validity, and an index construction are discussed in Appendix B.[2] In the following chapter, we will examine the historical roots that provide a foundation for the contemporary treatment of elderly in our society.

Notes

1. The inferential statistical techniques used in the following chapter should be considered as descriptive techniques for describing the data. Tests of significance are using the test of a random model measuring the probability of chance occurrence. No assumptions of representativeness or generalizations to other populations are being made.

2. As in any manuscript there are differences of opinion on the arrangement of chapters and materials that should be relegated to the appendix. In the first version, which opened with the methodology chapter, it was suggested that this was a deadly way to begin the book. In a later draft, the methodology was contained in a separate chapter, Chapter

three. Reviewers were concerned about the lack of clarity regarding the source of quoted materials in the previous chapter. In this final version, the methodology chapter was split—the basics were contained in the first chapter, and more elaborate details on response rate, confidentiality, and so on were relegated to the appendix.

2

PRESTIGE AND POWER OR
PITY AND POVERTY:
A HISTORICAL OVERVIEW OF
THE ELDERLY IN AMERICA

I don't think that old people should be put out to pasture. I think that it is very important to feel that they are a part of the family. [#103—43-year-old-daughter who has been caring for her 90-year-old mother-in-law for 7 years]

A Historical Overview of Family Violence

History has clearly illustrated that any group that is perceived to be politically and economically weak is unlikely to receive adequate attention and an equitable allocation in the distribution of scarce resources. Often it requires dramatic and disturbing images to overcome our selective inattention—a mechanism by which we simply choose to overlook that which we find upsetting. The phenomenon of elder abuse has suffered from selective inattention as have other forms of violent family interaction—such as spouse and child abuse and incest and marital rape—all of which counteract our desire to view the family as an oasis of love and caring.

The autonomy and private nature of the family—"the man's home is his castle" ideal has permitted and almost encouraged abuse of those family members considered to be submissive and vulnerable. Thus a family with a tradition characterized by submission of the wife to the "head of house" and children to the authority figures (parents) probably expects those in the submissive role to obey without question. Unfortunately when the authority figure is disobeyed, abuse, and violence often occur in an attempt to reestablish the authority and restore the family system to the desired state.

Although we know that children have been abused throughout history (deMause, 1974), it was not until the 1960s that we acknowledged, publicly, the phenomenon of child abuse, sponsored legislation, developed services to provide help to victims and their families. Likewise, it was not until the 1970s that wife abuse became a recognized problem, and attempts to understand and provide services to women became a public concern (Steinmetz, 1986). In 1978, it was suggested that the decade of the 1980s would "herald in the 'public' awareness of the battered aged—elderly parents who reside with, are dependent on, and battered by their adult, caretaking children" (Steinmetz, 1978: 54).

There are several parallels between the battered child and the battered parent. First both are in a dependent position, relying on their caretaker for basic survival needs. Second, both the child and elder are presumed to be afforded protection because of the love, gentleness, and caring that society considers to be a family's major role. A third similarity is that both the dependent child and the dependent elder can be a source of emotional, physical and financial stress to the caregiver. Although the cost of caring for one's children is a socially recognized responsibility and burden, the emotional and economic responsibility for the care of one's elderly parent over a prolonged period of time—a problem not likely to be faced by most families in the past—has not been acknowledged.

As formal institutions such as the church, the school, and the work place replace the functions once performed by the family, the family's major responsibility becomes one of fulfilling the expressive needs of its members. The way care is provided, not just whether or not it is provided, has become the standard by which we measure the health of the family environment.

In our attempts to glamorize the family of yesteryear, we have often overlooked the failure and idealized the strengths. We have tended to blame contemporary family problems on the rapid, post World War II changes such as the two-car and two-career family, increased occupational and geographic mobility, the high divorce rate and the "pill." However, evidence to the contrary abounds that refutes the notion of the idyllic, multigenerational family of the past. Haraven (1977) notes, in her examination of family over time that:

> Families shared their household space with other kin only as a last resort during periods of housing shortages or severe economic constraint [p. 65].

Kent (1965), in a discussion of the multigenerational family of the "golden past," notes:

> The three-generation family pictured as farm idyll is common, yet all evidence indicates that at no time in any society was a three-generation

family ever the common mode, and even less evidence that it was idyllic [p.55].

We recognize that child, spouse, and sibling violence, as well as sexual abuse of children and wives has probably occurred throughout history. Contrary to Massachusetts law during the Colonial period, which required cohabitation to be peaceful, all spouses were not loving. The First Church of Boston excommunicated Mary Wharton "for reviling of her husband and sticking of him and other vile and wicked courses." One man in Plymouth Colony was punished for abusing his wife by "kiking her off from a stoole into the fier," and another for "drawing his wife in an unciveil manor on the snow." Joan Miller was charged with "Beating and reviling her husband and egging her children to healp her, bidding them to knock him in the head and whishing his victual might choke hime" (Demos, 1970: 93).

Attempts to help parents control their rebellious children was the goal of a 1646 Colonial law. This law stated:

If any child [ren] above sixteen years old and of sufficient understanding shall curse or smite their natural father or mother, they shall be put to death, unless it can be sufficiently testified that the parents have been very unchristianly negligent in the education of such children, or so provoked them by extreme and cruel correction that they have been forced thereunto to preserve themselves from death or maiming [Bremner, 1970: 37].

The industrial revolution, which helped shape nineteenth century America, was an era in which children endured long hours of work, extreme physical hardships, and numerous beatings to ensure that they would exhibit no laziness. Sarles (1976) has suggested that the contemporary euphemism "beating the dickens out of the child" persists today as evidence of the child abuse Dickens witnessed and wrote about. We should note, however, the Oxford Dictionary states that "dickens" refers to the devil, and the phrase was used as early as the eighteenth century.

In 1874 there was strong public reaction to the story of Mary Ellen, the 9-year-old who was being physically abused by her parents. Since there were no laws protecting children, protection was afforded by defining Mary Ellen to be a member of the animal kingdom and appealing to the Society for the Prevention of Cruelty to Animals. This incident was instrumental in the founding of the Society for the Prevention of Cruelty to Children (Fontana, 1973).

Because we tend to consider abuse between children as normal childhood-peer interaction, we have overlooked the child's first attempt to use the forms of interactions witnessed between others in the family, neighborhood, or media and experienced directly. Thus, sibling violence should be considered as one of the first attempts by children to perpetuate the cycle of family violence since it represents the first attempts to practice the violence they have observed or directly experienced (Steinmetz, 1977; 1981; 1987).

An eighteenth century diary written about the time of the American Revolutionary War, accurately reflects the contemporary view of sibling violence:

> Before breakfast Nancy and Fanny had a fight about a shoe brush which they both wanted. Fanny pull'd off her shoe and threw it at Nancy, which missed her and broke a pane of glass . . . they then enter's upon close scratching &c. which methods seem instinctive in women (Fithian, 1945: 349-350).

During the early nineteenth century, the "appropriate" treatment of wives, like the "appropriate" treatment of children, went unquestioned. The husband's right to chastise his wife "in case of great emergency" and with "salutary restraints" was upheld by the Mississippi court in 1824 (Bradley v. State, Walker, 158, Miss., 1824).

However, by the last quarter of the nineteenth century, the position that a husband had the right to use physical means to control his wife was challenged. A North Carolina court, in 1874, ruled that the "husband has no right to chastise his wife under any circumstances," however:

> If no permanent injury has been inflicted, nor malice, cruelty, nor dangerous violence shown by the husband, it is better to draw the curtain, shut out the public gaze, and leave the parties to forget and forgive (State v. Oliver, 70 N.C.60,61, 1874).

A few years later, in 1885, the cost of incarcerating wife beaters and providing for their families was of such great concern that the Pennsylvania legislature suggested public whippings as an alternative punishment (Steinmetz and Straus, 1974: 45).

Elder Abuse: An Old Problem in A New Package

We now have become sensitized to another form of family violence—abuse of the elderly by their adult caregiving kin. This form of abuse and neglect is also not without historical precedent. As Haber (1983) has noted, the classification of elderly had clear and important criteria for distinguishing useful old age from superannuation. Those who were able to retain their authority maintained the respect of the community, that is, useful old age. Those who lost status, power, and wealth, the superannuated, were ridiculed.

There are a number of myths that need to be explored in order to present a more accurate picture of care of the elderly during earlier times.

CONTEMPORARY ELDERS AND THEIR FAMILIES HAVE NOT CHANGED OVER TIME

The first myth to be discussed revolves around the idea that our contemporary elderly population and their families are similar to elderly and their families during some earlier era. There are several factors that serve to discredit this myth. First, a large number of the elderly are currently living beyond their economically productive years and, until recent changes in federal retirement legislation, were forced out the labor market. Second, the dependency ratio, the number of individuals under 18 and over 64 as compared with those in the work force has increased. Third, with the invention of antibiotics and other medical advances, elderly persons can live for longer periods of time in a state of deteriorating physical and mental health.

Increased life expectancy. About a century ago, 1870, only about 3% (1.2 million) of the population was 65 years of age or older (S. Brody, 1978). By the turn of the century, the percentage of individuals over 65 had more than doubled to 6.4% (3 million). This figure has now increased to over 12% (26 million) and is projected to be 21.1% of the population by 2030 (U.S. Bureau of the Census, 1983). Life expectancy has increased tremendously. We have, for the first time, a large number of vulnerable elderly who are 75 years of age or older (the life expectancy of those individual born in 1985). Currently, 10 out of every 100 people are 65 years or older. However, by the end of this century, a mere dozen years, approximately 20 out of every hundred individuals will be 65 years or older.

Although this represents a dramatic increase in the aged population, an even more dramatic increase will occur among those living beyond the age of 75, a group that will experience a rate triple that of the 65 to 70 age group. The impact of this growth rate among the oldest segment of our population on the demographic profile can best be illustrated by comparing the rates of the very old with those of middle-aged groups. Between 1970 and 1976, the population in the 40-64 age group increased just under 2%, while those 85 years or older increased by 40% (U.S.Bureau of the Census, 1986).

Currently, there are about 26 million persons over 65, a number that will increase to nearly 67 million by the year 2040. During the same period, those over 85 years of age, currently about 2.2 million, will increase to 13 million. Unfortunately these individuals are at risk both as caregiving perpetrators of abuse as well as later becoming the dependent elderly at risk of being abused.

Changes in roles with increased life expectancy. The dependency ratio refers to the number of adults considered to be in their economically productive years (ages 20-59) as a ratio of "nonproductive" individuals—children under 18 years of age and adults over 65 years of age. With the abolishment of age-specific mandatory retirement for most occupations, a methodological problem now exists because census data and most national research have used the previously mandatory retirement age of 65 to define "noneconomically productive" elderly. These trends will need to be reevaluated, especially in light of the financial penalties assessed to those who retire early. Another problem is the different ages used when computing dependency ratio, which can present a somewhat different picture.

Treas has estimated that the dependency ratio of persons 60 years and over to those in the 20 to 59 years of age category has grown from a low of 13 dependents per 100 economically productive persons in 1900 to 29 per 100 in 1975, with a projected ratio of 44 to 100 in the year 2030 (Treas, 1977). While the number of dependent children is showing a slight decrease, the number of elderly persons is increasing.

Analyzing demographic life cycle data from 1650 to 1950, Fischer (1977:228) has noted the sharp contrast in the roles fulfilled by the elderly during those years. In 1850, women, whose life expectancy was about 61, would have been in their late fifties or early sixties before their last child came of age. By the turn of the century, with a life expectancy of 71, women concluded these responsibilities while in their mid-fifties. However by 1950, with a life expectancy of 81, women could expect approximately 33 "roleless" years. The term *roleless,* is being used in these studies to define a period of time during which women are not involved in the traditional female tasks related to motherhood. Women in pre-industrialized America did not have to face the "empty nest" stage. They spent the majority of their old age in their *own* nuclear family, not in the family of their adult child.

The above statistics can best be illustrated by Haber's (1984) analysis of the Willing family over three generations:

Thomas Willing, a Philadelphia merchant and politician was born in 1731, the oldest of eleven children. His youngest sister, Margaret, was born in 1753, 23 years and an entire generation later. . . . From 1764 (a year after his marriage) to 1781 (the year of his wife's death), Willing and his wife had thirteen children. . . In 1781, the year their daughter Anne married William Bingham, Thomas Willing and his wife had their final child. . . . In 1799, Anne and William Bingham became grandparents for the first time; a year later, their own son was born [pp. 10-11].

Thomas Willing's parents would have spent 40 years raising a family, had they survived. Thomas approached his seventh decade before his last surviving child reached adulthood, and the birth of his daughter's first and last child was separated by nearly two decades. Clearly parental roles and responsibilities remained until advanced age, and, in fact were often not completed before death.

Today a sizable number of persons over 65 have one or more living parents; one in 10 elderly have a child over 65. S. Brody (1978) reports that approximately 82% of the elderly have at least one surviving child; 70% have grandchildren; 30% have great-grandchildren. She notes:

In the future, not only will those who are dependent be older and therefore will require more services than older people in general, but those on whom they depend . . . their family members . . . also will be older . . . more often those depended on will be middle-aged, aging and even old themselves, with their capacities to be supportive diminished [1978: 16].

Furthermore, although the availability of role models, educational experiences, and services for families with dependent children are extensive, those for adults 65 and older, who will soon constitute one out of five individuals in the United States, is frighteningly low, and nonexistent in some areas.

Another demographic factor that contributes to the vulnerability of elders is the trend toward smaller families and the decreasing size of the younger generation. Although the aging population is growing, a decreasing birth rate means that there will be fewer younger kin to provide support for their elders (Treas, 1977). Even women who marry earlier, often postpone childbirth until later in life and limit their family size to one or two children. These lower birth rates restrict the older generation's access to younger kin who could provide assistance (S. Brody, 1978; Treas, 1977). Thus we find families in which there are several members still living into advanced age while there are relatively few members of the child and grandchild generation available to provide assistance.

Finally, we are a society characterized by serial marriage. For every marriage that currently takes place each year, one divorce or annulment is granted (U.S. Bureau of the Census, 1983). However, we also strongly believe in marriage, and approximately 66% of those divorced will remarry (Glick, 1986). Furthermore, more than half of these divorces (55%) involved children (Knox, 1985), thus increasing the likelihood that in-law/grandchildren interaction will prevent a complete severing of former marital ties.

When we consider the additional relatives added to a family by widow or widowers who remarry, as well as by those who remarry after divorce, it is clear that the total number of relatives for which a middle-aged couple may feel some sense of filial responsibility is likely to considerably exceed one set of parents and in-laws. More likely it will also contain a step-parent, and (step-in-laws) as well as other relatives from each of the caregivers' former relationships.

Today it is not uncommon for one or two brothers or sisters to bear some level of responsibility for four or five family members over 75 years of age who are no longer able to live independently. When one adds to this burden the relatives of one's spouse from current as well as previous marriages, the number of potentially dependent elders grows considerably. The problem faced by adults with few or no siblings or other close relatives is illustrated by a caregiver who is an only child married to another only child. When she was asked if she had any relatives that could help, she replied:

> No, I am an only child. I did have a great deal of support and help. My husband's parents are equally as old. They are both living and they are very helpful . . . They would stay with [my] mother so that we could go away for a few days [#11—60-year-old daughter, who had been caring for her 84-year-old mother for 3 years].

These relatives, the only source of "help," are an 85-year-old mother-in-law and her 83-year-old husband.

As the existence of multiple generations featuring generationally inverse families grows, the impact of "parent caring" on these middle-aged offspring must be addressed (Archbold, 1983; Shanas, 1979; Silverstone and Hyman, 1976). The question of who takes care of the caregivers, when the caregivers need taking care of, needs to be raised.

HEALTH STATUS

Although we have increased the life expectancy it has mostly resulted from decreasing infant mortality and childhood illness. Although we have considerably more individuals reaching the eighth, ninth, and tenth decades, it is still extremely rare for someone to live much beyond this age.

More importantly, the frail elderly, as a group, may not all be experiencing the same general physical health that might have been experienced by those who survived to this age in an era during which only the fittest survived. As a group, those over 65 use more medical services with an average of six visits to doctors for every five visits for the younger group, use twice as many prescription drugs, and experience twice the number of hospitalizations with twice the length of hospitalization (U.S. Bureau of the Census, 1983; Brotman, 1978).

Most of us cannot remember a time when antibiotics were not available. It is hard to imagine that flu, pneumonia, and minor infections, until recently, were life-threatening. However, pneumococcal pneumonia, before the introduction of penicillin in the 1940s, had a mortality rate as high as 85%. It was not until after World War II that antibiotics became readily available to the general public. Another life-threatening disease, diabetes, one of the leading illnesses among elderly, was fatal until the development of the commercial extraction of insulin in 1926 (American Peoples Encyclopedia, 1968).

Until relatively recently, the frail, less fit, and those suffering chronic illness had little chance of survival. In fact, as recently as the late 1940s and early 1950s, an individual suffering from a heart condition, stroke, hardening of the arteries, or a variety of related diseases, was unlikely to recover. Today these medical conditions are fairly common, and individuals suffering from these illnesses do recover and are often restored to full capacity. In other instances, individuals survive, but regain only limited use of their faculties requiring constant care and even mechanical devices to enable them to live.

During our forefathers' time, only the very fit survived, in a true Darwinian sense. Today we have prolonged the life expectancy for all, but have paid little attention to the quality of life afforded those who have experienced physical or mental deterioration. There is a desperate need for research and education that will enable us to increase the quality of life as well as quantity of life.

Consequently, the numbers of frail elderly have increased dramatically, but they often suffer severely diminished physical or mental capabilities that prevent them from living independently.

Our image of yesteryear includes vignettes with grandpa working in the fields on Monday, becoming ill on Tuesday, the family gathering for round-the-clock vigils on Wednesday and Thursday, and staying for the viewing and burial on Friday. This picture of love and devotion, possible for a brief period of time, is not possible today. Contrast the above vignette with that of today when expensive care in hospitals and nursing homes extends the dying process, causing the patient prolonged suffering and stripping families of emotional and financial resources.

This is assuming, of course, that the family is able to afford the cost of nursing home care.

EXCELLENT FAMILY CARE OF ELDERS

The second myth to be discussed is that of the excellent, now almost unattainable care of the elderly provided by the family in some earlier time. The evidence to refute this position includes diary and court accounts of abuse; examination of property transfers requiring provisions for elderly parents; and patterns of migration of the young people who settled the frontiers leaving their kin behind.

Records of abuse. Although old age was venerated in early America, veneration was construed to mean reverence, respect, and worship—not affection or love (Fischer, 1977). The Biblical commandment "Honor thy Father and thy Mother that their days be long upon the earth" (Exodus 20: 12), required respect of one's parents, however this respect or veneration did not automatically come with aging. Growing old in Colonial America was a mixed blessing. The special powers assumed to be held by elders might be from either God or the Devil. Elders were venerated and respected, but also feared, isolated, and despised.

An examination of the ages of 118 persons accused of witchcraft in Essex County, Massachusetts, revealed that over 40% of the women and 30% of the men were 50 years of age or older (Fischer, 1977). Since life expectancy was about 50, these individuals would certainly represent the oldest citizens.

Elderly citizens who had maintained authority and power were awarded the most prestigious pews as "elders" of the church, however, those elders lacking money and power constituted the predominant group of paupers, a status that has not changed over time. In 1910, the elderly constituted 60% of the residents of Ohio State Pauper Institutions, 62% in Pennsylvania, 87% in Wisconsin and 92% in Massachusetts (Fisher, 1977). Today older women who have limited money or power constitute the majority of nursing home residents. Furthermore, of those relegated to institutional care, 50% of these elderly have no living kin who might provide them with resources (Nursing Home Care in the U.S., 1982).

The loss of power and prestige with advancing age has also been lamented throughout time. Increase Mather complained of loss of esteem after leaving the pulpit; his status of veneration and adoration now categorized as useless and outdated. He noted: "It is a very undesirable thing for a man to outlive his work." (Mather, Two Discourses p. 134). His son, Cotton Mather, in A Brief Essay on the

Glory of Aged Piety, publicly berated the elderly for refusing to voluntarily retire from important positions. He wrote:

> Old folks, often can't endure to be judged less able than ever they were for *public appearances,* or to be put out of offices. But good, sir, be so wise as to *disappear* of your own accord, as soon and as far as you lawfully may. Be glad of a *dismission* from any post, that would have called for your activities.

There is considerable evidence that the elderly were neglected and abused in Colonial America. Cotton Mather, in Dignity and Duty, complained that "There were children who were apt to despise an Aged Mother." More than a century later, in 1771, Landon Carter noted in his diary:

> It is a pity that old age which everybody covets and everybody who lives must come to should be so contemptible in the eyes of the world [Cited in Smith, 1980: 275].

The poor elderly fared most miserably. They were treated badly and brutally. Throughout the court records of the Colonies are instances of attempts to bar these people from entering a given town, since they would increase the population of the alms houses. For example, 1772 New Jersey law required the justices of the peace to search arriving ships for old persons, as well as other undesirables, and to send them away in order to prevent the growth of pauperism (Smith, 1980). Neighbors "warned-out" poor widows and forced them to wander from one town to another.

The Minutes of the April 15, 1737 meeting of the Boston City Selectmen reported the following:

> Whereas One Nicholas Buddy an Idle and Poor Man has resided in this Town for Several Years past, and is in danger of becoming a Charge to the Town in a Short time, if not Transported. And There being now an Offer made by some of his Friends of Sending him to Jersey (his Native Countrey) Provided they might be Allowed the Sume of Five Pounds towards defraying the Charges of his Passage thither. Voted, that Capt. Armitage, and mr. Clarke be desired to Treat with the Person or Persons making the said offer, and to pay them a Sum, not Exceeding Five Pounds, Upon Condition that they forthwith Cause the said Nicholas Buddy to be Transported as above [Records of the Boston Selectman, 1836: 33].

If a poor elder was considered to be a native of a community or State or had served his country during a war, there appeared to be a greater feeling of generosity toward the individual. The September 28, 1737 entry of the Selectmen's meeting noted:

> Richard Watford, a Disbanded Soldier from Pemaquad, being weak in Body and extream Poor, Sent to the almshouse Recommended to the Overseers of the Poor, there to be kept at the Province Charge [Records of the Boston Selectmen, 1836: 73].

However, other poor were not considered to be the town's responsibility. Such was the fate of James Hamilton, as recorded in a November 24, 1742 entry:

> James Hamilton a Soldier from Rhode Island came from there about twenty Days since is very poor, & not, able to help himself has been a Soldier twenty years. Ordered, that mr. Savell procure him a pair of Shoes & Thirty Shillings Old Tenor upon Condition that he depart the Province [Records of the Boston Selectmen, 1836: 368].

This maltreatment of the elderly in the seventeenth and eighteenth centuries was continued into the nineteenth century. In 1898, the Board of Commissioners of Brown County, Minnesota were presented with a bill for the boarding of a poor, sickly old man who had been driven off by his son, who no longer wanted to support him (Fischer, 1977: 152-153). Unfortunately this type of situation still exists. The local paper reported the story of an elderly couple who deeded their home to a grandson with the understanding that they would be able to live out their remaining years in the home. Later, they discovered their home had been sold from under them, and the grandson had skipped town with the money (Wilmington [Delaware] News Journal, 1985).

As noted earlier, the status of being poor and elderly falls most heavily on women. When the status derived from being married was lost, the effects were often devastating. The accounts presented to the Boston Selectmen by the assessors and collectors at the December 14, 1742 meeting revealed:

> We also Apprehend there is about 1200 Widows included in the above numbers of Souls One Thousand whereof are in low Circumstances & a great Number of other Persons so poor that they are not taxed [Records of the Boston Selectmen, 1836: 369-370].

In a review of mid-nineteenth century reform movements and

charitable organizations, Haber (1983) notes that the ideologically justified refusal of these organizations to assist the old were based on:

(1) intractability of the character of the old (they would never change and therefore would never be worthy of charity), and
(2) they had outlived their years of maximum productivity; thus charity would not restore them to productive, worthwhile lives.

Property transfers. An examination of wills, property transfers, and deeds of gifts reveals a tug of war over economic control and security between the parent and child. It is obvious that a concern to provide for their own security as well as that of a surviving wife, was an important consideration in the economic decision making of these aging fathers as well as an attempt to maintain their power and authority. Parents often used economic coercion to control the family property, and thus assure allegiance of their children. Many wills, for example, included elaborate provisions requiring that the adult child furnish food, clothing, and shelter as well as other services, such as a ride to church on Sunday, or else they risked forfeiture of their inheritances.

Henry Holt, through a deed of gift, for example, gave the original homestead to his unmarried son when he reached 30 years of age. The deed required the son to: "Take ye sole care of his father Henry Holt and of his natural mother Sarah Holt " (Grevan, 1970: 143).

Adam Deemus of Allegheny County, in 1789 gave his wife:

the privilege to live in the house we now live in until another one is built and a room prepared for herself if she chuses, the bed and beding she now lays on, saddel bridle with the horse called Tom: likewise ten milch cows, three sheep [Haber, 1983: 20].

Josiah Winslow left all his movable properties to his wife for her to distribute to the children after death according to their performance of filial duties (Mayflower Descendants XXXIV, as cited by Demos, 1970: 75).

Timothy Richardson, of Wolburn, Massachusetts, according to his father's will of 1715, would not be granted his father's estate until he agreed to:

Give, sign, and pass unto his mother, the widow of the deceased, good and sufficient security . . . during her widowhood [Haber, 1983: 20].

Clearly these precautions would not have been deemed necessary unless there existed examples of maltreatment of elders by their children after property had been transferred. By incorporating these requirements of filial duty, elders who transferred property to an adult child retained the right to revoke the transfer and regain the economic ability to pay others for their care.

However, parental use of economic resources to control their adult children was not without repercussions. Because of Robert Carter's inability to obtain economic independence, he was forced to live until the age of 52 under his father Landon Carter's roof and rule. Bitter arguments resulted from this continued economic dependence of the son on his father—many of which nearly resulted in physical blows. One evening Robert invited friends over for an evening of gambling. The elder Carter peremptorily ordered the cards and tables removed. Landon later recorded in his diary that "I was told by a forty-year-old man he was not a child to be controulled." Fearing for his life, he armed himself with a pistol and noted in his diary:

> Surely it is happy our laws prevent parricide or the devil that moves to this treatment would move to put his father out of the way. Good God, that such a monster is descended from my loin [cited by Fisher, 1977: 75].

Although the examples presented above do not represent a scientific survey of the abuse and maltreatment of the aged, they do suggest that the myth of the excellent care of the elderly that was automatically provided by their kin in bygone eras needs a careful reexamination. This position is provided still further support by examining mobility patterns.

Mobility patterns. Geographic patterns of settlement and the high rates of mobility have affected intergenerational support patterns in the past. Whether one agrees with or disputes the argument that the contemporary nuclear family is more isolated today than in the recent past (Sussman, 1959), we do know that for the first time, almost all children are growing up with grandparents and many have great-grandparents. Contemporary society is highly mobile with one out of every five families moving each year. Yet, in spite of geographic distance, visiting and helping patterns between the generations remain vigorous and extensive.

Our view of the past is colored by those relating its history. The small town or village in the "old country," is often remembered with warmth, affection, and praise to a degree that considerably exceeds reality. Likewise, the sentimental ideal of the close knit families of the past, which are used as models of past filial performance, are often a distortion of reality—a tendency to glamorize the strengths and minimize the weaknesses. We need to scrutinize the accounts spun by these purveyors of the nostalgic perspective of Western family life.

Many individuals who are currently enjoying their "golden years" were part of the large waves of immigrants (or their descendants) that flocked to our shores during the end of the nineteenth and beginning of the twentieth century. They left the old country when they were young adults or came as infants or small children with their young immigrant parents. These families were following a pattern that has persisted in the settlement of the United States; the adventurous youth moved to the "frontier," the elderly remained at home. The only care these individuals provided to their elderly kin in the old country was financial and emotional support through letters.

Apparently, we hold as ideal a behavior that was not typical of actual behavior. In fact, we know that the multigenerational family, long viewed as the predominant (and most desired) form, existed more as an ideal to be achieved than a reflection of reality (Bane, 1976). Therefore, to suggest that in an earlier era we cared for our elders and today we are unwilling to do so is unrealistic, because a totally new situation is facing multigenerational families today.

THE MEDIA AND ELDER ABUSE

The third myth examines the media portrayal of elder abuse versus reality. The media has simultaneously portrayed the unrealistic view of multigenerational families most famously in *The Waltons* while attempting to gain our attention by also focusing on the shocking incidents of family abuse of elders such as the 35-year-old alcoholic son who beats up his 60-year-old mother to get her to sign over Social Security and pension checks.

Though dramatic, such cases do not typify the large number of families in which stress has pushed the caregiver to the point of abusive or neglectful behavior. Unfortunately, while drawing our attention to this problem, it inhibits the identification of oneself as a potential abuser, in a manner similar to the way that parents who repeatedly strap their misbehaving kids rationalize their behavior as different from that of the parent who burns a toddler's fingers or punches an infant. If we do not identify the stress and its effect on our ability to continue to provide care then we are not likely to seek help until the situation is out of hand.

The print media has also tended to ignore the role of caring for elderly kin. Although books abound on the care of children, virtually no books for the general population on how to care for an aging parent appeared until the late 1970s and these have focused almost exclusively on interpersonal relationships and finding alternatives to family care. Still lacking are books that provide information on day-to-day problems of providing care, such as transfers, bathing, food and nutrition, redesigning spaces and improving the home environment. Market analysts have finally recognized the mature profile of the consumer. *Modern Maturity* recently overtook *National Geographic* in numbers of issues sold to become the third most purchased magazine.

Conclusion

It seems clear from this brief foray into the historical view of elderly and their families that many myths about family care of the elderly, all with a kernel of truth, seem to have survived in spite of overwhelming evidence. Perhaps in the hustle-bustle of contemporary society, the idyllic view of family life in the past, no matter how untrue, provides us with a measure of serenity. If things were that good in the past, perhaps they will be that good in the future.

Though such a view might be functional for a sentimental journey into an imagined, and perhaps desired reality, it forces us negatively to compare our own attempts at providing care for our elderly kin with an unrealistic and unattainable model. This only adds additional stress, conflict, and guilt to what is often an unbearable responsibility for the caregiving children.

For the first time in history, there are a large number of multigenerational families, approximately 1 in 36, in which a dependent elder must rely on his or her kin for prolonged physical, social, psychological, and financial aid. These aging offspring and their frail elderly parents are faced with this emerging family form. Unfortunately, we lack historical precedents or role models for dealing with dependent and often disabled elderly family members over a prolonged period of time (Steinmetz, 1979, 1981).

In the next chapter a review of research on dependency, stress, and feelings of burden resulting from providing care to an elderly relative will be examined. The existing research on neglect and abuse of the elderly will also be discussed.

3

PARENTING YOUR PARENT:
A CONTEMPORARY ANALYSIS
OF THE PROBLEM

My family believes in taking care of their own. It's usually the youngest child in our family taking care of the older parent. It has been like that for the past 100 years in our family. It seems like some tradition passed down. My mom took care of her mother and she took care of her aunt. My aunt took care of her mother and father. It has just gone straight down the line. It just seems natural to me . . . a part of family life . . . your parents are somebody you are supposed to respect. I just couldn't see turning them out and letting them fend for themselves if they can't do it [#19/20—27-year-old daughter, who had been caring for her 62-year-old mother and 64-year-old father for 6 years].

What Do We Call These Families?

Although the media has made us aware of the problems of elder abuse, a careful examination of the stresses, dependencies, and conflicts that arise in multigenerational families, which are characterized by middle-aged children who are caring for an elderly parent, is needed.

Generationally inverse families. Unlike most other dependencies that family members assume, our elderly, because they can neither be cured nor overcome their infirmities, will not return to independent life-styles. However, before we can embark on any discussion of these families, we must address the lack of terminology to describe adequately this rapidly growing family form. The fact that such terminology is nonexistent is further indication of the relative newness of this phenomenon as a prolonged experience that is faced by growing numbers of families.

Historically, as Laslett (1972) noted, there were few grandparents and parents as an active force for long periods of time within the family. By 2030, however, approximately 1 in 33 Americans will be over 85, which means that a considerable number of old people will themselves have a surviving parent (Carey, 1985).

Although we are aware of subtle changes in roles that occur as we progress through the life cycle from the stage characterized as a young married couple with small children to that of an elderly, widowed individual being cared for by his or her adult children, the exact nature of these role changes and even what to call them is imprecise. This stage in the life cycle has also erroneously been called the "roleless" years to suggest that there is no meaningful (or valued) role for these individuals to play in our society. It is possible that this viewpoint prevails because most socialization prepares us to learn increasingly more difficult, complex tasks. We have virtually no socialization that prepares us for the graceful acceptance of diminished functions.

These changes in roles from caregiver to dependent elder has been labeled *role reversal* primarily because studies of family interaction (Gelfand et al., 1978; Rautman, 1962) saw the reversal of roles as an inevitable developmental task for both the aging parent and the adult child.

The problem with the concept of role reversal is that it is based on the assumption that competency in all areas ceases simultaneously at a certain point in life; that parents revert to childlike behavior; and that adult children accept this childlike behavior, which is often associated with senility. Most important, however, "role reversal" is reversible.

Researchers such as Brim (1974), Goldfarb (1965) and Nye and Berardo (1973) consider the maturation of the two generations to be a continuation of the socialization process. The first step in this process of socialization at the older end of the life cycle is Blenkner's (1965) concept of filial maturity. For a healthy intergenerational relationship to exist, adult children must be able to cast off the parent-child roles of their youth, and view their parents as individuals. Likewise, the parent must provide a role model that enables the adult child to achieve maturity and develop the capacity to be depended upon and later to assume the caregiving role.

One caregiver explained this process and the care it took on both the adult child's and elderly parent's part:

She was used to being in charge. I had been in the professional world and didn't know very much about cooking for one thing. The changing of the guard took a while. I wouldn't say that I was always my best and she probably wasn't either because it was hard for her to give up her role and try to make a compromise. . . . Sometimes I would just, on purpose, ask her about something, not for her to tell me what to do, but to let her know that her opinion was valuable. It was hard work to be able to do that. You know, two women sometimes can't get along in the same house. I think that we did remarkably well [#92—60-year-old daughter, who had been caring for her 92-year-old mother for 26 years].

To resolve this dilemma in terminology, the term *generational inversion* has been suggested (Foulke, 1980; Steinmetz, 1979, 1981, 1982). Because the roles played by both the parent and adult child will change as the elder's dependency increases, generational inversion more subtly captures the essence of these changing roles.

In her thesis, Caring for the Parental Generation: An Analysis of Family Resources and Support, Foulke (1980) differentiated role reversal and generational inversion in the following ways. Role reversal can occur at any time in the life cycle, however, generational inversion can occur only during the latter portions of the life cycle.

Role reversal does not require reciprocity. It may be experienced by only one member, for example, the widow who returns to school or a career; or it may be reciprocal, for example, the young divorcee who returns to the home of her parents, at which time she reverts to the daughter role and they resume their former parenting role.

Generational inversion is predicated upon changes in both caregiving and care-needing roles. Role reversal does not necessarily *require* a degree of dependency; generational inversion can not exist without it. Finally role reversal does not automatically imply finality in fulfilling these new roles. Generational inversion does assume that once the inversion has taken place, these new roles and the relationship predicated upon them, will become final.

As Randall (1977: 60) notes, "To every mother there comes a day where her role is no longer the same—it comes, too, to every child." Thus the term *generational inversion* will be used to define families in which an elderly parent is dependent upon the child generation for social, financial, physical, or psychological support.

Dependencies In Caregiving

The problems created by increased longevity are not confined to the elderly, but encompass all members of the family and continue throughout the family life cycle. Middle-aged children are often unable to cope with problems arising from within their own nuclear families (Kirschner, 1979; Silverstone and Hyman, 1976). Caregiver role overload and confusion, variable motivation, and deficiencies in the skills necessary to care for an elder are seen as precursors to elder abuse (Rich, Eyde, and Runyon, 1982).

The additional burden of shouldering a parent's problems may represent the proverbial "straw that broke the camel's back" increasing the potential for abuse and neglect of the elderly parent. The changes in the roles between those needing care and those providing the care may build feelings of resentment and misapprehension in both generations (Hooker, 1976; Knopf, 1975). Feelings of love and respect can easily turn into disappointment, guilt, and hatred as children attempt to function in their new roles as caregivers.

Unresolved conflict between parents and adolescent-age children often continue throughout the life cycle with the result that contact between the generations remains at the level of the obligatory vacation or holiday visit. It is possible that while the caregiver may perceive that role reversal is occurring, the elderly parent might not share this perception—a phenomenon labeled *asymmetrical transition* (Fischer, 1983).

It is unlikely in these families that the child will shoulder the responsibility of caring for an elderly parent with open arms and a warm heart. Consequently the motivation to care for the older kin may arise not only from love and concern, but also from a sense of responsibility, duty, or guilt.

Generationally inverse families, in which the elderly parent is dependent upon the child generation for social/emotional, financial, or physical support, are no longer unique. In these families, not only are roles inverted, but a complex set of generationally linked rights, responsibilities, obligations, and ways of viewing oneself and others are affected.

Since these middle-aged (or elderly) caregiving offspring are often coping with their own children's college and wedding plans, their impending retirement and age-related physical and social/emotional changes, the additional burden created by being responsible for a parent's problems can become a source of crisis with the potential for abuse and neglect (Steinmetz, 1979, 1981, 1983; Steinmetz and Amsden, 1983).

DEFINING DEPENDENCY

There are a number of ways that dependency has been defined. For Blenkner (1969), dependency is: "a state of being not a state of mind, a state of being in which to be old—as to be young—is to be dependent." This is similar to Clark's (1969) cultural perspective on dependency. Both researchers view age-related dependency as a normal, expected developmental dependency—or as Clark suggests, the dependencies resulting from "permissible" crises such as widowhood, illness, and retirement.

Blenkner defines four types of dependencies: economic, which stems from the loss of the productive worker role, requiring one to become dependent on income transfers from the currently working generation; physical, resulting from a decline in physical power and diminished functional ability to carry out the tasks of everyday living; mental, characterized by diminished cognitive functioning, forcing reliance on their caregivers to perform this function; and social, produced by multiple losses in roles, affection, companionship, status, and power.

The degree of deterioration that the elder experiences determines to what extent the elder will need to relinquish independence and accept dependency. Three stages of transition are suggested by Otten and Shelley (1977). The first entails the relinquishing of tasks requiring physical strength; the second—half independence/half dependency—may encompass shopping, light housework, writing checks; the third, full dependency, requires that personal care as well as social tasks be performed for the elder.

Knopf (1975) has identified three categories of dependency that are quite similar to those suggested by Otten and Shelley (1977): interdependency, characterized by voluntary assistance between adults; survival dependency, characterized by traditional forms of aid, and usually limited to the very young or very old; and excessive dependency, in which the aid demanded exceeds normal expectations and often builds resentment.

Foulke (1980), in a preliminary analysis of a subsample of respondents contacted for this research, identified four stages of dependency. The first stage, independence, is characterized by autonomous individuals who exchange favors. The second stage, reciprocal dependency, is characterized by an equal flow of assistance between adult child and parent, but there is some evidence of the elder's diminished physical strength and functioning. Asymmetrical dependency, the third stage, is characterized by the parent being more dependent than independent and an increasing amount of support and aid being provided by the adult child. The final stage, survival dependency, is one in which the adult child is providing almost total personal care, as well as social/emotional and financial tasks for the elder (Foulke, 1980: xi).

Although there appears to be numerous ways one can attempt to define dependency and its different stages, the effect of the elder's dependency on the caregiver, regardless of the names given, has important implications for this increasingly larger group of elders.

The myths of "alienation" or "isolated nuclear family," which allege that elders are abandoned by their families, have been amply disputed by Sussman and Burchinal (1962), Shanas (1979), and Brody et al. (1983). Intergenerational support systems remain strong and it is the family, not institutions or social service agencies, that still fulfills the major task of caring for the elderly. The institutionalized elderly represent only about 4%-5% of this population, and more than half of those in institutions have no living kin or close friends because they have outlived them (Nursing Home Care in the U.S., 1974). There are a number of dependencies that need to be examined in terms of their impact on the elder and the caregiving family. These include household tasks, personal and health care, mobility, social and emotional support, mental health, and financial dependencies. The degree of dependency as well as the type of dependency will depend on the health status of the elder, the length of time the elder has been dependent, and the alternative resources available in the family and the community.

WHO PERFORMS THIS ROLE?

Filial responsibility becomes operational when the adult child acknowledges the aging parent's dependency on him or her. This process may occur suddenly as the result of an unexpected crisis (e.g., death of one parent, acute illness, or accident):

> My father fell and hurt himself and they, the doctor and my sister, decided that he shouldn't live alone anymore. He was delegated to me [#95—66-year-old daughter, who had been caring for her 86-year-old father for 4 years].

The process may occur slowly over time (for example, a gradual debilitation of physical or mental health, or declining financial ability to maintain an independent living environment).

> I went every two weeks to take her shopping and do her errands. It was 100 miles away . . . She had been hospitalized and came home from the hospital and stayed by herself for one week. Then I realized that she was not feeding herself or getting her medication straight. I realized that the time had definitely come. I had been uneasy for a long time about her living alone, but that precipitated it [#4—60-year-old daughter, who had been caring for her 80-year-old mother for 4 months].

The past parent-child relationship need not have been positive for an adult child to accept the caregiving role. As Horowitz (1978: 6) notes, "It appears that children respond not only to a loving parent but to a parent in need . . . if anything care is given in spite of, not because of, the past relationship."

Family obligation emerged as a major motivator for providing care, in a study of 203 primary caregivers (Horowitz and Shindelman, 1983). Although close affectional relations were the norm, caregiving could occur in their absence. However the absence of affection was correlated with higher levels of perceived stress. George and Gwyther (1986) compared 510 family caregivers who were caring for a memory-impaired elder (most of whom lived with the caregiver) with data from the Harris Survey of Myth and Reality of Aging, and the General Accounting Office Survey of the Well-Being of Older People in Cleveland, Ohio. Although caregivers appear to be similar to other populations in terms of physical health, they average nearly three times as many stress symptoms, have lower life satisfaction scores, and a higher use of psychotropic drugs. The researchers suggest that the caregiving burden is experienced primarily in the areas of mental health and social participation, but little evidence of a decrease in physical health or financial security.

Brody et al. (1983) studied the responses of 403 women who were either elderly grandmothers (n = 131), middle-generation daughters (n = 165) or young adult granddaughters (n = 107). They were asked what they thought adult children in other families should do to help a dependent parent, and whom they would prefer to help them in their own old age. A large majority of all generations felt that adult children should adjust their family schedules in order to help the mother, especially if this were a nonworking married daughter. They also believed that financial help should be provided, especially among working children. However, about half of the eldest generation and about two-thirds of the other two generations believe that work schedules should be adjusted—especially the work schedules of daughters.

Although a majority of each generation did not recommend that adult children share a household with the elder, the youngest generation was most favorable, the middle generation least favorable, to living together. The oldest generation clearly preferred the child to perform a wide range of tasks than have others do these tasks, whereas the middle-aged generation was the least likely to prefer having their child provide these services. Brody et al. (1983: 744) note:

> This is consistent with the overwhelming evidence that old people want to live near but not in the same household with their adult children. Only among the youngest women did a majority favor joining households,

probably reflecting their youthful idealism and lack of experience in either receiving or providing help to elderly adults. Further, the findings clearly differentiate between the desirability of the child providing financial assistance for services and being the preferred provider of these services.

Brody et al. (1983) also found that although significant generational differences were found on attitude items relating to gender appropriate roles and sharing the care of the elderly, child care, and household tasks by women and men, the majority of all generations favored such sharing. They conclude that values regarding family care have not eroded despite demographic and socioeconomic changes over time.

Circirelli's (1983) path model for predicting the adult offsprings' helping behaviors indicates that the child's helping behaviors are a function of the child's attachment behavior (such as living close to the parent, telephoning, letter writing, visiting) and the parent's dependency needs. Filial obligation (acceptance of societal norms of helping one's parents) and feelings of attachment or close bond with the parents have only an indirect influence on helping patterns.

Although adult children are willing to provide the care, filial responsibility also requires the acknowledgment by the elderly parent of the new statuses of both parent and child. Unfortunately, while the adult child may recognize his or her increasing responsibilities, this change in statuses may never be acknowledged by the parent. This theme is noted by several caregivers:

I find differences in the . . . personalities of my mother and mother-in-law. My mother-in-law didn't rock the boat, whereas my mother tells me what to do. She treats me like I'm 10 [#140/141—62-year-old daughter, who had been caring for her 83-year-old mother for 1 year and her 90-year-old mother-in-law for 18 years].

She tells me what to do all the time as if I were a 5-year-old. She always tells me not to forget this and that. She tries to dominate me [#108—61-year-old daughter, who had been caring for her 93-year-old mother for 15 years].

Another respondent, discussing the issue of her mother's refusal to respect her privacy, reported:

I'm her daughter and there is nothing she shouldn't know about. . . . She's just thoughtless. She doesn't realize what she is doing. She was raised with "honor thy father and mother." Parents are right and always are, up to the hour of death. You don't talk back. One day she told me I talked back to her. Here I am a great-grandmother, talking back. She says, "You're the only child I had that talked back to me." My brothers all do, but she doesn't notice that [#31—58-year-old daughter, who had been caring for her 82-year-old mother for 2 years].

These quotes are amazingly similar to Landon Carter's account in his diary discussed in the previous chapter, in which he and his son almost come to physical blows over his refusal to acknowledge the 40-year-old son's right to independence and autonomy. Although the contemporary saying "You only go around once" may accurately describe a philosophy in which an individual's pursuit of happiness reigns, the folk adage "What goes around comes around" more accurately describes inter-generational relationships over the life cycle and throughout the centuries.

HOW IS THE CAREGIVER SELECTED?

The method by which each family selects the member who will bear the responsibility of caring for the elder is of interest. Since families rely primarily on their members for support and help in caring for their elders, this selection process often reflects a history of intergenerational family relationships over the life cycle. Is the eldest selected because of his or her leadership role among siblings? Is the daughter selected, reflecting the close mother-daughter bonds (Circirelli, 1981)? Is the son or daughter who heads a single adult home (either never married, widowed, or divorced) selected because caring for the parent won't interfere with caring for one's husband or wife? Is a particular child selected because of a special skill—the nurse, nun, social worker?

It appears that in each family, someone is identified as having, as a nursing student so aptly labeled it, the "nurse mentality." This individual is identified by the family as the best member to care for anyone needing help—be it the pregnant, adolescent niece or the elderly parent (Steinmetz, 1982). As one caregiver stated:

I took care of foster children for years before I took in my mother-in-law and mother. I adopted this last girl that I had. I like to take care of people. I like to be of service to a person. I'd rather be of service to someone than go to a senior center and do ceramics. . . . I feel good about it, that I'm doing something for somebody whether it is appreciated or not. [#140/141—62-year-old daughter, who had been caring for her 83-year-old mother for 1 year and her 90-year-old mother-in-law for 18 years].

Another caregiver who demonstrated the nurse mentality was caring, at the time of the interview, for the 1-month-old grandchild of her 32-year-old unwed daughter who "deliberately got pregnant," her own mother, and a great aunt. Her record of providing care has characterized her lifetime.

> My husband was away in the service after we were married and my father had been injured and was unable to drive or work. I cared for him for over 30 years . . . Mother has lived with me "forever" 55 years! When [mother's] uncle passed away five years ago, her aunt came to live with us also. [#110/111—55-year-old daughter who has lived with and later cared for her 74-year-old mother for 55 years and 89-year-old great aunt for 5 years].

Unfortunately, this level of caregiving is not without cost. When the great aunt moved in, the caregiver's husband left, and this caregiver reported "feeling a great sadness" over her husband's decision.

Having cared for her 97-year-old mother for 11 years, one daughter, when asked about the most difficult part of caring for her mother, responded:

> I can't say that any one part is difficult. Like I said before, I wish I had a bit more freedom. I don't consider it a burden. Maybe it's the type of person that I am. My brother has said that I think that nobody can take care of my mother but me. So, you see, that it's the type of person that I am.

> Interviewer: You want to take care of her?
> Caregiver: I'm going to—I'M GOING TO! [#90—66-year-old daughter].

Another caregiver responded in a similar manner:

> I don't think that there is anything wrong with the children knowing that there are other people in the world who love them and care for them and belong to them. I don't think that it has caused a problem between my husband and myself. We have all gotten along pretty well. My husband's mother moved in with us for six months, and that was interesting. My husband's brother moved in with us. Everybody moves in with us because I don't say no. I am a softy. [#7-36-year-old daughter, who had been caring for her 65-year-old mother for 2 years].

In some instances, the interviewers were not truly aware of the total family composition until the end of the interview when additional demographic information was requested. When asked who lived in her home, one caregiver reported:

> My spouse, he is 53. Then there is my son, Paul, he is 16. My son Lars, he is 14, Kirston is 11, Greg is nine, and three shelter kids.

Interviewer: Are they foster children?
Caregiver: This is emergency shelter, so they stay here for a month, temporary shelter. Emergency temporary shelter . . . three beds for any kid between the ages of 11 and 18.
Interviewer: What are the ages of the children who are here now?
Caregiver: Right now we have three, 15, 16, and Billy is 15 [#103—43-year-old daughter, who had been caring for her 90-year-old mother for 7 years].

Several families were providing adult foster care in addition to caring for their own elderly parent. For example, one family cared for their own elderly kin, as well as providing an adult home for three elderly males; in another family, adult foster care was provided to one elderly adult.

Erikson (1964) sees emotional satisfaction being provided in mid-life through nurturing, teaching, and serving others—a continuation of the child rearing- mothering role, which has been completed by this time. Thus we are not surprised to see this role almost always being fulfilled by women.

Other factors have been suggested that might explain the mechanism by which family members are selected to fulfill caregiving roles. Silverstone (1976) suggests that the one who elects to fill this role might be the one least loved child who is trying to establish a once-desired special relationship with the parent.

Aldous (1978) notes that the sibling with fewer family-of-procreation responsibilities, the unmarried or childless sibling, or the sibling whose children are grown and on their own, is often assigned the obligation for "seeing the parents through their last illness." She further suggests that, inasmuch as divorced siblings often assume this responsibility, deviation from traditional norms, as well as not being responsible to a husband, may act as a mechanism for delegating this responsibility to a particular sibling. Sometimes brothers and sisters have so many family problems that it is just understood that they could not help. One caregiver, with several sisters, explained why they were not able to help.

One sister [helped] except for the last year and she refused. One sister is getting a divorce, another just remarried and the new husband could not cope with mother. Another sister's husband has a stroke and she could not take care of both husband and mother. One sister has severe arthritis [#121—58-year-old married daughter with grown children, who had been caring for her 96-year-old mother for five years].

The provision of assistance to aging kin, according to Treas (1977), rests upon a balance of delicate sentiments such as affection, gratitude, guilt, or desire for parental approval. Thus those deviating from the traditional norms of family life may see their caregiving as a way to overcome parental displeasure or disapproval. Of course, as Levande (1980) suggests, the assumption of the caregiver role might simply be out of deep affection and compassion.

Lopata (1973) and Treas (1977) have also noted that a sex role division of labor exists in the provision of care of aging kin. Instrumental tasks—managing money or making funeral arrangements—are more likely to be provided by sons, whereas the expressive tasks—providing services, personal care, and social/emotional support—are more likely to be provided by daughters. Female elderly are more likely to expect filial support than do their male counterparts (Seelbach, 1977).

Johnson and Spence (1982), noting that women give the most ongoing support to parents, raise the issue of the impact of women entering the labor market on the availability of persons to serve as caregivers. With more women entering the labor market, one might expect greater role conflict, especially since the level of task performance related to the elder's care was not significantly lower among employed caregivers (Reece et al., 1983).

Elderly women receive significantly more social, emotional, and instrumental (task oriented) support from family members than do elderly males according to Longino and Lipman (1981), which may reflect males' unwillingness to accept the dependent status. The impact of the elder's gender was noted by a respondent who had cared for both her father-in-law and her mother:

I think that it is very important to know whose parent it is and what their sex is. It has worked very, very well for us because Dad [in-law] is a male. What he does, the chores he does, and he does chores, are not chores that I would do. I'm finding that with my mother, and of course there was always the thought that she would someday live with us, I think twice about that now just in the three months that she's been here. There has been a lot of tension between the two of us. The things that she will do overlap the things that I would do . . . I've often wondered about it. Personalities have a lot to do with it and is something to take into consideration. My father-in-law was a very domineering man and if he had been my father instead of my father-in-law, would I still be his daughter and would there be conflict there? I don't know. It has worked perfectly with my father-in-law. I can see where there will be things to work out when it is my mother's turn [#12/13—39-year-old daughter, who had been caring for her 84-year-old father-in-law for 11 years, and her 84-year-old mother for 3 months].

What tasks are performed. In a cross-cultural study of intergenerational helping patterns, Shanas (1967) found reciprocal patterns of support based on need and opportunity, a finding also supported by Riley and Foner (1968). Shanas (1979: 169) has noted that "Family help, particularly in time of illness, exchange of services and regular visits are common among old people and their children and relatives whether or not these live under a single roof."

Hill et al. (1970), in their study *Family Development in Three Generations,* assessed both the beliefs and actual behaviors regarding intergenerational visiting. They found that 60% of the grandparent generation, 42% of the parent generation, and 36% of the child generation agreed that "a young couple and their parents-in-law should go their separate ways and see each other only occasionally."

Furthermore, gender differences (women were the "kin keepers") and social class differences (working class men more involved in intergenerational interaction than white collar men) were found. When asked to whom they turned for family or personal problems during the past year, 48% of the grandparent generation, 34% of the parent generation, and 48% of the child generation turned to the family as a source of help. It is obvious that this middle generation is the "sandwich" generation caught between two generations in which the flow of support given exceeds the flow of support received.

When 3,781 actual transfers of support were recorded, 65% of the help received by the grandparent generation was familial as contrasted to 53% for the parent and 44% for the married grandchild generation. However, 47% of the help given to others by grandparents, and 44% of help given to others by parents, was given to "other" generations, whereas only 28% of help given to others by the grandchild generation was given to other generations. Overall, 70% of exchanges of help in these families was familial, and as Hill et al. (1970: 66) note:

This is hardly support for the assertion that urban families are living in vulnerable isolation shorn of kinship supports. For none of the three generations does this assertion hold. In mutual aid as well as in visiting patterns and sharing common activities the three generations are linked together in a symbiotic network of multiple services.

SOCIAL/EMOTIONAL DEPENDENCY

The emotional bond studied most frequently between the young child and parent also affects parent-child relationships throughout the life cycle. Brody (1966) suggests that this bond enables families to accommodate the changing roles and needs of the elderly kin. Maintaining psychological ties might be, according to Boszormenyi-Nagy and Sparks (1973), of greater importance than the actual services provided. They note:

> The major connecting tie between the generations is that of loyalty based on the integrity of reciprocal indebtedness . . . expressed in the form of physical caretaking, telephoning, visiting, writing, showing interest, respect and concern [p. 217].

Although this emotional bond serves a positive function in keeping the family together, it can also be dysfunctional when competing problems vie for emotional time, since the social/emotional dependencies are considered to be extremely stressful (Steinmetz, 1983; Steinmetz and Amsden, 1983). Control over one's environment and lack of privacy pose additional conflicts for both generations. To have a smoothly running home one assumes that all members must function interdependently. Yet it is often difficult for an older person who has been transplanted from his or her home to find an appropriate role in the new setting. Since this problem is predominantly faced by women, it takes on an additional dimension: rivalry between mother and daughter over appropriate ways to manage households, husbands, and children (Farrar, 1955; Johnson, 1978). As one respondent noted:

> She's right there washing dishes while I'm trying to cook dinner. These are the things that drive me bugs and some other times she never bothers me. She is always wishing that she could do more, and if she would just stay seated at the table it would help me so much. I do think it is hard for two women to be in the same house, and she did have one of her own [#148—46-year-old daughter, who had been caring for her 84-year-old mother for 2 years].

Because the decision to have an aging parent move in with an adult child is often made during a period of crisis, this decision is often based on haste, guilt, love, and a sense of responsibility, rather than a careful evaluation of all options and an acknowledgment of what is best for the elder, the adult child, and the family.

In a preliminary analysis of the data for this book, we found that often the elderly kin moved in under previous rules of "guest" status (Steinmetz, 1982). For example, the family members bow to the wishes of a guest, rising early on the weekends to fix breakfast when the family usually sleeps in. The host family always asks the guest what he or she wants to eat and tries to fix his or her favorites regardless of the family's taste. The family is constantly mindful of the need for the children to play quietly or the teens to keep the stereo low, when one has house guests. This idea was expressed by one caregiver:

> When a parent comes to live in your house, they are like a stranger. I didn't want her to be a stranger, but my mother was always just a visitor. She wasn't one who would walk in and do what I do in my daughter's house. I can walk in my daughter's house and take over and do whatever I please. I go to the refrigerator and I'll cook and do. My mother would just wait to be waited on. So it made it kind of hard at first. I had to tell her, "sit down mom, you live here and this is where you are going to stay" [#22-60-year-old daughter, who had been caring for her 80-year-old mother for 14 years].

Although these accommodations may be possible for a week-long, or even month-long visit, this disruption of the caregiving family's life-style often becomes unbearable when continued for prolonged periods of time, especially when the family recognizes that this situation is permanent. The elder's demands now become stressful to the family and are interpreted as selfish. However, any attempts to change this routine are likely to be perceived by elders as an indication that the caregiving family no longer wants them. They feel that something else is being taken away from them, when they have already lost so much—a spouse, their home, friends, their independence and autonomy over their environment. Unfortunately, this reaction is likely to increase the guilt and stress felt by the caregivers and is likely to intensify further the family's resentment. This aspect was noted by a son-in-law who described the following disruptive behavior by the mother-in-law:

> She knocks on my door at 7:00 every morning to see what she is supposed to do. Saturday and Sundays are the same. My wife would say, "You don't have to ask me, do what you want . . . the knock on the door every morning bothers us. We are not ready to get up yet, and that bothers us"

[#23/24—61-year-old son, who had been caring for his 92-year-old mother for over 15 years and his 90-year-old mother-in-law for 9 years].

A respondent, whose mother had lived with her for 16 years until she died at 87 years of age, "did not quite realize what one did to an elderly parent by taking them out of their environment."

I assumed, wrongly assumed, that my mother would assimilate herself into the household. My mother was always like a guest in the house. I realize now that she was afraid to move in. It really wasn't her house. It was not her kitchen. It was my kitchen. . . . She was not the type who would walk in and take over. . . my mother's [needs] were always first, which may have been wrong. It would never occur to me to do otherwise [#26—50-year-old daughter, who had been caring for her 87-year-old mother for nearly 15 years].

The loss of independence is a problem for both generations. The aging parent must face a continually constricting social space (the physical areas that define's one's social life), one that slowly contracts from the community, to the immediate neighborhood, to the home, and finally the bedroom. This is also a time of adjustment for the adult offspring. As Kirschner (1979) notes:

At a time when the parent needs help adjusting to the aging process, the adult children are facing problems of menopause, the climacteric, and retirement; grandchildren are being born, and are claiming the attention of the family (Kirschner, 1979: 209).

This is an unexpected part of the mid-life crisis, or as Silverstone and Hyman (1976) label it:

The special generation caught in the middle—being pulled in three directions, trying to rear their children, live their own lives, and help their aging parents, all at the same time (p. 4).

Social/emotional problems experienced by the elderly are a considerable source of distress to the caregiving children. The parent's feelings of unhappiness, depression, and loneliness are likely to produce feelings of guilt in the adult children. In fact, the social isolation and loneliness that their elderly parents might be experiencing were major sources of concern to adult children in studies by Archbold (1980) and Simos (1970).

Using a subsample of the families interviewed for this book, Foulke (1980) reported that the social/emotional and mental health dependencies were the most stressful and that physical dependencies, even when they resulted in increased health-care responsibilities, were easier for caregivers to handle, and produced less stress than did social/emotional dependencies. This finding was further substantiated in a preliminary analysis of the completed interviews (Steinmetz and Amsden, 1983).

PHYSICAL DEPENDENCY

Physical deterioration through loss of hearing, failing vision, or decreased strength, and severe or chronic illness, which often accompanies aging, places additional burdens on the caregiving family. This matter is further complicated by the fact that the elder may refuse food or medicine and resist following the doctor's orders. The stress of meeting the physical needs of the elder is intensified because the caregiver realizes that inadequate care could easily produce a life-threatening situation for the elderly parent (Knopf, 1975).

Families often delay the institutionalization of the elder at considerable emotional and physical cost to themselves, resorting to the placement of the elder in a facility only when the mental and physical condition produces stress beyond the caregiver's ability to cope (Wershaw, 1976; Robinson and Thurner, 1979).

In a study of six families caring for stroke victims, Archbold (1980) found that providing needed medical care was especially difficult, creating an atmosphere of concern, worry, and constant crisis for these families.

HOUSEHOLD DEPENDENCY

Numerous studies (e.g. E. Brody, 1979; S. Brody, 1978; Shanas et al., 1968) have noted that family members are responsible for providing most of the care for impaired older people over a prolonged period of time. This care, especially for the bedridden, includes meals, housework, and personal care.

A national survey of the noninstitutionalized population 65 years or older (Shanas, 1979) found that the husband or wife of the invalid was the main source of help, followed by paid helpers, then adult children. A comparison of the services provided by spouses and adult children of invalids revealed that 44% of spouses versus 26% of children prepared meals; 38% of spouses versus 22% of children performed household chores; 30% of spouses did the shopping, whereas 34% of children shopped. In fact only 20% of the families paid for household help; 18% for meal preparation; and 8% for shopping.

One wonders how these percentages would change when the spouse is no longer present. It seems likely that children would absorb a major portion of these services. Brody et al. (1979) reported that 80% of all medically related care, such as bandage changing and injections, as well as personal care, such as bathing, dressing, toileting, and feeding, is provided by families. Furthermore, about one-third of the recipients of care need constant rather than partial or intermittent care (Brody et al., 1979).

The demands made on caregivers, especially those involving food preparation and meal schedules can be demeaning and stressful for the caregiver. Often the elder is unable or unwilling to eat during the normally scheduled meals and feels the need to have numerous, carefully prepared items that conform to medical as well as self-imposed diet restrictions. The studies reviewed seem to agree that the first assistance offered to elders by their children tends to be specific and replaces tasks requiring stamina and physical strength. Thus shopping, housework, and cooking tend to be performed before financial tasks.

ECONOMIC DEPENDENCY

Historical and legal ramifications. The burden of responsibility for an elderly parent has not always rested with kin. Children were held accountable for care of their parents under Medieval Church Law. However, the Elizabethan Poor Laws engendered the concept of community care of the elderly. In America, being poor is often considered to be an indication of laziness or incompetence. During the turn of the century, the inability of men to prepare adequately for their wives resulted in large numbers of elderly women being committed to live in pauper institutions, or poor houses (Fischer, 1977).

Social security, in addition to "forcing" men off the labor force in order to make jobs available to the young during the Depression, developed the concept of intergenerational support, whereby those in the labor force support the older, nonworking generation (Kreps, 1965). Social Security, was, in effect, a societal recognition of at least minimal community response toward elders.

The economic impact on families who care for elderly kin cannot be overlooked. This impact has special implications for women, who not only constitute the majority of elders needing care, but who also predominate as caregivers. Not only has the life expectancy for all

Americans increased, but women outlive their spouses (a life expectancy of 77 for women; 71 for men). The continuing spiral in the cost of living has forced many of these widows to continue working or to return to work until poor health or mandatory retirement at age 70 pushes them out of the work force. The women are caught in a double bind: they need to work for their own economic survival; yet if they work, who will care for the elder parent?

An annual Federal tax credit, with a maximum of $720 allowed for the care of a dependent child or elder (1987 U.S. Master Tax Guide, 1986: 95), hardly compensates for the actual cost of care, yet this credit is predicated upon the notion of "need to work." When Medicaid legislation was passed, many states changed their relative-responsibility laws, especially with the passage of the 1977 amendment prohibiting the requirement of or even permitting relatives other than a spouse or dependent child to contribute to the cost of nursing home care.

The 1983 Federal budget, however, proposed to "Allow States flexibility to recover long-term care (LTC) costs from beneficiary estates and relatives" by removing Federal Laws and regulations that "pose barriers to State collection from beneficiaries' families" (U.S. Government Annual Budget, 1983: 56). This clearly signaled a different philosophy, one in which the government was placing the burden of care of the elderly on families, without recognition that most elderly do not want to be dependent on their children and would prefer care from a stranger. Most adult children do provide support and care at whatever level is possible; and those adult children, to which this reinterpretation of relative responsibility applies, are themselves elderly (or nearly so) by census definition.

As Streib (1972) has suggested, studies on intergenerational relationships among older families have tended to overlook the rights and needs of adult children, and to blame them if they have not provided a comfortable, happy arrangement for their aged parents during this crisis that may last for 10 to 15 years. Although states have limited the liability one bears for a child—18 years of age in most instances—the relative liability laws that were passed in a flurry of activity did not, for the most part, recognize an upper age limit (see Steinmetz, 1985, for a fuller discussion of these laws and their implications). Most of this legislation was withdrawn, defeated, or overturned on legal technicalities, yet the degree of liability presented in these bills indicates the potential devastation faced by these families if legislation of this type were widely adopted.

For example, Massachusetts would have required each adult child *residing* in the state and having a taxable income of over $20,000 to pay up to 25% of the costs. Although payments were to be mandatory, elders would not lose their eligibility for services if the relative did not contribute to the cost (Nursing Home Law Letter, 1982a). However, legislation drafted by Mississippi stipulated a loss of entitlement to nursing home care if relatives did not pay the amount assessed based on a sliding scale of $25-$250 per month on incomes exceeding $8,000 per year (Nursing Home Law Letter, 1982b).

Idaho developed a voluntary plan, but the anticipated revenues fell considerably short, with only $14,000 being contributed. This resulted in the development of mandatory laws that were overturned in 1984 (Nursing Home Law Letter, 1984a). Hawaii had repealed their laws in 1965 because of anticipated conflicts with the Medicaid legislation, and a recognition of the potential for intergenerational trauma and financial burden. Although Hawaii acknowledged governmental responsibility, recent financial difficulties forced the state to reinstate their relative-responsibility laws. Colorado's draft bill would have made the children of an elderly parent responsible for the total cost of care, thus removing all responsibility for care of the elderly from the state (Nursing Home Law Letter, 1984b).

Since child abuse and neglect as well as foster care or other guardianship arrangements might dissolve any emotional ties between biological parent and child, the issue of an adult child's responsibility for an elderly parent who had been a less-than-adequate parent was addressed by two states. Indiana limited responsibility to:

(1) Children between 21 and 60—thus eliminating the elderly "child" from this responsibility; and
(2) Children who were provided with food, shelter, clothing, medical attention, and education until age 16 (Nursing Home Law Letter, 1984b).

Wisconsin's bill, defeated in 1982, excused from responsibility:

(1) Children who had been abused by their parents, and
(2) Children who had had little or no contact with the elder since the child became an adult (Nursing Home Law Letter, 1982c).

Although only Delaware's law remains unchallenged because it meets the test of general applicability (i.e., is not limited to those receiving Medicaid), the increased number of elderly individuals, decreased number of relatives available for care, and the reduced, and in some instances eliminated, federal funds guarantee that these states will reintroduce relative-responsibility laws that will withstand the challenge (Steinmetz, 1985).

Economic impact on families. We are likely to be faced with situations in which elders have refused medical assistance, hospitalization, and institutionalization in order to avoid becoming a financial burden on their children. We may see other instances, characterized as "latch key" elders, in which an elder is left unattended during the day while the adult children work because suitable, affordable alternatives are not available. The concern over the need to continue her job and provide a safe environment for the elder was especially important to a caregiver who lived in a rural area without neighbors or friends close by:

> I started with this program because she was going to be left home alone. I put her on Meals on Wheels—not that she needed the meals so much, but so that I would have somebody to stop in to see if she was all right. This was a very selfish reason. I felt that even if she didn't eat the meals (I was paying for them) the kids would eat them when they got in. It wasn't a total waste. I had the satisfaction of having someone stop in at noon time . . . They go and knock on the door . . . they don't leave the meal unless someone is there. I would know that she was all right. It was an easy way to do it. It eased my conscience [#43—54-year-old daughter, who had been caring for her 81-year-old mother-in-law for 14 years].

Another daughter noted:

> The hardest thing is worrying about them when you're not home. If you are out and you know that they are here . . . When she was able to be alone and I went to the store, I would find myself going to the phone and calling her up. If I was going to be gone for two hours, I would want to call her [#22—60-year-old daughter, who had been caring for her 80-year-old mother for 14 years].

Economic dependency produces a loss of control, loss of self-esteem, and thus a loss of power and prestige for the elderly person. Furthermore, the caregiving family often experiences economic drain and conflict over competing goals for the use of their limited resources. At the very time that their family income will soon be leveling off because of their own retirement, and college loans and weddings are being financed, these adult offspring are faced with financial responsibility for an aging parent.

A five-year longitudinal study of lower-middle-class and middle-class caregivers revealed that financial management, that is, writing the check or paying the bill, was more likely to be provided than direct financial *aid* (Robinson and Thurner, 1979). More than 20 years earlier, Shanas (1957) had found this to be true among ill elderly. However, financial aid can be provided in many indirect ways, such as extra heating, food, and laundry costs associated with having an additional member in the home. These costs tend not to be separately calculated in one's budget. For others, however, uncompensated or undercompensated medical costs add up. For example, those with Alzheimer's disease are not eligible for Medicaid services.

Simos (1973) in her study of 50 Jewish-American families found that adult children expressed considerable bitterness over medical expenses that had wiped out their parent's savings. Horowitz and Shindelman (1980) studied 201 primary caregivers in New York City and found that 23% had experienced a worsened financial state as a result of this caregiving responsibility, but only 4% considered this to be a serious problem. It is not clear whether the difference in these two studies can be attributed to a difference in the samples—the improved financial status of the elderly and caregiving families.

There is a need to provide financial incentives for families to provide care for their elders in home, as well as making it financially attractive to contribute to the cost of care when they become institutionalized.

The Impact of Stress on Caregiving

The roles and concomitant life-style changes that result when an elderly parent experiences a transition from independence, to interdependence, then to total dependence can produce a crisis and tension for all generations. The additional needs of the elderly, unless a large number of resources are available, will mean that resources such as physical energy, time, emotional strength, space, and money will need to be redirected to provide for the elder.

A change in status, role loss (Hanson, 1974), deprivation of material goods and resources (Streib, 1972), and organizational change in family structure and boundary ambiguity (Boss, 1986; Boss et al., 1979), can produce stress. When families become generationally inverse, all of the above stressors are experienced by both the elder and the caregiving family members.

When these stressors exceed the tolerance level, family dysfunction in terms of individual disorders or abuse and neglect of the elder or other family members results (O'Malley, 1979). In a survey of third-party service providers, Douglas et al. (1980) found that a lack of training, lack of sensitivity to the needs of the dependent elder, resentment and unwanted responsibility for this elder, and a lack of awareness of community resources and supportive services contributed to the maltreatment of the elderly. In discussing the stressful effects of caregiving, S. Brody (1978) cites a study done in England in which 50% of the second-generation caregivers had symptoms of excessive anxiety, and 30% of the children experienced insomnia, headaches, depression, and other disruptive symptoms.

Lack of privacy and the increased amount of personal time required to care for an elder often absorb any time available to fulfill the caregiver's own needs. As the elderly person grows older, they lose friends and relatives and become more dependent on the immediate family (Circirelli, 1981). This narrowing of the elder's social space forces the family into becoming the center of the elder's universe. This increased dependency on the adult child caregivers for economic, social, and psychological needs increases the stress being experienced by the caregiver (Cormican, 1980).

Often considerable resentment by other family members arises when the elder attempts to be the center of attention and direct all activity. In an effort to restore balance, families often plan specific parent-child or husband-wife activities that exclude the elder. These activities, such as the husband and wife spending an evening alone or with their friends, or engaging in an activity with their children that would be too rigorous for the elder, tend to produce further resentment by the elder and conflict over being "ignored" (Steinmetz, 1983; Steinmetz and Amsden, 1983; Steinmetz, 1988).

Stress also results from a conflict in values. Where do these middle-aged caregivers place their priorities—in the parents who reared them or the children who may still need emotional and financial support? As one caregiver so poignantly noted:

We always have one more to consider. When your children are growing, you and your husband have a tendency to live your life around your children, and anything that we do or try to do is in the direction of our children . . . but now you have that additional person that you have to include somewhere in there and it is not always easy . . . we are dealing with an elderly person who does not have her own life, her whole life is intertwined with ours and it is difficult to deal with . . . I want the freedom to be able to do for my children and to do things with my husband and not have to consider another person every day of my life [#9 / 10—38-year-old daughter, who had been caring for her 74-year-old mother for 6 years and a 76-year-old male friend of the family for about 5 years].

Caught in this dilemma, the caregivers may find that there is no physical, psychological, or financial cushion for themselves.

A SENSE OF BURDEN

Neugarten (1978), in an interview with Brubaker and several colleagues, identified the sense of burden expressed by middle-aged children as a critical issue in caregiving. A sense of burden can be characterized as a complex set of subjectively perceived issues that involves the family, the elder, and the family's situation. When caregivers are asked whether they feel a sense of burden by caring for an elder, their answers reflect their perception of the total effect that this experience has had on them.

Since this perception of being burdened may reflect coping abilities and therefore alternative strategies to violence, this variable may provide important insights. Steinmetz and Amsden (1982) found that the degree of the elder's dependency, which is an objective measure of additional tasks and responsibilities provided by the caregiver, was not related to a sense of burden, which is a subjective expression of the caregiver's feelings about these tasks and responsibilities. Poulshock and Deimling (1984) noted the importance of the subjective meanings attached to feelings of burden by caregivers. Inasmuch as a person's perception of a situation is often a better predictor of behavior than objective criteria (Lester, 1968; Neimi, 1974; Steinmetz, 1977a), caregivers who report a sense of burden may have a greater potential for using abusive or neglectful behaviors.

Burden can be defined as the emotional costs in terms of overload (Thompson and Doll, 1982). It can also be defined in terms of the costs resulting from specific changes in the caregivers' day-to-day lives such as the need to provide a greater amount of daily services (Steinmetz and Amsden, 1983), or financial difficulties, role strain, and physical health deterioration (Robinson, 1983; Zarit et al., 1980).

ELDER ABUSE—THE CURRENT STATE OF KNOWLEDGE

Elder abuse, as a topic of research, has had an extremely short history—barely a decade. Cronin and Allen (1982) trace the beginnings to the 1978 Congressional hearing on domestic violence that included information on elder abuse as part of the testimony provided by Steinmetz on the "overlooked aspects of domestic violence." They note that although the Congressional Hearings was not the first published reference to elder abuse, it was the "first to gain such national prominence, and was the sole portion of the Hearings to earn coverage in the New York Times, as well as a mention from Walter Cronkite."[1] The concern generated from this hearing, according to Cronin and Allen, resulted in the Administration on Aging's request for proposals to explore the incidence of elder abuse and the subsequent funding of two studies (Block and Sinnott, 1979; Douglas et al., 1980).

The first academic article devoted to the topic was "Battered Parents" (Steinmetz, 1978) in the July/August 1978 issue of *Society*. This article, mostly a theoretical treatment with selected case studies gathered from the Delaware Public Guardian's office, was followed by an article based on an examination of cases drawn from a hospital clinic (Lau and Kosberg, 1979).

Two congressional hearings: A House of Representatives Select Committee on Aging, June 1979, and a Senate Select Committee on Aging, May 28, 1980 brought further attention to the problem. In addition to the two studies funded by the Administration on Aging, a smaller study (but in many ways a more solid piece of research) funded by Legal Services for the Elderly in Boston (O'Malley et al., 1979) represented the major sources of data.

Although there have been a number of studies of institutional abuse of elders, or their victimization resulting from street crimes, the study of abuse of elders by informal caregivers is a new area of research.

Unfortunately, these studies, and other local studies that gathered their data from agency records, provided little more than rough estimates of demographic profiles, based on third party records of service providing agencies. The methodology used did not enable the researchers to eliminate multiple reporting of the same case by different agencies and different personnel within an agency. Most suffered from fairly low response rates. Furthermore, these studies were not limited to family caregivers and included friends, distant relatives, and paid caregivers. These early studies, as well as the most current studies, have been categorized as: surveys of professionals, agency data, studies of awareness and attitudes, and interviews with elder or caregivers. They will be discussed below.

Surveys of professionals. In one of the first studies of elder abuse, a mail survey of 1,044 medical personnel, social service professionals, and paraprofessionals in 1979, 183 reports of elder abuse, occurring over an 18 month period, were received. Some 70% of the reports noted that the abuse occurred twice. Furthermore, 75% of the reported victims lived with the abuser, and in over 80% of the reports, the abuser was a relative

(O'Malley et al., 1979). Nearly three-fourths of the families were experiencing some additional form of stress such as alcoholism, drug addiction, medical problems, or long-term financial problems. However, it was also noted that the elderly victim was a source of stress to the abuser primarily because of the physical, emotional, or financial care required.

In another study, only 13% of service providers who responded to a mail survey reported that they knew of a case of elder abuse. However, 88% were aware of the problem and knew of a case within the last six months, even if they had not handled an elder abuse case (Block and Sinnott, 1979). The abused elderly in this study had extremely high levels of impairment: 94% were physically impaired; 62% could not prepare their own food; 54% needed help with medication; and 47% were mentally impaired. Overall, 64% of these elderly lived with their children, 23% lived with their spouses, and 39% lived with other relatives. One point that needs addressing is the redefinition of the act when the individual becomes 60. Is the spouse who has been physically abused during the marriage, now, upon reaching 60, a victim of elder abuse? Because of an extremely low response rate, only 31%, these findings must be viewed with caution.

Douglas et al. (1980) conducted 228 semistructured interviews with a variety of professionals: clergy, police, lawyers, doctors, social service and mental health workers, and coroners. They stated that 17% of their respondents reported a case of physical abuse of an elder and 44% reported verbal or emotional abuse.

Chen et al. (1981) surveyed 90 practitioners requesting information about elder abuse and found that the public was largely unaware and unconcerned about the problem, which might account for their low return rate—33%.

An examination of the typology of 29 elder abuse studies (Hudson, 1986) revealed that most were based on professional samples; in only one study (Gioglio and Blakemore, 1983) was information requested that would enable the researchers to control for duplication of citings.[2] Most of these studies found that although abuse occurred across all age groups of the elderly, it tended to be concentrated among those 75 or older—the frail or vulnerable elderly. It is possible that because of the elders' frailty, even minor acts of physical abuse can produce visible, serious injury.

Agency data. Unlike the professional sample, agency data is based on actual records collected by a particular agency. These might be social service, adult protective service or law enforcement agencies, or hospital records. In some studies the data are collected retrospectively, by examining case files (Lau and Kosberg, 1979; Hall and Andrews, 1984; Andrews and Hall, 1984; Rounds, 1984; Giordano and Giordano, 1984).

One of the first of these studies was conducted by Family Services Association of Greater Lawrence, Massachusetts. They collected data for a three month period, during which 50 cases were handled. Of these, eight were suspected abuse by a family member, four were suspected physical abuse by a nonrelative, and three were referred for possible neglect by a family member who was caring for the physically dependent elder. However, a follow-up of the 50 original cases revealed that 21 elders were experiencing harm or were seriously threatened with harm by the actions of individuals upon whom they were dependent (Langdon, 1980).

During 1978, the Baltimore City Police Department reported 149 assaults against individuals 60 years of age or older. Nearly two-thirds of these assaults (62.7%) were committed by relatives other than spouses (Block, 1980). In the first eight months after passage of the Connecticut Elderly Protective Service Law (June 1978-January 1979), 87 cases of physical abuse, 314 cases of neglect, 65 cases of exploitation, and eight cases of abandonment were reported (Block, 1980). By April 1979, the total number of reported cases was 937, which included 651 neglect cases (both self-neglect of the elderly, as well as neglect by the caretaker); 166 cases of physical abuse (a majority of which had been inflicted by grown children of the abused victim or by a spouse); 127 cases of exploitation; 32 cases of abandonment; and 89 cases needing other kinds of assistance.

In an examination of 39 cases collected during a one-year period from the Chronic Illness Center in Cleveland, Ohio, Lau and Kosberg (1979) found that over three-fourths of these abused elderly cases involved physical abuse and over half involved psychological abuse. Three-fourths of the elders suffered from at least one major physical or mental impairment.

Sengstock and her colleagues (Sengstock, 1984; Barrett and Seng-stock, 1982) surveyed elderly abuse victims in Detroit in 1981. In half of the families in which elder abuse had occurred, 10 or more problems were noted; 20% had 20 or more problems. Family members predominated as perpetrators, and in half of the cases the family member was an adult offspring. They found that sons tended to be physically assaultive whereas daughters tended to neglect.

The most recent and most comprehensive survey of agency data, conducted by the American Public Welfare Association and National Association of State Units on Aging (1986), gathered reported suspected or alleged elder abuse data for 1983 and 1984 from the state agency mandated to collect these data. They obtained reports from all but six states, however only 29 states were able to provide data on reports of abuse/neglect involving *only* those 60 or 65 and older (American Public Welfare Association and National Association of State Units on Aging, 1986: 23). The incidence rates per 1,000 elderly persons (either 60 or 65 and older) by informal caregivers in domestic settings for fiscal year 1984 ranged from a low of .02 for Minnesota to a high of 1.9 for California (Table 5, p. 29). Overall, 13 states included self-abuse/neglect as well as abuse and neglect perpetrated by informal caregivers. As could be expected the incidence rates were considerably higher ranging from a low of 0.9/1,000 reported by Mississippi to a high of 8.0/1,000 reported by Missouri (Table 6, p. 31). Seven states included institutional abuse as well as that perpetrated by informal caregivers and self-abuse/neglect. These states reported incidence rates that varied from Alaska's rate of 1.6:1,000 to Idaho's rate of 8.5:1,000 (Table 7, p. 30).

Of course, comparisons among states are difficult. Different agencies are responsible for collecting the data and the statutes define "elder abuse" to include a wide range of ages as well as abuse occurring in different settings and perpetrated by others as well as by elders themselves.

Studies of awareness and attitudes. In a poll conducted by Louis Harris and Associates (*Sourcebook of Criminal Justice Statistics,* 1982, Tables 2.68 and 2.69), 15% of the black respondents and 19% of the white respondents reported that they knew a victim of elder abuse. However, 58% of the blacks but only 36% of whites who were interviewed considered elder abuse to be a "very serious" problem.

This finding is particularly interesting since women predominate as caregivers and elders needing care; black women are more likely to live in multigenerational households; a greater percentage live in poverty (42% of black women versus 16% of white women over 65 years of age); and older blacks are in significantly poorer health, even when income, gender, and social class are controlled (Dowd and Bengston, 1978). All of these factors might predict higher abuse rates (and less concern over elder abuse because of numerous competing concerns) among blacks.

When a caucus of 80 older persons representing various areas of Los Angeles County, California listed their concerns, they noted abuses committed against senior citizen by nursing home staff, children of the elderly and others as a major issue (Greenberg and Wertlieb, 1983).

Pratt, Koval, and Lloyd (1983) mailed questionnaires to service providers and requested that they respond to vignettes that described verbal abuse: pushing, hitting, and severe beating. They were also asked to provide data on cases of elder abuse that they handled during the last year. The researchers reported that the victim-abuser relationship, rather than victim's age, affected the type of intervention chosen by service providers.

Dozier (1984) had social workers field test an assessment instrument on 52 clients referred to them by their supervisor. The assessment tool revealed that over 46% of the cases listed self-neglect as the primary problem; self-referral occurred in about 8% of the cases; few referrals were obtained from physicians or clergy. More than 90% of the clients had at least one chronic physical or mental problem, yet 23% refused services. Alcohol and mental illness among caregivers and elders was a prominent stressor.

The ethical issues of mandatory reporting also have a direct impact on the type of data collected and the likelihood that this data will be reported in a consistent manner. A comparison of 16 state elder-abuse reporting statutes (Salend et al., 1984), revealed a failure to provide consistent information about elder abuse victims. The researchers note that neglect is more often reported than abuse and that within the "neglect category," self-neglect predominated. Complicating this problem even further is that although most state have some sort of "mandatory" reporting, penalties for failure to report are absent or minimal, rendering the "mandatory" aspect problematic. Faulkner (1982) and Krauskopf and Burnett (1983) contend that mandatory reporting laws not only infantilize the elderly by basing competency on age instead of cognitive or physical ability, but they also have the potential for further abuse by taking away the elder's rights. Salend and colleagues (1984) state that consciousness-raising and education directed toward increasing the public's sensitivity to the problem of elder abuse are better approaches than mandatory reporting.

Interviews with elders and caregivers. Several studies interviewed abused elders, usually identified through agency personnel. Liang and Sengstockk (1982) combined mailed questionnaires to agencies, interviews with agency personnel, and interviews with 20 abused and 50 nonabused elders. The profiles of the abused were similar to other studies, 33% were over 80 years of age; nearly three-fourths were female; nearly half were abused by adult offspring with slightly more sons than daughters as abusers (26% versus 23%). In all, 80% had incomes of $10,000 or less. The rates of abuse varied: 82% experienced psychological abuse, 55% experienced financial abuse, and 43% experienced physical abuse.

It is important to recognize that the criteria for selecting the individual to be interviewed critically defines the parameters of the findings. For example, Liang and Sengstock (1982) selected only verified cases of abuse, thus the high levels of physical abuse they report, when compared with other studies, is not unexpected. Likewise, Pillemer and Finkelhor (1987) in a case study of elderly abused victims, found that the abusing caregivers were often dependent on the elder, which is contradictory to other studies that correlated increasing dependency to increasing abuse (Circirelli, 1986; Steinmetz, 1983;1987; Steinmetz and Amsden, 1983).

Phillips (1983) divided referrals from the active caseloads of public health nurses into "abused" and "nonabused." Interviews were conducted in the elders' own homes and the interviewers were unaware of their abuse status. Phillips found that the abused subjects had lower expectations for their caregivers, lower perception for the caregiver's actual behavior, significantly fewer friends, suggesting a measure of social isolation, and a greater degree of depression.

Pillemer and Finkelhor (1987) interviewed a representative sample of 2,020 individuals 65 or older by telephone. Based on this study, they estimate that in the Boston area there are between 8,646 and 13,487 abused elders. They project that approximately 3.2% of all elders over 65 may be experiencing abuse or neglect. The abused elders were three times more likely to be living with someone, whereas the neglect victim was more likely to be living alone and isolated from support systems. Some 58% of the elders were abused by their spouses as compared to 24% who were abused by an adult child.

Notably missing from this categorization and review of the studies in elder abuse are studies based on interviews with informal caregivers, and national incidence and prevalence studies.

COMPARISONS AND INCONSISTENCIES IN STUDYING ELDER ABUSE

Given the diversity in definitions of abuse, methodologies used for collecting data, and samples selected, the lack of congruence between findings is not surprising. Unlike other forms of domestic violence, it is the age of the victim, not the act or the relationship between the victim and perpetrator that defines elder abuse. For example, is the spouse who has been physically abused during the marriage, upon reaching 60, now a victim of elder abuse?

The typical definition of elder abuse used by adult protective service (APS) agencies, the agency designated to handle elder abuse cases in most jurisdictions, includes financial exploitation, neglect, emotional, sexual, and physical abuse, as well as self-abuse and self-neglect. These agencies serve the needs of all adults over 18 years of age, not just those 60 years of age and older. The primary objective is protecting the adult from abuse or neglect. The victim-perpetrator relationship or form of abuse is secondary. Thus data collected by APS agencies not only include adults between the ages of 18 and 60 as well as those over 60, but also self-abuse and self-neglect cases, which constitute a significant amount of cases handled.

Pillemer and Finkelhor (1987) used the conflict tactic scales (CTS) to measure abuse among a random sample of individuals over 65 residing in the greater Boston area. They note that the interviews conducted by telephone and in person most likely did not tap those most vulnerable—the frail elderly with physical and mental impairments—those most likely to become data in an agency-based sample. They also found that nearly three-fifths of the perpetrators were spouses, and a large proportion of these victims were husbands (a 1:1.6 ratio of wives to husbands as victims).

As noted above, are we measuring spouse abuse among couples who are over the age of 60? If so, elder abuse in these instances is simply a category of family violence applied to another age group. Likewise, would we consider as child abuse instances in which an elder physically attacked their care-taking adult child? What about two siblings over 60 who use physical, verbal, or psychological abuse on each other—is this sibling abuse? In other words is elder abuse a distinct category of family violence or is it simply an adjective, denoting the age of the victim, and modifying a variety of other categories of family violence?

Straus and Gelles (as cited in Pillemer, 1987) also collected spouse abuse data for 520 couples over 65. Their rate of spouse abuse, 5.2:100 was considerably higher than the rate of 2.5:100 computed by Pillemer and Finkelhor. However, Pillemer and Finkelhor's sample contained those living alone or with children, in addition to those living with spouses, groups with considerably lower rates of abuse. Although Pillemer and Finkelhor explain the difference in terms of regional difference, a more plausible explanation is the difference in samples. Among agency-based samples, self-abuse and self-neglect predominate as the largest part of their case load—a form of abuse that was not considered in the above studies. Earlier analysis of the data that form the basis of this book (Steinmetz, 1981, 1983, 1987; Steinmetz and Amsden, 1983) strongly supports a somewhat different set of findings when the sample is based on dependent elderly who are residing with caregiving adult offspring. Thus when interpreting the findings of this book or other research, it is important to recognize the impact that the definition of abuse, the characteristics of the sample, and the individuals providing the data can have on the findings.

Conclusion

It is clear, even given the limitations of the research noted above, that abuse of the elderly by family members is widespread. Furthermore, the potential for abuse is likely to increase. As a result of the extended life expectancy, decreasing family size, the elimination of mandatory retirement and concomitant expectation that one might chose or have to work beyond the age 70, and the large numbers of women entering the work force, fewer people will be available to care for increasingly larger numbers of elderly.

Thus this emerging phenomenon in which approximately 1 in 3 families may face generational inversion and the long-term family care of an elder is a direct product of our aging society. Neugarten describes this phenomenon as

> not the actual physical care of the parent (although that, too, is also a critical issue) but the decision making in which the adult child or grandchild participates, the social and emotional supports required (and given), and the sense of burden expressed by so many middle-aged, especially middle-aged women [Brubaker et al., 1978].

Caregivers' ability to assume this role will be dependent on but not limited to the following:

(1) the family's willingness and ability to provide emotional/social, physical or financial support;
(2) their ability to cope with the various stages of independence and dependence that the parents experience;
(3) availability of resources, such as money, time, transportation, adequate housing, sources of help (labor), not only from other family members but from the community at large;
(4) health of individual members;
(5) the family adaptation to stress resulting from a series of crises or near crises;
(6) filial expectation of the older generation;
(7) the historical perspective of the intergenerational relationship;
(8) the attitude and functional capabilities of the elderly parent (Foulke, 1980: 6).

This role may be provided through daily or weekly contact, or may involve less frequent contact. Contact may be through phone calls, letters, and visiting, with services being limited to financial assistance and brokering of services for the elder. One elder may need little or no assistance with "activities of daily living" (ADL), while on the other end of the care spectrum, which is the focus of this book, another elder will depend on his or her family to provide most tasks.

The following chapter will examine the dependency tasks that are provided for the elder. The relationship of level of dependency to stress and the control maintenance techniques used will be explored.

Notes

1. Butler, in his book, *Why Survive, Being Old in America* (1975) briefly refers to the battered older person syndrome; in the same year, Burston, in a letter to the editor of the British Medical Journal, discussed granny-battering.

2. The studies reviewed by Hudson (1986), based on interviewing or mailing a questionnaire to professionals, included: O'Malley et al., 1979; Beachler, 1979; Block and Sinnott, 1979; Douglas et al., 1980; McLaughlin, Nickell, and Gill, 1980; Boydston and McNairn, 1981; Chen et al., 1981; Pepper and Oakar; 1981; Crouse et al., 1981; Wolf, Strugnell, and Godkin, 1982; Pennsylvania Department of Aging, 1982; Liang and Sengstock, 1982 (they also interviewed victims); Levenberg, 1983: Gray Panthers of Austin, Texas, 1983; O'Brien, Hudson, and Johnson, 1984; Elder Abuse Task Force, 1984; and Phillip and Rempusheski, 1985.

4

ELDERS AND THEIR CAREGIVERS:
A PROFILE

No matter how much you love a person, sometimes age differences can present problems. I know they say there is a generation gap between teenagers and their parents, but there is one between an older person and their aged parents. Living together, especially when you are close in one house can cause problems [#42—50-year-old woman, who had been caring for her husband's 87-year-old aunt for 8 years].

The goal of this chapter is to describe this sample of generationally inverse families and examine the impact that certain demographic variables, such as a small number of males or blacks, might have on the findings.

In order to test for these possible effects, the sample was divided into the appropriate categories and the mean scores for dependency, stress, feelings of being burdened, and the control maintenance techniques used by the caregivers and elders were compared. Tests of significance were computed using the SAS program for ANOVA and t-test. The .05 level of significance was considered to represent the highest acceptable level of probability. A summary chart indicating the probability levels for scores that differed significantly, Table 4.1, is included in this chapter; the specific values for each variable are contained in Table C.1 in Appendix C.

Family Variables

These variables describe characteristics of the family rather than specifically relating to the caregiver or elder. They include race, location of the residence, length of caregiving, the relationship of caregiver to the elder, and the number of elders being cared for in the family. (See Figure 1.1 for the frequency of selected demographic characteristics, and Table 4.1 for significance differences by demographic characteristics for measures of stress, dependency, burden, and control maintenance technique scores.)

RACE

Overall, 95% (n = 99) of the families were white, and the remaining 5% (n = 5) were black. No Asian or Hispanic families were represented in this study. Because of the small representation of minority families, it was especially important to test for any racially related differences. No significant differences were observed between black and white care-givers, although black caregivers reported slightly higher scores on all dependency measures except financial dependency. This was surprising since one might expect minority status to be associated with lower socioeconomic status, which would result in less access to economic resources with which to purchase services.

Although there were only slightly higher dependency scores for blacks, black caregivers experienced more resultant stress than white caregivers. However, the level of the family stress (e.g., small children, alcoholism, no spouse, and physical or emotional problems) was lower for black families.

The control maintenance techniques (CMT) scores for caregivers and elders showed that black elders were somewhat more likely to: refuse to eat or take medication; call the police; hit, push, or throw things at the caregiver; yell; cry; or not respect the caregiver's privacy. However, none of these differences approached significance.

To summarize, there does not appear to be significant race-related differences. Black caregivers had slightly higher dependency scores and experienced somewhat higher level of stress associated with providing these tasks, but these differences were not significant. Black families appear to reflect a greater intensity in all interactions between the caregiver and the elder. The only CMT scores in which white caregivers exceeded black caregivers was for the variable "give advice"; the single variable for white elders was "to pout."

Again, it must be noted that this nonprobability sample contained only five black caregivers. Thus differences between blacks and whites on many measures could be a result of idiosyncratic responses. There-fore, caution is needed in interpreting these findings; generalizing these findings to other black families, or using these findings to explain race-related adult offspring-elderly parent interaction would be ex-tremely questionable. These findings do provide a measure of confidence that the data from black families can be combined with that from white families for purposes of analysis.

RESIDENCE

Differences in the availability of services, especially between rural areas and cities, might affect the options that adult children have both in terms of the actual decisions to care for the elder in their homes and also the availability of in-home or senior center support services that can ease the burden of responsibility. An attempt was made to have geographic representation from a city, suburbs, small towns, and rural areas.

Delaware is a small state, both in size and population. There is only one large city, Wilmington, and only a few "towns" that are not overwhelmingly rural. Therefore, typical Census designations were not used. Wilmington, characterized by a high density, high mobility rates, a diverse ethnic population, a high concentration of elderly population, and a sizable minority population represented about 11.5% of the families. Suburban areas, primarily those in New Castle County, which surround Wilmington, comprised 30.8% of the families. Small towns, Newark, where the University is located, and Dover, the state capital, located in a primarily rural Kent County, represented 30.8% of the sample. A total of 17.3% of the families were residing in rural areas in middle and lower Delaware.

An additional 9.6% of the sample consisted of families that we were not able to classify by geographic area. Since many of the caregivers contacted us from their place of employment and were interviewed in places other than their home, asking where they lived, after emphasizing anonymity seemed unreasonable and probably would not have added information.[1]

Residence appeared to have little effect on stress indices. Although families residing in urban and suburban environments tended to have slightly higher stress levels than did families residing in small towns or rural environments, these differences were not significant. Mobility and social/emotional dependency differed significantly by residence; however there were no observable patterns in these variables. Likewise, although significant differences in caregivers' use of CMT were observed for yelling, ignoring, and forcing medicine or food, no patterns related to residential location were discerned. Neither significant differences nor trends by residence were observed for the elders' use of control maintenance techniques.

It appears that geographic location, in this study, had little patterned effect on the variables under study. No significant relationships were found between the stress level and elders' use of CMT and residence. Mobility and social/emotional dependencies, caregivers' use of verbal abuse, ignoring, and forcing food and medication were significant but no observable trends for other dependency or CMT categories were found.

LENGTH OF CAREGIVING

The length of time that caregivers cared for an elderly kin ranged from one family that, at the time of the interview had been providing care for two months to another family that had been providing care for 660 months (55 years). In the latter case the elder had never been separated from the caregiver, although we have to assume that at least for the first decade or two the elder fulfilled the parenting role.

The sample was divided into five groups based on the length of time the family had been providing care at the time they were interviewed. The first group consisted of 21 elders who had resided with the caregiver 12 months or less. The second group (n = 19) lived together 13 months to 36 months. A third group, the largest, with 42 elders, lived with the caregiver from between 37 months and 108 months—roughly 3 to 9 years. The fourth group, the smallest with 14 elders, had lived with the caregiver for between 10 and 14 years (109-168 months). The length of caregiving for the final group (n = 23 elders) exceeded 14 years: 8 elders had resided for about 15-16 years; 6 had resided between 18-20 years; and 6 elders had resided between 22 and 34 years. One caregiver had provided care for 48 years; another for 51 years; and a third for 55 years. Thus caring for an elder can be a long-term investment in time and energy, as well as in personal and family resources.

The division of the sample by age groups was based on naturally occurring breaks in the frequency distribution. In any artificially assembled grouping it is always possible to blame the lack of significant findings on the composition of the group. However, the lack of any significant findings for any of the stress indices, dependency indices, and CMT for caregiver and elder when coupled with the lack of any discernible trends or patterns strengthens the conclusion that the length of time that the caregiver has been responsible for the care of the elder apparently has no direct influence on the major variables being considered in this study.

THE RELATIONSHIP OF ELDER TO CAREGIVER

The study design was based on interviewing caregivers who had assumed the responsibility of caring for an elderly parent. We discovered that *parent* is in the eye of the beholder and defined in terms of parentlike relationships that have endured over the years. We were concerned not only with the possible effect that being an in-law versus parent might have, or the result of caring for a mother versus a father, but also any effect that these "nonparent" elders might have on the results.

One also has to recognize that with multiple marriages and women living longer, a caregiver may be faced with simultaneously providing care to a mother, stepmother, and mother-in-law. The sample was recoded into mothers (and step-mothers), fathers (and step-fathers), in-laws, and "other."

There was a tendency for caregivers who were caring for mothers to report higher stress levels than caregivers who were caring for fathers or other relatives; and those caring for fathers to report the lowest levels of stress. None of the findings, however, were significant. The slightly higher scores that in-laws and "others" received as compared with fathers, may reflect the overwhelming female composition of those groups. It is possible that providing care to a woman, regardless of the relationship, is more stressful. These gender differences will be examined in greater detail below.

When the dependency scores were compared by relationship of elder to caregiver, the only apparent pattern was that mothers required more tasks performed for them. However, none of these findings were significant. Caregivers did feel that it might be more difficult to care for their mothers or mothers-in-law. Since women are almost always the primary caregivers, the competition between mother (or mother-in-law), and daughter seems inevitable. As one caregiver noted, "living with her father-in-law worked nicely because he is a male and there was no competition in performing chores." However, she believed that living with her mother was not going to be as easy:

> I'm thinking twice about that now just in the three months she's been here. There has been a lot of tension between the two of us. The things that she will do overlaps the things that I would do [#12/13—a 39-year-old woman, who had been caring for her 69-year-old mother for 3 months, and her 84-year-old father-in-law for 11 years].

Despite the plethora of mother-in-law jokes and the comments of respondents alluding to the ease or difficulty of certain relationships, differences related to gender and the relationship of caregiver to elder appear to be individualistic, based on personalities and role relationships.

A lack of either statistically significant differences or trends characterize the association between the elder's and the caregiver's CMT and the type of relationship. Since there was some evidence that the "female" composition of "other" and "in-law" categories might have some effect on the data, mother and mother-in-law were compared and father and father-in-law were compared. Although caring for a mother-in-law is perceived to be more stressful and require more tasks then caring for a mother, the differences were not statistically significant.

Caregivers tend to have higher levels of interaction with mothers than with mothers-in-law, ignore them less, and are less likely to "threaten to send them to a nursing home." These differences are small and did not reach statistical significance. Mothers are more likely to use verbal or physical abuse, pout, manipulate, or call the police than are mothers-in-law. Mothers-in-law are slightly less likely to respect the caregiver's privacy and more likely to cry. However, only the mothers' more frequent use of verbal abuse reached significance.

A comparison of fathers with fathers-in-law suggested that caregivers provided more help to fathers and that caregiving was considered to be more stressful in caring for a father than a father-in-law. A greater level of financial support provided to fathers was the only difference to reach significance. With the one exception of greater amounts of talking with fathers-in-law, caregivers tended to report higher levels of interaction with fathers. These differences were not significant, nor was the tendency of fathers-in-law to use higher levels of control maintenance techniques when interacting with the caregiver.

MULTIPLE CAREGIVING ROLES

In all, 15 of the caregivers in this study were caring for two elders (or had done so in the recent past). Although we treated each caregiver-elder dyad as a unique case, the impact of caring for more than one elder might be reflected in the level of dependency, stress, or CMT scores.

In hindsight, it can be admitted that we were completely unprepared for the large numbers of families that were caring for or had in the past cared for several elders. We limited the number of elders being cared for by restricting the referent period for data collection to the past three years. In many instances, this did not accurately reflect the lifetime of caregiving that characterized these families.

One woman reported that she was "caring for an 87-year-old mother." It became clear that this caregiver was also responsible for the elderly, infirm housekeeper/companion (who had no family), who had been hired 20 years earlier to help the mother. This caregiver had also assumed responsibility for her father-in-law after it was discovered that an alcoholic sister-in-law had been neglecting and abusing him. The combination of her husband's death and the father-in-law's stroke forced this caregiver to place her father-in-law in a nursing home. This respondent, however, was directly queried only about the care of one elder, although she had been caring for three elders in the recent past and was still responsible for two of them.

The differences between caring for one elder and caring for two elders were not significant for any of the variables examined. It was surprising, given the exasperation, frustration, and stress verbalized during the interviews, that caregivers providing care for two elders actually experienced less family, dependency, and total stress than did caregivers who were responsible for only one elder.

Likewise, two-elder families reported lower dependency scores with the exception of mobility scores. It is possible that two elders, each doing a small amount of work, are able to lighten the housework for the caregiver and, with each other for company, are less dependent on the caregiver for social/emotional support.

A son who was caring for his 92-year-old mother and 90-year-old mother-in-law noted that the two of them got along "excellently."

> It's been more of a problem for us since my mother left the home than it was when they were both here. My mother-in-law is just lost. Even though there wasn't much communication between them, they were there. My wife's mother kept wandering into her room to sit down or get little things for her. They were company for each other. When one left, we found ourselves having to fill that role. That put a lot of stress on us (#23/24— 61-year-old son, who had been caring for his 92-year-old mother for over 15 years, and his 90-year-old mother-in-law for 9 years].

It is also possible that if we had items that measured the total amounts of dependency and feelings of stress and burden resulting from *all* caregiving responsibilities instead of that associated with providing care for a specific elder, higher levels of task provision and stress might have been reported. Unfortunately, our data collection procedures do not allow us to examine statistically the cumulative effect of caring for more than one elder.

Caregivers in two-elder families are more likely to talk, force food or medicine on the elder, or threaten to send them to a nursing home. They are less likely to use physical abuse, seek advice, or ignore the elder. However, none of these differences were significant. Likewise, the elders' use of control maintenance techniques do not show consistent trends, and differences were not significant.

TABLE 4.1
Demographic Variables that Differ Significantly

	Family Characteristics							Caregiver			Elder	
	Race	Residence	Length of Time Cared For	Relation	Father vs. Father-in-Law	Mother vs. Mother-in-Law	One or Two Elders	Age	Sex	Marital Status	Sex	Age
Stress												
family	—	—	—	—	—	—	—	—	—	—	—	—
dependency	—	—	—	—	—	—	—	—	—	—	—	—
total stress	—	—	—	—	—	—	—	—	—	—	—	—
Dependency												
household	—	—	—	—	—	—	—	—	—	—	—	.002
personal health	—	—	—	—	—	—	—	.02	—	—	.02	.03
financial	—	.03	—	—	.006	—	—	.05	—	—	.0004	.01
mobility	—	—	—	—	—	—	—	.009	—	—	.003	.04
mental health	—	—	—	—	—	—	—	—	—	—	—	—
social/emotional	—	.04	—	—	—	—	—	.0002	—	—	.007	.001
total dependency	—	—	—	—	—	—	—	.0009	—	—	.002	.0008
Burden	—	—	—	—	—	—	—	—	—	—	—	—
CMT (Caregiver)												
advice	—	—	—	—	—	—	—	—	.008	—	—	—
yell	—	.03	—	—	—	—	—	.04	—	—	—	—
ignore	—	.003	—	—	—	—	—	—	—	—	.02	—
medical abuse	—	.05	—	—	—	—	—	—	—	—	—	—
threats	—	—	—	—	—	—	—	—	—	—	—	—
physical abuse	—	—	—	—	—	—	—	—	—	—	—	—
CMT (Elder)												
yell	—	—	—	—	—	.003	—	—	—	—	—	—
pout	—	—	—	—	—	—	—	—	—	—	—	—
refuse food	—	—	—	—	—	—	—	—	—	—	—	—
hit	—	—	—	—	—	—	—	—	—	—	—	—
cry	—	—	—	—	—	—	—	—	—	—	—	—
manipulate	—	—	—	—	—	—	—	—	—	—	—	—
call police	—	—	—	—	—	—	—	—	—	—	—	—
invade privacy	—	—	—	—	—	—	—	—	—	—	—	—

NOTE: — = no significance.

Caregivers

The typical caregiver in this sample (n = 104) can be characterized as a 52-year-old married woman, with children still living at home, who is caring for an 83-year-old mother. Caregiver characteristics are summarized in Figure 1.1. As previously noted, the significance levels for differences in caregiver characteristics for stress, burden, dependency, and the control maintenance techniques are summarized in Table 4.1, and the actual values for these variables are in Table C.1 in Appendix C.

AGE OF CAREGIVER

The age of the caregivers ranged from a 23-year-old granddaughter to a 72-year-old daughter. The median age was 52; the mean age was 51.4. The caregivers were divided into four age groups: Younger than 39; 40-49; 50-59; 60 and older. About 11.5% of the caregivers (n = 12) were under 40 years of age, and 25% (n = 26) were in their forties. However, the largest group, 44% (n = 46), were in their fifties, and nearly 20% (n = 20) were 60 years old or older. Thus nearly two-thirds of the sample were elderly or nearing this age category. It needs to be noted that chronological age is often meaningless. Columnist Jack H. Smith in an article titled "Financial Problems Are the Down-Side of Longer Life," reported the following conversation about the increasing burden on mid-lifers who have to care for aged parents:

> "Mr. Smith," said the female member of a couple across the table, "We are both 70. And we are both caring and paying for a parent in the 90s. And, in addition to that we are asked to help a child in the 50s now and then" [Smith, 1986: G8].

Most caregivers in this study were in their fifties and sixties. In one family the major worry about an 82-year-old elder was her driving:

> Well, the only thing that gives me concern is her driving. That really sort of has me on edge. She had a little fender bender in Florida last year and it really upset her terribly because she's never had an accident in her entire life. Her friend that is always with her in the car can't see, so I guess when they looked they didn't see this man coming so fast, and she tends to pull out slowly instead of going right out. I think the one thing that really upsets me a little bit is when she takes off in the car, I worry about her [#3—56-year-old daughter, who had been caring for her 82-year-old mother for 3 years].

In another family, the 72-year-old caregiving daughter, when asked about her 103-year-old mother's diminished physical functioning, reported that her mother had lost

> both her hearing and her sight. I would say that her hearing began to deteriorate a lot when she was about 90 and her sight about 95. She couldn't enjoy TV very much.

> Interviewer: Was she able to get around?

> Yes, until after her hundredth birthday. She was able to get around quite well until after that with a walker. She had used a cane for a good many years before that. But she was not badly crippled. I remember we had a 100th birthday party and celebrated for two days. . . . Mother was sitting on the divan and she had her leg up under her and our doctor was so amazed and said, "Look at that for 100 years old." So she was quite mobile [#48—72-year-old daughter, who had been caring for her mother. 103, for 48 years].

The only consistent, but nonsignificant, trend observed was the slightly higher scores for family, dependency, and total stress among those 39 years of age or younger. This probably reflects both the stage in the life cycle of a group that also has major responsibilities for school-aged and adolescent-aged children as well as the demands of an occupation, and less preparations for taking on the role of caring for parents.

With this age group, severe, unexpected illness is most likely the reason that these elders have moved in with a child. The excerpt from one interview clearly indicates the impact of the medical condition of relatively young parents on the decision of their children to provide care:

> Dad is a diabetic, but that is under control. My mom has heart problems, cancer, diabetes, arthritis . . . she has had both breasts removed because of cancer. She has had 60% of her stomach removed because of ulcers. She has had four or five major heart attacks. They put a strainer, they call it an umbrella, into her blood veins to strain the clots and prevent heart attacks. She has had bowel troubles and just about everything [#19/20—27-year-old wife and 30-year-old husband with two small children, who had been caring for her 62-year-old mother and 64-year-old father for six years].

Obviously, the level of care required for the above mother exceeds that for older kin who need help because of diminished functions owing to age, not primarily because of a major illness. As aptly stated by one daughter:

> There is nothing wrong with my mother. Well not totally. She is just tied up with old age and not knowing where to go and where to belong or fit in [#7—36-year-old daughter, who had been caring for her 65-year-old mother for 2 years].

The dependency index scores also show a consistent trend, with increasing dependency needs accompanying an increase in age of the caregiver. All categories except mental health differed significantly. Since the increasing age of the caregiver reflects an increase in the age of the elder these trends were not surprising. Although dependency increased with increasing age of the elder, and the youngest group of caregivers experienced higher levels of stress, the data revealed no consistent age-related linear or curvilinear patterns for dependency stress. It is possible that increasing dependency needs might be offset by the older caregiver's lessening of family and work responsibilities.

When asked if caring for her mother, whose major medical problem was that she was legally blind, was a burden, a fairly young caregiver suggested:

> Not really, I guess I would hate for it to go on for years and years, as I am getting older too. My husband is getting older too and we do need to take a trip once in a while to get away too [#112—36-year-old daughter, who had been caring for her 77-year-old mother for 6 years].

One daughter, when asked if she experienced a sense of burden replied:

> Yes, I sure do! Being confined is part of it and part of it is because of the age I am. I don't feel physically able to cope with it. I have my own physical problems—my emotional problems. I am 66 years old. If I were 43 like my sister I could better handle it. When he goes there, she can enjoy him because to her he is company and she is a lot younger, physically stronger than I am and she has a husband who brings in a good living and doesn't have to worry where the next tank of oil is coming from or how she is going to pay the phone bill or electric bill or all this . . . It makes a big difference [#95—66-year-old daughter, who had been caring for her 86-year-old father for 4 years].

Only the greater use of verbal abuse among the youngest caregivers differed significantly. Weihl (1979) proposed that better relationships among older adult children and their parents might result from the adult child's clearer understanding of the problems attendant in old age. It is possible that the greater use of verbal abuse among the youngest caregivers reflects not only competing demands, an unwillingness by both the elder and adult child to relinquish former roles and accept new ones, but also the caregivers lack of understanding of, and experience with, the aging process.

The elders use of CMT are randomly distributed and show no patterns related to the age of the caregiver. It is quite possible that both elders' and caregivers' use of these techniques is more related to personality and firmly entrenched ways of resolving problems than to age related circumstances.

It appears that older caregivers perform significantly greater dependency tasks. However, the age of the caregiver has no significant effect on family stress, dependency stress, total stress scores, or the CMT used by elders and caregivers (except for caregivers' use of higher levels of verbal abuse).

SEX OF CAREGIVER

The traditional view of women as being more nurturing, assuming the kin-keeping responsibilities, and having more flexible time (when they were primarily homemakers) are usually cited as reasons for daughters dominating in assuming the caregiving responsibilities for elderly parents. Horowitz (1985) in a study of 131 adult children identified as primary caregivers, found that 22% of sons compared with 28% of daughters shared their households with older parents. However, when they lived separately, daughters were significantly more likely to live in the same neighborhood. Sons and daughters were fairly similar in the amount of telephoning and visiting, and differed primarily in the allocation of responsibility to spouses. Over three-fourths of the married sons (77%) named their wives as a major provider of care. In fact, Horowitz (1985: 615) notes:

> Women often voiced appreciation that their husbands remained neutral toward the caregiving involvement; in contrast, men expected and depended upon both emotional and concrete support from their wives. Thus caregiving as a primary female role clearly extended to daughters-in-law as well as daughters.

Only when there was an absence of available female siblings were males likely to become caregivers. In this study, six males (6%) identified themselves as "caregivers," all of whom were living in intact marriages.

However, three of these male caregivers lived in families in which two elderly parents or kin were being cared for. A fourth caregiver's family served as an adult foster care home for three elderly males in addition to the elderly parent. This suggests that perhaps the presence of more than one elder necessitates more direct help from the husbands. As a result, they are more likely to feel comfortable discussing the daily tasks and interaction. It also should be noted that in several families both husband and wife participated in part of the interview. Although the adult that initially agreed to be interviewed, or who actually provided most of the information, was coded as the caregiver, household chores as well as those related to caring for the elder were reported to be shared by husband and wife in a few families. In these maritally intact families, we are most likely obtaining a measure of the male's or females's *perspective,* that is, one's subjective view on caregiving rather than an objective measure on *actual* caregiving activities.

A male caregiver who was caring for two elders responded to the question of sharing tasks as follows:

Interviewer: Who does the light housekeeping?
Caregiver: We share in it. Because my wife works she does the cooking and I clean up the dishes. We share heavy housekeeping and laundry . . . grocery shopping. I guess I supply what transportation is needed . . . and run errands [#28/29—a 44-year-old son who has been caring for his 79-year-old mother for nearly 20 years, and his 90-year-old aunt for two years].

This caregiver also reported that he helps with the mother's bathing, dressing, and shampooing her hair.

Another caregiver responsible for the care of his 92-year-old mother and 90-year-old mother-in-law explained the distribution of responsibility for his mother's care as follows:

My wife cared for her in the afternoon and I cared for her at night. I'd feed her her supper and get her into bed for the night and hope that she'd stay all night. I had a noisemaker so that I could tell when she needed help [#23/24—61-year-old son, who had been caring for his 92-year-old mother for 15 years, and his 90-year-old mother-in-law for 9 years].

In other families, chores seem to be assigned according to gender, with women performing most social/emotional, housekeeping, and personal grooming/health tasks. Since preliminary analysis (Steinmetz and Amsden, 1983) revealed that social/emotional, and personal grooming/health dependencies are considered to be extremely stressful, it is possible that even when chores are assumed to be equitably assigned, those assigned to women are the more stressful tasks. As one husband noted in response to the question on providing the elder with help in personal grooming:

> That's no big hassle for me because Ruth [the sister] does it. But it sure does bother her though. It wears her out. It's very hard on Ruth. She has two full-time jobs [#5—52-year-old son, who had been caring for his 74-year-old mother for 1 year].

Although not significantly different, female caregivers report experiencing greater amounts of family stress, and slightly lower levels of dependency stress than do male caregivers. It is possible that males are less adequately prepared to take on the caregiving role and thus find it to be more stressful. This finding is especially interesting since male caregivers were considerably less likely to provide verbal descriptions of stressful events.

Male caregivers reported higher levels of financial, personal grooming/health, mobility, mental health tasks, as well as higher levels of overall dependency. The differences were not significant. Female caregivers provided greater amounts of household tasks and significantly greater social/emotional support. In summary, gender did not significantly differentiate the tasks provided, stress experienced, or the control maintenance techniques used by caregivers. Female caregivers tended to report higher family stress but lower dependency scores than did male caregivers, but these differences were not significant. Male caregivers reported somewhat lower scores for most CMT's except for providing more advice to elders than did female caregivers. The gender of the caregiver produced no observable trends for the elder's use of CMT.

MARITAL STATUS

In all, 80 of the 104 families (77%) were maritally intact families. In a number of these families a decision for one of the couple to reside in the elder's home, often located in another area, had been made. For example, the husband in one family had been caring for his mother and father while his wife and adolescent-aged children remained in Canada. This commuter marriage had existed for over four years at the time of the interview. Although there were sisters in the area, this caregiver felt that it was his responsibility as the son to care for his parents and oversee the family business. He noted his feelings of being torn between the desire to be with his wife and children and the need to care for his dependent parents:

> I feel like I can't go where my heart wants to go. But then, again, I can't get out of this [#106/107—44-year-old son, who had been caring for his 70-year-old mother and father for 4 years while his wife and children were residing in Canada].

A husband-wife interview revealed the conflicts arising from competing parent and marital demands:

Husband: Before [mother moved in] I had to go to her, spend 2 to 3 nights a week up there and not get home until 8 or 9 o'clock. No dinner, no nothing.

Wife: Every little thing, she called. Change a plug, change a fuse . . . I didn't even know it. He would call and say "I have to go up to mom's, I won't be home". . . everything was a catastrophe.

Husband: I didn't know what was going on so the only way I could be sure was to go and see . . . Up there is Dad's house and I was supposed to take care of Dad's house, the grass cutting . . . I had two lawns to take care of instead of one . . . two driveways to get the snow off . . . I was maintaining two properties and I had to maintain it at the standards that had been set by Dad [#5—52-year-old husband and his 48-year-old wife who have been caring for his 74-year-old mother for 1½ years].

Thus although maritally intact, many of these families experienced temporary residential separateness. In order to examine the effects that marriage might have on the caregiver/elder interaction, the sample was divided into married and nonmarried, which contained divorced and widowed caregivers. Being married might provide an additional adult to help with the care of the elder. If, however, the spouse was disabled or needed additional care, then being married might provide an additional source of stress.

Slightly higher levels of dependency stress were reported by married caregivers, but this difference was not statistically significant. Family stress levels were quite similar between married and nonmarried caregivers. Nonmarried caregivers reported slightly higher levels of household, financial, mobility, social/emotional, and total dependency. Married caregivers reported slightly higher personal grooming/health dependency and mental dependency. None of these differences were statistically significant. Nonmarried caregivers scored higher, but not significantly so, on all the control maintenance techniques than did married caregivers except for forcing food or medication. Except for crying, elders cared for by a nonmarried caregiver were reported to use greater amounts of all control maintenance techniques.

It appears that the wisdom of assuming that the unmarried (or no longer married) adult child is best able to care for the elderly parent because of a lack of competing family (i.e., husband) demands needs reconsideration.

Evidence from this study suggests that the caregiver's perception of competing demands might be more a reflection of an unwillingness to meet the demands of a spouse. One fairly young caregiver, whose husband, their 4½-year-old son, and 15-month-old daughter lived with her parents, noted that a major conflict between her and her husband was over moving. Her husband kept saying that he wanted a place of his own.

Interviewer: Given the fact that your mother has all these physical problems do you feel that you might be abandoning her if you moved out?

Caregiver: No, I just feel that if we moved out we would not be able to survive. It's just that simple. Where can you get an apartment for $200 a month and a baby sitter and everything for just $200. There is just no way. I guess that I would feel completely insecure if we moved out.

Interviewer: Overall, what do you think is the most difficult part of living in the same household with your parent?

Caregiver: Really, we don't have that many difficulties. My husband! Sometimes, I think that if we got rid of him we'd be better off. He will want to do something like go to his mother's and I won't want to go. Mom will say "You should go up and visit her." Really there are no difficulties [#19/20—27-year-old daughter caring for her 64 year mother and 63-year-old father for 6 years].

Circirelli (1983) found that adult children in "maritally disrupted" (defined as widowed, divorced, or remarried) situations provided significantly lower amounts of help to their parents. He also discovered that the caregiver's perceptions of the elder's needs differed significantly. Maritally intact caregivers saw a greater need to provide help to their elderly kin, and reported greater filial obligation as compared to caregivers in maritally disruptive families. A final difference was that 29% of adult children in intact marriages, but only 16% of those with marital disruption, felt they could continue to provide care under any circumstance. However, in his study, the elderly were not living with their adult children, thus they did not face the day-to-day caregiving responsibilities and stress.

Unfortunately, as the interview data clearly indicate, those with the fewest resources, the widowed and divorced female caregiver, are also those least likely to be able to secure alternative care for the elder.

The total dependency scores were quite similar between the two groups and showed no consistent patterns. However married caregivers reported higher levels of stress associated with providing these tasks, supporting, at least on a limited basis, the notion of competing demands. The nonmarried caregivers exhibited higher uses of verbal and physically aggressive control maintenance techniques, suggesting that the lack of alternatives from providing care may result in higher levels of potentially abusive caregiving.

The Elders

There were 119 elders in the sample. Of these, 15 elders were living with caregivers who had the responsibility of caring for two elders. (See Figure 1.1, for frequencies of elder characteristics and Table C.1 in Appendix C for actual scores.)

SEX OF ELDER

The sample of elders consisted of 19 male elders and 100 female kin. An examination of the data reveal that caregivers reported slightly higher family stress when caring for a male elder and somewhat higher dependency stress and total stress when caring for an elder female. However, none of these differences were significant.

Caregivers caring for an elderly woman consistently reported higher levels of dependency for all of the dependency measures than caregivers caring for an elderly male. Only household and mental health dependency did not differ significantly. This was consistent with Longino and Lipman's (1981) finding that elderly women received significantly more emotional, social, and instrumental (task oriented) support from family members. The question that needs to be raised is how much of this difference is a reflection of actual need, help offered, and help accepted.

There were no gender related patterns between the caregiver's or elder's use of control maintenance techniques. However caregivers were significantly more likely to force food or medicine on female elders. Female elders were more likely to pout, cry, and attempt to manipulate through guilt—characteristics that appear to be stereotypic behavior of women—whereas males used more yelling, hitting, and refusing to respect privacy. None of these differences, however, reached statistical significance.

AGE OF ELDER

The age of the elders ranged from 59 to 103, with a mean age of 82 years and a median of 82.5 years. About 10% of the elders (n = 12) were younger than 70, the remaining 90% were 70 years or older (n = 107). In all, 23% (n = 27) of the elders were between 70-79 years of age; but the largest group, 46% (n = 55), were in their eighties. The other 21% (n = 25) were in the ninth or tenth decade of life.

There appear to be no statistically significant relationships between the elder's age and the family, dependency, and total stress experienced by the caregiver. The relationship between the age of the elder and the levels of dependency show a strong and statistically significant increase in dependency levels with increasing age for all but the mental health dependency.

When combined with the findings for the age of the caregiver, it appears that the increasing age of the caregiver, which usually indicates an increasing age of the elder (their correlation was r = .56) intensifies the relationship. Older caregivers, those with the fewest financial, physical, and emotional resources, are responsible for the oldest elders, those requiring greater amounts of financial, physical, and emotional support.

There were no observable trends or patterns in the caregiver's use of control maintenance techniques and none of the relationships between the age of the elder and CMT were significant. Although an elder's use of CMT was not significantly related to the elder's age, there was a somewhat consistent trend of decreasing use of most techniques with advancing age.

The questions of overall feelings of burden also failed to be significantly related to any of the family, caregiver, or elder variables. Furthermore, few trends were noted: urban dwellers, blacks, male caregivers, and those under 39 years of age were slightly more likely to feel burdened, and single caregivers were slightly less likely to feel burdened. One area in which age may have some effect is the increased competition for the role of head-of-house/parent. This loss of "head-of-house role" often results in subtle, or in some cases overt, conflicts between the two generations. The costs to both the caregiver and her (or his) family, as well as to the elderly parent in these generationally inverse families are considerable. A caregiving daughter with a relatively young mother noted:

I truly mind turning my children over to my mother . . . I don't like being back on the job with small children at home, but it is a financial thing and I have to be working. She [her mother] is still the mother. I've lost my mother status around here. . . . My mother and I are basically very different and through my growing years it was no touch, no kiss, no nothing. I'm very much like my father. My mother and father were divorced. I'm completely the opposite, I kiss, hug, love, touch. That has come to a stop. She doesn't really approve of it, so we don't. It just doesn't happen when my mother's there.

Interviewer: This bothers you very much doesn't it?
Caregiver: It certainly does. It is very, very difficult. My mother is very loving . . . but she doesn't touch or hold. She has her set of rules and they [the grandchildren] live by them . . . I have literally stepped aside, you know, rather than have an unhappy home where we are always in conflict [#7—36-year-old daughter, who had been caring for her 65-year-old mother for 2 years].

Another caregiver reported a similar problem when her father interfered in the disciplining of the child.

Interviewer: Did he ever exhibit explosive behavior?
Caregiver: Yes, especially at times towards my husband. He would have spells of not shouting, but if things didn't go his way, he wasn't too willing at times to accept changes. With the children (ages 11 and 13), it was hard sometimes in disciplining them because he was always watching, so to speak. For instance, my son, who was just about two was having a good old temper tantrum and my husband sort of whacked him a little bit on the bottom. My father got very upset and was going to report him for child abuse [#16—52-year-old, who had been caring for her 89-year-old father for 14 years].

Summary

Although differences were observed, relatively few of the findings reached statistical significance. The lack of systematic patterns or trends provides support that the sample is not skewed for the major demographic variables examined. Out of 182 possible relationships based on family characteristic variables, only 10, just over 5%, were significant. This suggests that variables such as race, residence, the length of time one has been providing care, the caregiver-elder relationship, and caring for more than one elder have little if any direct effect on the provision of dependency tasks, the stress produced by performing these tasks, family stress, caregivers' and elders' use of control maintenance techniques, and overall feelings of burden.

There were 78 caregiver variables examined, with 8% (n = 6) of the relationships differing significantly. Of the 52 elder variables, 23% (n = 12) were significant. It does appear that the sex and age of the elder is highly predictive of the elder's level of dependency on the caregiver. In fact all but one of the significant differences observed were in the dependency categories.

Overall, out of 312 possible relationships, only 8% (n = 25) differed significantly as a result of a particular demographic characteristic. Given the nonrepresentativeness and small sample size, the relatively few differences in these variables provide a measure of confidence in the applicability of these findings to other families who are caring for an elderly parent in their homes.

The following chapter will focus on the issues of independence and dependency and the prevalence of specific dependency tasks. The processes involved in the decision to care for an elder in one's home as well as the delegation of the caregiving responsibility is discussed.

Note

1. In all, 15 families were caring for two elders, thus the residency of *elders* did differ somewhat from the percentages based on *families*. For elders there were 12.6% residing in a large city; 29.4% residing in suburban areas; 31.9% residing in small cities; 17.6% residing in rural areas; and approximately 9.6% of the sample could not be accurately classified.

5

IN THEIR BEST INTEREST:
TO CARE OR NOT TO CARE

I think that it can work. I wouldn't say don't do it or you'll be sorry or one of those things. I think you have to try and see what happens. It depends on a lot of things. If my mother were not financially able to take care of herself [in a nursing home], I guess we would have to manage. This is what happens to poor people, isn't it? They don't have the choices we do [#11—60-year-old daughter, who had been caring for her 84-year-old mother for 3 years].

This chapter will focus on the issues of independence and the loss of independence that the elderly face when they must live with and rely on their adult children to perform increasingly greater amounts of tasks for them. We will examine six specific categories of dependency, and the impact that these dependencies had on stress, feelings of burden, and the control maintenance techniques used by caregivers and elders.

Dependence Versus Independence

Probably the major loss to one's independence comes when one is no longer able to live independently and alternative arrangements for care are required. The impact of this most disruptive transition, for both the elderly parent and the adult child, produced considerable discussion and reflection during the interviews. Although many caregiving offspring justified their decision as the correct and best one for all family members, this was not necessarily the belief held by caregivers in other families that were interviewed.

In a society such as ours, maintaining one's independence is extremely important. Many elderly parents resented giving up their independence and went to great lengths to retain even the smallest indication of their ability to still provide help to others.

One caregiving daughter explained that it was very important for her mother to "play the piano at the nursing home, to entertain and play for the patients." Making the necessary arrangements so that her mother could feel needed was considered to be most important especially because her mother was beginning to evidence early signs of senility. This caregiver noted the impact that the mother's senility had on the family:

> My husband is bothered a lot by my mother asking the same questions over, and she knows the answers as she has been answered on the same question before. Mother appears to know more than she lets on [#115—52-year-old daughter, who had been caring for her 79-year-old mother for 9 years].

This is in direct contrast to the contribution of another mother who has maintained a high level of cognitive and physical functioning:

> My mother does all of my laundry. Every day I go to my closet and every single stitch of clothes I own and the children own are always in place. She takes this on as her job in the household. It has not been asked of her to do that, but she has always done that . . . it is not something that I expect her to do, but she feels this is a way of repaying us when she does that [#7—36-year-old daughter, who had been caring for her 65-year-old mother for four years].

Unfortunately, in other families, this need to retain some semblance of independence or autonomy resulted in a virtual tug-of-war between the caregiver and elder. The hardest part of caregiving was, according to one caregiver:

> Getting her to relinquishing the reins to me. Getting her to give up her dominance. She's a matriarch. She feels that the whole family should bow to her and give her all the support and all the attention. It is very difficult to get her to give that up—to allow me to take the full responsibility because I do everything anyway [#110/111—55-year-old daughter who has been caring for her 74-year-old mother, who has always lived with her; and an 89-year-old great aunt, who has lived with her for 5 years].

Elderly parents who were perceived to be excessively demanding and who always wanted to get their own way, perhaps in a final attempt to maintain control over a small part of one's environment, were a very disruptive element in many families. The exasperation experienced by the caregivers was considerable. As one daughter reported:

> Mother does her own cleaning and has no idea what her house looks like. She would be humiliated if she saw the accumulation of dust, crumbs, and this sort of thing, but I do not dare go in and do anything for her. She would get angry. I have offered and she will not accept help.

Interviewer: And she will not accept help from outside either?
Caregiver: Oh, no. That would be worse. Her house is too precious to let
               anyone in to do housework . . . Mother is fiercely independent
               and she is going to stay that way until she becomes blind or
               bedridden [#104/105—58-year-old daughter of an 88-year-old
               mother and 93-year-old father living in an adjoining home].

These comments illustrate the importance of one's home to an elderly
person. Having to move out of their homes and get rid of most furniture
and personal belongings representing a lifetime of memories is devastating. For some elderly, the need to assert their will in an attempt to be
master of their child's home is a direct outgrowth of their need to
attempt to fill the void resulting from this personal loss. Unfortunately,
these parents actions were a source of conflict. "She is the owner of my
house, the boss" noted one daughter.

It is her house simply because she is my mother . . . and it is hard to accept.
Our taste in decorations are different . . . she likes pretty dishes and every
inch of every table and every piece of furniture has to be covered with a
dish or a doodad of some kind and this bothers me tremendously. I'm
constantly irked by it. If I said "Mother my house is not geared to this
decoration. Your house was, but my house isn't and I don't like all of
this," I get tears and "I don't see why I can't have what I like just for this
little bit of time that I've got to live." She's quite an actress, she should
have been on the stage, there's no doubt about it [#31—a 58-year-old
daughter, who had been caring for her 82-year-old mother for 2½ years].

She has excessive demands and wants to do things her way and we want to
do them our way and it's hard. It is a conflict between her decision making
and the family's decision making. It's not that we don't want to do it; it is
just that we are under stress to do it. She still wants to be independent, yet
she still wants people to stop everything and do things for her "right
now" [#109—49-year-old daughter, who had been caring for her 80-year-
old mother for 14 years].

MAKING THE DECISION

As the parents grow older, their ability to care for themselves safely
became a constant source of worry for these adult children. The ever-
present danger of falling or becoming ill and having no one there to deal
with the crisis precipitated the move for several families.

One night she fell getting into bed and laid there all night until the next
morning when she dragged herself to a phone to call for help. I was away

that day and didn't call her, which I usually did every morning, and no one else bothered to call. Ever since that day we have not left her alone [#142—48-year-old daughter, who had been caring for her 83-year-old mother for two years].

I went to work one morning and she had gotten up to go to the bathroom and she had a stroke. They called me at work. My father had Parkinson's and was a little senile—we had to watch him. When she had her stroke, my husband said that there was no sense in me paying someone to come and stay with them . . . and they were not financially able to pay for it . . . their social security would not have paid for someone to come and stay with them. My husband said to quit work and stay home and tend to them. . . . After my father passed away, I told her that "I was going home and you are welcome to come live with me." [#44—51-year-old daughter, who had been caring for her 86-year-old mother for 7 years].

The decision to take an elder into the home in other families resulted from the elder's or caregiver's dissatisfaction with nursing homes.

I had her up at Rivertown Nursing home for a while. My nerves were affected and it was nice [to have her there for a while]. Then I was able to get her into Hillview, but I didn't feel that she was getting proper care so I took her out of there and kept her at home [#37—50-year-old daughter, who had been caring for her 72-year-old mother for 8 years].

Another family reported that they had

put mother in a nursing home for one month. My sister and I did not like it, and mother cried the whole time she was there, so we brought her home [#142—48-year-old daughter, who had been caring for her 83-year-old mother for 2 years].

Granting the final wish—the death-bed promise to provide care—is often the reason for this decision.

We promised our father before he died that we would do that [care for mother]. That was the last thing that our father asked us when he was dying. He was in the hospital 10 days before he died. He had a bad heart. My mother took care of him for 20 years. He wasn't always down in bed. The last thing my father asked was, "watch out for your mother." So you have to do that [#22—a 60-year-old daughter, who had been caring for her 80-year-old mother for 14 years].

The decision to have the caregiver and perhaps the caregiver's family move in with the elder was another alternative. This solution was used when the elder adamantly refused to move and yet was unable to live alone. This forced the caregiving family to relinquish furniture, decorations, and control over the home, as well as having to put up with constant reminders that they were guests in the elder's home. The reminders that this was the elder's home were used as a power chip. Elders frequently threatened to oust the caregiving family if their demands were not met.

It is possible that some elders did not fully understand the circumstances behind their child's decision to move in with them. For other elders, senility probably played a part. Nonetheless, the difficult decision that caregivers and their families made in order to prevent the trauma that would probably result if the elder were forced to move, was intensified when the elder interpreted this as invading his or her home, or as "evidence" that the adult child was not able to maintain a home.

It is also quite clear that these generationally inverse families are different from the families that Pillemer (1986) studied in which the adult offspring moved in with the elder because the offspring lacked the resources to live independently.

Who is designated "caregiver"? The decision to take an elderly parent into one's home is usually made during a crisis such as hospitalization, serious illness, or death of a spouse. Even when adult children acknowledge their parents' declining mental or physical status, there is a tendency to avoid taking action until the situation is defined as a crisis.

When caregivers were asked how the decision was made to take the elderly relative into their homes, their responses indicated that a considerable range of decision-making processes had been used. In some families one child, usually a daughter, was delegated. A caregiving daughter noted:

> I don't believe that there was ever any decision. It was automatically assumed that when my father died she should come and live with me because the daughter takes the mother . . . I guess that in many ways I just assumed this would happen [#33—56-year-old daughter, who had been caring for her 83-year-old mother for over 3 years].

Another caregiving daughter was delegated to care for her father because she did not work, was on social security, and, unlike her considerably younger sister, had no spouse or children to care for. This decision occurred when

> my father fell and hurt himself and they, the doctor and my sister, decided

that he shouldn't live alone anymore. He was delegated to me [#95—66-year-old daughter, who had been caring for her 86-year-old father for 4 years].

The above caregiver reported that her sister enjoyed dad's visits because the sister was much younger, in better health, and had a husband to help with the additional responsibility.

In another family, a daughter was selected because she was the last to leave home, therefore most familiar with the parent's needs, and was less likely to have established an independent life-style.

It was more my brother and sister who felt that physically she should be with us. First, we lived in a big city and when I got married, I was the last one to leave . . . she moved in . . . and she lived above my sister's [apartment] . . . then she became very sick and this is what brought it all on. She had been in and out of the hospital at my sister's and we had no idea what was wrong. She began to have these fainting spells and it turned out to be from her gall bladder. In a sense it was a medical problem. I had to spend so much time watching her that we thought it was better if she were here. But in the meantime she had come downstairs to live with my sister because of these fainting spells [#112—44-year-old daughter, who had been caring for her 77-year-old mother for 6 years].

Sharing the care. Sharing the care of the elderly parent appeared to be a workable solution in some families. However, in other families shared responsibilities were disturbing to both the elderly parent and the caregiving families. Being responsible for the elder, even when the level of responsibility is confined to part-time care, can be a drain, especially when this pattern exists over a number of years. The transfer of the responsibilities for an 84-year-old mother from one daughter's home to another after five months was described by the respondent:

Last weekend we drove her down to Lynchburg, Virginia to stay with my older sister for an indefinite length of time. It may turn out to be what we are doing is taking turns [#127—47-year-old daughter, who had been caring for her 84-year-old mother for 5 months].

This pattern seems to be similar to that which developed in another family:

We share mom half and half . . . I have her in the winter time for 3 months, but we change more often—six weeks or two months as a rule [#130—50-year-old daughter, who had been sharing the care of her 81-year-old mother for 7 years].

Still another daughter noted that her 96-year-old mother had lived with her for

> eight years for six months of the year, and the last year, all the time . . . She stayed . . . with my oldest sister for three months and came down to us for three months and went back and forth like that [#121—58-year-old daughter, who had been sharing the care of her 96-year-old mother for 5 years].

"That's the nice part, we all share my mother," stated another caregiver, who added:

> My two brothers, sister-in-law, and sisters all share her. She would spend two months at my sister's in Penn Acres, then a month with my brother in Swanwyck. We would visit around. My other sister has her now in Claymont, because I was in Ohio until the end of February. She is getting along good. I expect when the summer sets in, my husband should be done with his job, he will move back home, and we will all be together again [#22—60-year-old daughter, who had been sharing the care of her 80-year-old mother for 14 years].

In a bit of irony, the above caregiver later noted that her mother acts like a visitor rather than a permanent member of the family. One could certainly understand why the mother might feel this way. She really was a visitor—a welcome, loved, and cared for visitor—with no place really to call her own home.

After her husband, died one mother, although quite healthy and capable, began spending about six months a year with each of her daughters. After 15 years of this arrangement, the daughter noted:

> I think the [hardest part] is the emotional part. Just her being present in the house, an atmosphere. It takes me about a week to adjust to her when she comes back from my sisters. . . . I should have told her [15 years ago] to cope on her own. It would have been better for everyone. Mother doesn't do anything. She just sits around waiting for her death [#130—50-year-old daughter, who had been sharing the care of her 81-year-old mother with her sister for 15 years].

Both the caregiver and elderly parent in other families find that even short visits to another daughter's home were upsetting.

> I'm upset because mother is upset, apparently at my sister. Mother wants to come back to my house right way. I want to go and get her. My sister wants to take care of her and wants to share in her problems. It's almost

like having a child with me. I don't think anyone else can do quite as well with mamma as I can with her. I worry when she is away from me and I worry when she is with me . . . I am reluctant to let her go . . . In some ways it is easier when she's with me because I know how she's doing. Not knowing how she is doing is sometimes a bit harder [#4—56-year-old daughter, who had been caring for her 86-year-old mother for 4 months].

FINDING ALTERNATIVE CARE

Obviously when the costs become too high for the caregiving family, and they outweigh any rewards or benefits from providing this role, decisions regarding alternative housing need to be made. Although the reasons varied, these decisions were obviously painful. One daughter reported the reasons for seeking alternative care:

He started wandering. He got up at 2-3 o'clock in the morning, got dressed thinking he was going to a meeting. The morning that we took him to the hospital, that is before he went to the nursing home, his room was in shambles. He had overturned the TV. Somehow he must have fallen, because he had a slight gash on his forehead. He had opened a storm window that even my husband and I can't open with a lot of strength. He had taken things and wrapped them up, and put them in his wastebasket. We called the doctor and she said to bring him to the hospital. The ambulance took him. He was disoriented there . . . They said that he would require custodial care and advised us not to take him home . . . I did bring him home before Thanksgiving. He'd be sitting in the kitchen and would think that the dishwasher was moving. Or he would see animals. He started referring to my [deceased] mother; he had seen her . . . he could remember things 50-60 years ago, but he couldn't remember what happened the day before [#16—52-year-old daughter, who had been caring for her 89-year-old father for 14 years].

A mother in her mid-thirties with two grade-school aged children discussed the feelings of guilt associated with her decision not to bring mother to live with her after she was hospitalized. She noted that the hardest part was:

The emotional burdens of making the decision of whether or not to make the offer to have her live with us. The guilt I felt when I realized that I could not make that offer and I knew that she was expecting it and would be terribly hurt when I didn't. It did hurt her terribly.

Interviewer: Did you find that difficult to deal with?
Caregiver: Oh yes. Horrible, the worst daughter in the world. What kind of daughter am I that I will not take my poor sick old mother

into my home . . . compounded by the fact that one of my cousins offered to have her come and live with him. That made me feel even worse because a nephew is offering to do what I, as a daughter would not do.

Interviewer: Do you feel that you could have done more?

Caregiver: Yes . . . I could have had her come to live with us and devoted the [remaining] years of her life to her rather than to my family and myself [#30—38-year-old daughter, who had been caring for her 64-year-old mother for 6 months].

A clear conscience was listed as the rewards of caregiving for one daughter, who had been caring for her mother for 3 years:

My conscience is not bothering me . . . She expects to go into a nursing home. She would be there [already] if it weren't for us. She has a healthy mind . . . If she were physically unable we could put her in a nursing home. . . . You can do just so much [#131—52-year-old daughter, who had been caring for her 95-year-old mother for 3 years].

This respondent believed that a nursing home would be better able to care for a parent requiring extensive care, however other respondents wondered if they might provide better care than a nursing facility. One caregiver, whose mother is on a waiting list for a skilled nursing facility noted:

I have very mixed feelings about the nursing home. I don't know if I'm just telling myself that they can take care of her better than I can or whether they really can . . . am I reneging on my duty to not keep her at my house? [#4—60-year-old daughter, who had been caring for her 86-year-old mother for 4 months].

Another caregiver was more certain of her actions recognizing that her mother would have difficulty following the daughter's orders:

Caregiver: She thinks I am a little girl and not capable of doing things.

Interviewer: Would she rebel?

Caregiver: She wouldn't have any confidence in my being able to do anything. She would not cooperate at all [#37—50-year-old daughter, who had been caring for her 72-year-old mother for nearly 8 years].

In one family the mother and her husband had lived with her brother for 5 years. The mother became very depressed after her husband died.

She later developed emphysema and her condition deteriorated. The daughter noted that at this time her mother would not be able to live alone, but she also recognized that this was not the time to make permanent arrangements.

> It was clear that she could not live alone, but she could not go back to her brother's home, so she came to live with us on the basis of staying until she decided what was best. . . . In both her mind and ours it was a trial period . . . to see if it would work out. . . . It didn't, and after six months she moved into a retirement home . . . about two miles from our home [#30—38-year-old daughter, who had been caring for her 64-year-old mother for 6 months].

Not only is the decision to seek alternative care emotion-laden, finding suitable nursing facilities within the limits of one's insurance coverage is fraught with frustration. A caregiver employed by a large University-affiliated hospital, noting that she was probably more familiar with the type of services that might be available, still encountered numerous roadblocks.

> Because they said he required custodial care, there was no help whatsoever financially. It was very frustrating. I think I called about 30 people in the State of Delaware trying to get information. It was very frustrating. My husband and I both wound up resentful of some things . . . [My father's] social security was over the cut-off amount: He didn't have a suitable income as far as pension. In the nursing home, you knew that there were people there who were entitled to it . . . but you knew that there were people who never did a day's work in their life or cared about other people. Here was a man who did for others all his life and when it came his turn, and we tried to get some help, there was none.

> Interviewer: When you say you were bitter, were you bitter against the system?
> Caregiver: The system. Yes, resentful towards it [#16—52-year-old daughter, who had been caring for her 89-year-old father for 14 years].

Many families recognize that they will have to make this decision in the near future. Decisions regarding the care of one's dependent, elderly parents are often short-term arrangements and as an elder's physical or mental health deteriorates alternatives will have to be found.

> I think there are some [rewards]. I am taking care of her and I think that I

am doing a pretty good job keeping her cheerful. We get along. She is good company when she isn't depressed. My husband enjoys her. He loves her very much. Ordinarily we can laugh when she butters her napkin. She can laugh at us too. The rewards when she is not depressed are there. But there is a lot of worrying about what the future will bring [#4—60-year-old daughter, who had been caring for her 86-year-old mother for 4 months].

LEVEL OF DEPENDENCY TASKS

In order to assess the elder's level of dependence on his or her caregiving child, caregivers were asked how often they provided a variety of tasks that had been organized into six dependency categories. It was assumed that in order for the caregiver to provide these tasks, he or she recognized the elder's inability to perform these tasks. This assumption was supported during the interviews, when caregivers carefully outlined the tasks they *had* to provide for the elder versus those they did in return for a favor or just as a nice gesture.

Foulke (1980) in a preliminary analysis of a subsample of these data, described four stages of interdependency: Independence, when neither the parent or the adult child is dependent on the other, and they conduct their lives autonomously; reciprocal dependency, a stage characterized by aid flowing equally between the generations; asymmetrical dependency, the stage at which one generation, the elder in this study, is receiving more aid than he or she is providing; and survival dependency, the stage at which the elder is dependent on the adult child for all needs. The criteria for sample selection for this study eliminates families currently in the independent and reciprocal dependency stages. Although a number of caregivers, usually after becoming divorced or widowed, initially pooled their resources with their mothers to be able to enjoy a better standard of living, by the time of the interview, the elder was clearly dependent on the adult child for many of her needs.

Regardless of the current dependency stage, it is apparent from the interviews with the caregivers that most feel that over their lifetime the relationship with their parents has been characterized by a mutual sharing of resources. As one respondent noted:

I think that we learn a great deal from one another and the value of interdependence in all our relationships. Rather than dependence, it is interdependence. We learn to give and receive and sometimes I found in our relationships that it's more difficult for my parents to receive than it is for them to give because they've been extremely independent and the sense of pride really is uppermost in their minds. They don't want to become a burden to anyone [#38/39—54-year-old daughter, who had been caring for her 90-year-old mother and 88-year-old father for 11 years].

Although the tasks varied, elders in families in the asymmetrical dependency stage babysat, did light housekeeping or perhaps a special chore. In some families, the elder tried to do as much housework, cooking, or child care as possible in order to help the caregiver.

I would just tell her: "Mom, it is worth an immeasurable amount to me just to have you here. The boys come in from school and nothing could be more worthwhile than having you here and not having them come home to an empty house"[#43—57-year-old daughter, who had been caring for her 81-year-old mother for 14 years].

She likes to keep busy. I am a registered nurse and I work part time. It was ideal. She helped out and I kept working. I think she felt she had to help out [#151—46-year-old daughter, who had been caring for her 75-year-old mother, for 20 years].

I gave her two jobs to do and she pushed herself to do things, and a few days later she really was feeling bad and she felt that she *had* to do those things because I asked her and I wasn't home [#148—41-year-old daughter, who had been caring for her 71-year-old mother for 2½ years].

Often, families characterized as being in the asymmetrical or survival dependency stage, were performing numerous tasks "above and beyond the call of duty" in return for the elder's help to the family, for example, for having taken care of grandchildren, years earlier, while the mother worked. For some families, caring for another dependent person or watching another family member provide this care, served as anticipatory socialization for the role of caring for an elder. For example, several families that had a handicapped child noted that their mothers had helped with the care of this child. This provided them with a role model for the later care of an infirm elder as well as a recognition of the financial, emotional, and physical strain resulting from providing care. It also provided an opportunity for the caregiver and caregiving family to reciprocate for earlier assistance to the family.

As the following quotes indicate, there are life-long patterns of reciprocation of duties and tasks as well as mutual admiration between the generations:

My mother was very good to me when I had my children and when I needed her. She has been very good to my children and they have had the advantage of being close to their grandmother. . . . Some children never know their grandparents or they are strangers. She took care of them when we wanted to go away and they enjoyed her. She always helped me and now I can help her [#148—41-year-old daughter, who had been caring for her 71-year-old mother for 2½ years].

She moved in here to help with my son and help me . . . she wasn't feeling well at the time and about a year later she underwent an operation. . . . She's been very good to my son. She taught him a lot of things which I didn't have the time for because I went back to work . . . at first I began to substitute, and I was able to because she lived in the house. Every day she packs his lunch for him. She has some responsibilities. She really helps me out [#112—36-year-old daughter, who had been caring for her 77-year-old mother for 6 years].

She was a lot of comfort for the children. I have 10 children. They were living at home then too . . . she had been a school teacher [#150—58-year-old daughter, who had been providing care for her 88-year-old mother for 6 years].

My daughter has said that she is so thankful because her kids could be around an older person and learn something from an older person and be patient with them. She is my mother. She took care of a lot of old folks, her in-laws, stepmother, cousins, etc. Why shouldn't somebody do something for her? [#108—61-year-old daughter, who had been caring for her 93-year-old mother for 14 years].

The feeling of doing what I want to do, my duty to take care of her. I do feel that parents should be taken care of by their children, kind of a reverse cycle. Of course, it is not always great [#2—54-year-old daughter, who had been caring for her 87-year-old mother for almost 8 years].

The dependency tasks represented in this section were divided into six major categories: household, personal grooming/health, financial, mobility, social/ emotional, and mental health dependency, in order to examine the effect of elder's dependency. The sample was divided at the midpoint for each of the six categories, and the difference of means for family and dependency stress, burden, and the caregivers' and elders' CMT scores were computed.

There were some elders in each category who did not depend on the caregiver to provide these tasks. This should not be interpreted to mean that the elder did not *need* this task performed, but that the caregiver

Dependency Tasks

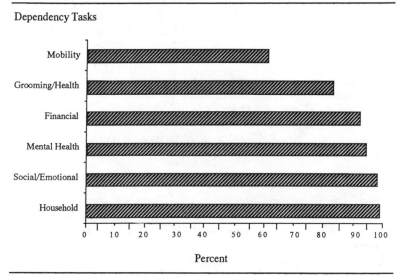

Figure 5.1 Dependency tasks, in percentages.

was not responsible for providing this task. Figure 5.1 presents the percentage of elderly requiring each type of dependency.[1]

HOUSEHOLD DEPENDENCY

There were seven items that comprised the household dependency score: Light housekeeping, heavy housekeeping, laundry, grocery shopping, cooking, provide transportation, and run errands; tasks that must be performed if an individual is to maintain an independent household.

The scores for household dependency could range from "0" (zero)—in which caregivers never provided any of the tasks (only one family did not have the caregiver providing *any* of the housekeeping tasks), to a score of "32." Six families reported that they provided all of the tasks at least some of the time. The mean score for the total household dependency scale was 22.4 and the midpoint was 24.5 suggesting that most elderly relied heavily on the caregivers for fulfilling their household dependency needs. (See Figure 5.1 for percentage of caregivers providing each dependency).

Light and heavy household chores seemed to predominate, although 84% of the caregivers noted at least one "other" chore that they provided.

In most families, at least during the initial stages of caregiving, elderly parents attempted to help with the household chores. In describing the reciprocation of tasks between her and her 68-year-old father-in-law, one caregiver noted:

> He is extremely helpful around the house. He does a lot of cooking . . . he is an excellent cook. It is just that he makes such a big production out of it. You have to adjust to his routine and his schedule and stay out of the kitchen and it has to be done his way. We do it primarily because he is so tickled to be helping [#133—44-year-old daughter-in-law, who had been providing care for her 68-year-old father-in-law for 1 year].

Other families represent the survival dependency stage. Such is the case of one 66-year-old daughter who described the level of care required by her 97-year-old mother for whom she has cared for 11 years as "I am completely her servant. Everything that gets done for her, I do it" (#90).

When the sample was divided at the midpoint into caregivers who provided high and low levels of household tasks, those who were characterized as providing high levels experienced significantly greater amounts of dependency stress and feelings of burden. No observable patterns in the caregiver's or elder's use of CMT were observed. However, elders experiencing higher levels of household dependency were significantly more likely to physically abuse the caregiver.

PERSONAL GROOMING/HEALTH

Seven items measured the degree of the elders' personal grooming/health dependency: help with bathing, dressing, hair care, doctor's orders, giving medication, bedding and diapering, and other. The scores ranged from a high of 66% of elders helping to carry out doctor's orders to a low of 34% who helped with bedding and diapering. The mean total personal grooming/health score was 10.91 and the midpoint was 8.0. The total scores could range from zero, a score obtained by 17% (n = 20) of the caregivers who did not provide any of the personal grooming/health tasks, to 28 points, a score obtained by 6 families.

Overall, 84% of the caregivers provided some assistance with personal grooming and health-related tasks. Helping the elder follow doctor's orders seemed to predominate with just under 66% of the elderly receiving this form of help.

Personal grooming. The concern one has for one's personal appearance and grooming is often an indication of one's emotional state and feelings of self-esteem. It is also a measure of the quality of care that a caregiver is providing for the elder. Therefore, caregivers took pride not only in their elderly parents' ability to attend to their own personal grooming needs, but also the caregivers' own ability to help their parents look presentable and feel comfortable.

One daughter who considered helping her mother maintain her sense of dignity and keeping her from becoming distraught to be extremely important, refrained from using diapers when her mother became incontinent

> because this is the last thing that she has got and that is something that she has a thing about . . . she doesn't like diapers. I either just wash the sheets or slip a bed pad under her which I don't mind doing. This is about as effective as diapers. We are trying to stay away from diapers so that we do not upset her [#103—43-year-old daughter-in-law, who had been caring for her 90-year-old mother-in-law for 7 years].

Although some caregivers had to make numerous accommodations in order to help their elderly parents maintain appearances and a sense of dignity, other caregivers marveled at their elderly mothers' (or mothers-in-law's) ability to keep up their appearance:

> She came to all our parties . . . she was more fun . . . we've always said that's what kept my mother going. Even at family parties where the old people were over here and the young people over there, my mother would never go and sit with the old people. She would sit with the young ones, talk, laugh, drink, and have a terrific time. You have to understand, this woman dyed her hair up until she was really ill. No one ever knew my mother had gray hair . . . the earrings had to be on, the lipstick had to be on, the hair had to be combed. She was a very young-looking woman. She didn't look a day over 60 [#26—50-year-old daughter, who had cared for her 87-year-old mother for nearly 15 years].

> It was a two way street—she helped us. When we were invited to dinner she was always included. She kept busy. She didn't just sit and expect to be waited on. That was the last thing in the world that she wanted. She was independent. She was remarkable. She helped with baking Scottish short bread. We did those things together. She was on a diet 26 years before she died and she managed to stay right with it. A little lady 5 feet tall and about 85 pounds who always wore youthful clothes [#92—60-year-old daughter, who had cared for her 92-year-old mother for 26 years].

Health needs. Difficulties in controlling the elder's emotional state was often a problem in these families. Explosive, demanding behavior, could be reflecting life-long patterns of behavior or personality changes resulting from illness (diabetes, stroke, hypertension). Doctors often treated these problems by prescribing tranquilizers. However, one family had to deal with loss of bladder control as a trade-off. The doctor had suggested giving medication because

> she was banging on the door to go out . . . It made her wet the bed every night. I couldn't take her emotional instability, but I couldn't take her physical problems either . . . I took her off the medicine [#143—46-year-old daughter, who had been caring for her 72-year-old mother for about one year].

The elder's disorientation caused another caregiver to suspend the medication.

> I have a prescription, that the doctor gave me . . . it is some kind of tranquilizer. I have tried it, twice . . . One time . . . he was at his wit's end . . . it had no effect on him. The next time it did help him go to sleep. But the next morning, he was so disoriented and so spaced out that I did not want to give it to him any more [#102—48-year-old daughter, who had been caring for her 82-year-old father for 3 years].

Probably the highest level of anger and frustration expressed by the caregivers revolved around the insensitivity of the medical profession and the red tape involved in obtaining services for a parent. The following quotes suggest that the doctors and nurses need to develop a greater sensitivity toward elderly patients:

> Hospitals and doctors write off the elderly. They literally write them off . . . I couldn't get anyone to help. It was really very frustrating. My attitude towards my mother was that she was 87 years old. Dammit, if she wanted a candy bar, let her have it. How do I know if she had two months, six months, or six years [#26—50-year-old daughter, who had been caring for her 87-year-old mother for nearly 15 years].

> It makes me angry that the doctor will not explain anything because he thinks that I wouldn't understand. Yet he expects me to care for her. I saw my husband through two major operations. The doctors explained everything and I understood. It really made me angry because she is my mother, one of my own, and if we are not going to help her, who is? [#101—34-year-old daughter, who had been caring for her 77-year-old mother for 2 months].

Another caregiver attributed this lack of concern for the plight of the elderly on the ageism of our society:

I got the feeling that even if this woman was a Ph.D. doing scientific research or any kind of research even in her own home and was contributing to the betterment of society, that they would still not have helped. The feeling was that how can anyone be of any use to anybody once they have reached 85 years old. In fact a nurse said to me, and I almost flattened her, "Well what are you going to do when the old person makes up his mind to die and they only have a few months?" The fact that I chose to have my mother under my roof worked against any kind of help that I could get for her . . . if I were to declare her destitute . . . say I can't have her, somebody would have come along and taken care of her—some agency. But the fact that I chose to do this for her in my own home worked against her. They were not interested [#26—50-year-old daughter, who had been caring for her 87-year-old mother for nearly 15 years].

When caregivers who provided high levels of personal grooming and health-related tasks were compared with those who provided lower levels, those providing high levels had significantly higher total dependency scores and dependency stress. The CMT scores for caregivers were similar between the two groups. For elders, no trends or patterns were observed and only one variable, elders' use of physical abuse among highly dependent elders, was significant.

FINANCIAL DEPENDENCY

Financial dependency was measured by five items and an "other" category. Most of the elderly in this study were not heavily dependent on their caregiver child for financial support. Scores could range from zero—no financial assistance was needed; to a score of 24: all financial assistance was provided by the caregiver. Only two elders needed to have total financial assistance from their caregivers, and 10 elders, about 8%, did not require any assistance. The midpoint for total financial dependency score was 9.5, and the mean score was 9.8.

Overall, 92% of the caregiving families provided help with at least one financial dependency task. Approximately 70% of the caregivers helped the elderly with writing checks or with managing resources, and over half reported that they paid for some essential items as well as for items they considered to be luxuries.

Some families noted that it would have been preferable to have the elderly parent remain in his or her own home with services provided as needed or to put them in a nursing home, but the cost was more than either the elder or their adult children could shoulder:

I wanted my mother-in-law put in a nursing home because of the care that she needed. In order to put her in a nursing home, my father-in-law would

TABLE 5.1
Relationship of Dependency Tasks to Stress, Burden and Control Maintenance Techniques: Significant Differences

	Household	Grooming/Health	Finance	Mobility	Mental Health	Social/Emotional
Dependency						
household	—	.0001	.0001	.0001	—	.003
grooming/health	.0001	—	.0001	.0001	.0001	.0001
financial	.0001	.0001	—	.05	.0001	.0001
mobility	.0001	.0001	.02	—	.02	.02
mental health	.0002	.0001	.0001	.02	—	.0001
social/emotional	.0001	.0001	.0001	.0001	.0001	—
total dependency	.0001	.0001	.0001		.0001	.0001
Stress						
family	—	—	—	—	.03	.006
dependency	.008	.004	.001	.05	.0001	.01
total stress	—	—	.008	—	.0001	—
Burden	.02	—	—	—	.002	—
Control Maintenance Techniques						
Caregiver						
talk	—	—	—	—	—	—
advice	—	—	—	—	.0001	—
yell	—	—	—	—	.0001	—
ignore	—	—	—	—	—	—
medical abuse	—	—	—	—	.001	—
threaten	—	—	—	—	—	—
physical abuse	—	—	—	—	—	—
Elder						
yell	—	—	—	—	.03	—
pout	—	—	—	—	.03	—
refuse food/medicine	—	—	—	—	.0001	—
cry	—	—	—	—	.0001	.03
hit	.04	.02	.006	—	.02	.02
manipulate	—	—	.05	—	—	.04
call police	—	—	—	—	—	—
invades privacy	—	—	—	—	—	—

have to pay $1,100 or whatever . . . He couldn't afford that [#45/46—45-year-old caregiver, who had been caring for her 86-year-old mother and 70-year-old mother-in-law both for about 3 months].

This caregiver did note, however, that her father-in-law probably "wouldn't have put her [his wife] in a nursing home whether he could have afforded it or not." Thus this caregiver was faced not only with providing the extensive care required for the mother-in-law, but also caring for the father-in-law.

Another caregiver suggested that her mother's ability to live independently was probably curtailed, in part, for financial reasons:

I'll let you have a copy of my harangue with the county when I told them that she can't afford to buy oil and that. She has enough money to live comfortably if she can live under my roof and I can pick up most of the expenses, which I'm already doing. So it's no burden. The alternative is the county can have her after two years because she'd be broke. She was spending $400 a month more than she was taking in. That doesn't last forever, does it? [#5—52-year-old daughter-in-law, who had been caring for her 74-year-old mother-in-law for 18 months].

Unfortunately the elderly parent's resources diminish and eventually run out, often at the time when the caregiver is also facing limited resources. The financial impact of long-term care is evident in the following account of the financial aspects of caregiving:

For the most part when she first came she had her own resources. But after 26 years they dwindled. She had a small monthly income and we tried to take care of her needs through the rest of the time she was here [#92—60-year-old daughter, who had cared for her 92-year-old mother for 26 years].

Although some caregivers, possibly because of their parents' financial resources, apparently did not consider it a problem to cover the additional expenses resulting from elderly kin living with them, others were not so fortunate. As the caregiver, usually a woman with limited means, observes her own resources dwindling, she realizes the impact of long-term financial responsibility. Not only are her elderly parents' resources shrinking, but as she assumes increasing financial responsibility for her parents she reduces her own resources. This hastens her entry into the next generation of impoverished women who will be forced to depend on their own children for financial support.

We can assume that when one 55-year-old caregiver took the full-time responsibility for her 86-year-old mother, she expected to be providing care for a relatively short time. Eleven years later, a 66-year-old caregiver, still providing care to her mother, who is now 97, finds that her own resources are depleted.

> I'm completely her servant, her support. She has her SSI which, if we put them together and are careful, we can get along. But we don't get clothes. But that is neither here nor there, it has nothing to do with my mother.... It bothers both of us that we. . . have only one bedroom. I sleep in the kitchen in the winter time. In the summer I sleep on the porch. It is a bother [#90—66-year-old daughter, who had been caring for her 97-year-old mother for 11 years].

Not only are there additional costs associated with caring for an elderly parent in one's home, but in many families it becomes necessary for the caregiver to leave paid employment in order to fulfill this caregiving role. The National Long-Term Care Survey of Caregivers (U.S. Department of Health and Human Services, 1982) revealed that 9% of the workers left the work force to care for an elderly person who required help with at least one activity of daily living (ADL). Furthermore:

> While less than 10% of the 2.2 million persons providing care to functionally impaired elderly relatives quit their jobs to care for someone, a sizable proportion of working female and male caregivers have had to rearrange schedules (29%), reduce work hours (21%), and/or take time off without pay (19%) to fulfill caregiver obligations [U.S.Department of Labor, Women's Bureau, 1986: 2].

This loss of income is tersely noted by a caregiving daughter:

> Let's face it. We don't have what we would have had, because he [the husband] doesn't make much money. I was a ward clerk in the hospital and had a good job [#44—51-year-old daughter, who had been caring for her 86-year-old mother for 7 years].

However, in other families, the elder's financial contribution to household expenses enabled the caregiver to stay home and provide care.

> We are making do, you know. I will say that if I didn't have the help from him, like board money, then I would be out working because there is no

way that we could make our house payments and buy the groceries and all without his check [#102—48-year-old daughter, who had been caring for her 82-year-old father for 3 years].

She gives me $150 per month. When you stop to think about it, that's not very much, but it is a help. With her not being senile we can discuss financial matters. As long as we could make it without us using our savings, I would do it. If we had to use our savings, she would have to start paying me more than what she is now [#44—51-year-old daughter, who had been caring for her 86-year-old mother for 7 years].

For employed women, who make about 60 cents for every dollar earned by men, or women living on social security, the financial burden can present considerable worry and stress.

Many elderly really seem to believe that their offspring owe them everything. Others believe that by not contributing to the cost of their care, they will be able to accumulate money. This money will enable them to maintain some control and power over the caregiver. The threat that the caregiver will be disinherited is the elder's way of attempting to assure compliance from the caregiver.

Although research on the black matriarchal families would seem to support closer mother-daughter sharing of resources, this research did not find any race-based differences. A comparison of the next two quotes—the first from a black daughter, the second from a white daughter—indicate that this sharing of resources appears to be an individual, personality-based response rather than an ethnic- or culture-bound tradition.

At first she would get her social security check in her name. She wouldn't contribute anything towards the household . . . no money to help buy food and everything. The social security man came and asked me how much she was giving me for board and everything [for tax purposes]. I had to tell him the truth—that she wasn't giving me anything. He asked her why, and she said "She is my child and I don't feel like I should give her anything." So he said, "That is why you are getting the check—it is because you have to pay so much for your board and food for your cost of living." Still she wouldn't give it to me. The next year he came back and wanted me to show him a receipt that she had been giving me money. I told him that I don't have one because she hasn't given me any. He put her name and my name on the check and made me sign a paper stating that I will take so much money each month out of her check towards living expenses. I signed the paper and she gave me hell about it [#98—58-year-old daughter, who had been caring for her 93-year-old mother for 8 years].

My mother won't share in paying the bills although she has money. I've had to rent two rooms out . . . simply because I couldn't make ends meet. This, of course, means less privacy for me, not for her, because she's on the other floor. Her privacy isn't bothered at all . . . for me this represents another sacrifice . . . Her social security check almost amounts to one of my pays. She cashes that check and runs right to the bank and justifies that by saying "When I'm gone, you're going to get it." I'm going to get one-fourth of it after the government comes in and takes its share. There are three brothers who are going to get some. It might seem small to even talk about it, but it is a consideration. One brother is an engineer and makes a fabulous salary, but she doesn't expect them to do anything. Yet they are going to inherit the same as I do [#31—58-year-old daughter, who had been caring for her 82-year-old mother for 2½ years].

When the sample was divided into caregivers who provided high and low levels of help with financial tasks for their elders, caregivers performing higher amounts of financial tasks experienced significantly higher levels of dependency stress and total stress. No differences were observed between the two groups for the caregivers' use of CMT; however, highly dependent elders used significantly greater amounts of physical abuse and manipulation to gain control.

MOBILITY DEPENDENCY

The sample as a whole was fairly mobile. In all, 39% of the caregivers reported that they did not have to help with any mobility tasks. Very few of the caregivers needed extended help with mobility problems. This might reflect the decision on the part of caregivers to seek alternatives when the elder's mobility becomes a major problem.

Some 55% of the elders needed some help with walking; however, only 42%, 33%, and 27%, respectively, needed help with stairs, getting in and out of a chair or in and out of a bed. The total mobility scores had a potential range of zero—39% of the sample (n = 46) reported no mobility dependency—to 16—a score received by 5% (n = 6) of the families. The midpoint was 2.0 and the mean score for all mobility dependencies was 4.06.

Loss of mobility was usually not mentioned as a major problem. In fact, most caregivers marveled at the elder's ability to get around.

Mother was involved in all family events. She went to our daughter's college graduation in a wheelchair, and she saw my son through graduate school and went to the wedding with a nurse at her side, and was part of the family. She was never isolated or sent to her room or any of these things—she was mother! [#92—60-year-old daughter, who had been caring for her 92-year-old mother for 26 years].

Nonetheless, the fear of falling and the likelihood of the elder becoming immobilized as a result was not overlooked by the caregivers. One respondent reported that her 80-year-old mother now walks with a walker, and needs help with a surgical girdle.

She wasn't here very long when she fell. She fell on my front lawn. It was a day she shouldn't have been out there. She went out to pick up the newspaper. It wasn't a bad fall, it was more like a slip. She had her bedroom slippers on, she stepped out on a slippery step and twisted her back. That did it; she fractured a disk [#22—60-year-old daughter, who had been caring for her 80-year-old mother for 14 years].

This daughter commented that during the last two years, mother needed constant care and that she had to request help from the police two or three times to help pick her mother up and put in bed after she had fallen. A fall is considered to be particularly hazardous because even a minor fall often results in hospitalization.

When she fell and broke her hip about two and one half years ago, and in January of this year, she fell and tore a ligament in her leg and was in considerable pain . . . She lost her balance on the way to the bathroom [#113—59-year-old daughter, who had been caring for her 78-year-old mother for 6 years].

Caregivers who are characterized as providing high levels of help with mobility experienced significantly higher levels of dependency stress. Although caregivers in the "high" category tend to have higher CMT scores for most all forms of interaction, these differences were not significant. The elders' CMT scores revealed no difference between the two groups.

SOCIAL/EMOTIONAL DEPENDENCY

This dependency taps the area of social life and emotional support. Taking the elder visiting, helping them make phone calls, write letters, reading to them, helping them to develop friendships and providing a social life for them were items in this index.

Overall, 98% of the caregivers reported that they provided some social/emotional support, and 87% felt that they were responsible for at least some of the elder's social life. Over half of this group, 52%, reported that they provided *all* of the elder's social life. Even when the elder was quite capable of going to a senior center or engaging in other activities, many did not want to take part in these activities.

The impact of having to provide for the elder's social life is two-fold. First, a considerable amount of time and energy is spent "entertaining" the elder, since the total responsibility falls on the caregiver and his or her family. Second, opportunities for the caregiver to have a social life separate from the elder are almost nonexistent. This becomes further intensified when there is no spouse or children to share the burden. The following quote, provided by a daughter who had been caring for her 97-year-old mother, clearly illustrates the bind that these caregivers experience.

> If I wanted to go anywhere, I would have to get a sitter. I never leave her alone, never. She is very frightened to be left alone at night. I have no social life of my own. Sometimes it bothers me. There is no place for a woman my age to go, anyway. I do have a few friends that I could or might go see. She is afraid to be left alone at night. I do sometimes leave her alone to go to the market. I make her promise not to go anywhere near the stove. She never does, she is a sensible woman, so far [#90—66-year-old daughter, who had been caring for her 97-year-old mother for 11 years].

In all, 74% of the caregivers arranged to have company visit or to take the elders visiting, and 68% encouraged them to develop friendships with people outside the immediate family. Only about 29% read to the elders, but 40% helped them write letters, and 64% helped them make phone calls.

Total social/emotional dependency scores had a potential range from zero (two families reported that they did not provided *any* social emotional tasks for the elder) to 32. The highest score obtained was 30, and only one caregiver reported this level of social/emotional dependency. The midpoint was 13.5 and the mean was 14.4. It appears from the frequency distribution that families' social/emotional dependency scores were distributed on a bell-shaped continuum with few elders exhibiting little or no social/emotional dependency and, likewise, few exhibiting extremely high levels of dependency.

Privacy. It is interesting to note that although the issue of privacy was often noted as a *major* disrupting factor, this variable was not correlated with emotional support. As will be discussed in the next chapter, many of these social/emotional dependency tasks were considered to be extremely stressful.

Elders who had been in a similar caregiving role recognized the need for privacy and family intimacy. These elders took special care to see that the husband and wife had the opportunity to be alone.

My mother had her sister living with us for 30 years. She kind of knows what it is like. So she tries to go to bed about 9 o'clock. She goes to her room, and if we ask her to come downstairs, she will [#148—46-year-old daughter, who had been caring for her 84-year-old mother for 2½ years].

The above families are fortunate. They have not experienced the fairly common problems noted in the following quotes:

Lack of freedom. You can no longer function as a family or do things together as a family because there is one more person to think of [#101—46-year-old daughter, who had been caring for her 77-year-old mother for 2 months].

She always wanted her bedroom door open and didn't want us to have any privacy. She was always there—even when we drove into the garage, she would be watching us from the door [#122—53-year-old daughter-in-law, who had been caring for her 84-year-old mother-in-law for 16 years].

He wants us to live our life and do whatever we want to do, but you can't just pick up and run uptown when you want to unless we can have someone here. The children have been helpful in staying with him [#102—48-year-old daughter, who had been caring for her 82-year-old father for 3 years].

Emotional support. The need to emotionally support the elder, through communication, listening to and attempting to help them solve social problems, and dealing with loneliness was difficult for many caregivers. A daughter suggested that she was trying to provide emotional support:

I'm trying to communicate with her and get through to her. I'm trying to keep her emotionally stable. It isn't easy when you get no response. It gets very discouraging. Sometimes she doesn't answer. She nods sometimes, which is the beginning of recognition—she knows it's me. That is the hardest thing to take emotionally. I asked about bringing in a therapist, but the doctor said that they were doing some [therapy] and it wouldn't do any good. He did not expect any progress. If she does start to form words, then I understand that there may be a therapist available through public health. Even before the stroke she always asked me to do everything for her [#101—46-year-old daughter, who had been caring for her 77-year-old mother for 2 months)

The items "lonely" and "demanding" were moderately and significantly correlated with emotional support (r = .23 and .24 respectively). It seems clear that emotional support involved a complex of tasks that are necessary in order to fulfill a wide range of needs. In some families emotional support was seen as trying to be everything to the elder.

Particularly distressing to caregivers was the recognition that the elderly parent was lonely. Longevity is not necessarily a blessing when you outlive your parents, your siblings, and your own children. Having to leave your home, friends, and neighborhood, all that is friendly and familiar—reduces the ability or even desire to reach out to make friends or even accept friendship that is offered. The caregiving family becomes the only source of human interaction.

In explaining her mother's loneliness, one daughter recounted the following recent deaths among close family members:

She is lonely. My husband, my sister's husband, my sister, and two of my brothers, and one of her [my mother's] brothers have all died. She says she doesn't want to live to see her children all dead. I can understand that (#90—66-year-old daughter, who had been caring for her 97-year-old mother for 11 years].

Describing the loneliness of her 84-year-old mother, another caregiver expressed helplessness. She recognized that her family had tried to relieve the elder's loneliness, but that there really wasn't any solution to the problem.

I guess it bothers me that she is lonely, but there is the practical side; all of her friends are gone. It bothers me but I can't do anything about it. There is no way to solve the problem. We try to be around as much as possible. It bothers me that she's lonely. Part of this, though, is the result of the illness. She can't help that she can't make new friends, and the old ones are all gone. We just feel real, real sorry for her, but don't know what to do. What do you do when someone is incapable of participating. You can be as loving and friendly with her, but she cannot do that to anybody else. It's almost like a self-imposed social isolation [#11—60-year-old daughter, who had been caring for her 84-year-old mother for 3 years].

Social life. Trying to provide a social life for the elder was considered to be time consuming and frustrating, especially when these attempts were resented. During an interview in which both the husband and wife participated, the husband noted the loss of social life encountered when the elder moved 100 miles to live with the daughter:

I try to have her call her friends. With me, she is away from so many friends. My wife and I have taken her back to visit . . . she is very reluctant [to be] with strangers and everybody in our area is strange to her [#4—60-year-old husband and wife, who had been caring for the wife's 86-year-old mother for 4 months].

When the interviewer asked another caregiver about her attempts to encourage her mother to make new friends in the area or perhaps have a minister visit, the daughter responded:

That was impossible. My mother was a first-generation Italian-American, and you don't do that. When my mother had her own home and I was a child, she discouraged this. Nobody ever dropped in on my mother. . . . No way, she was not a social person [#26—50-year-old daughter, who had been caring for her 87-year-old mother for 15 years].

Working in the field of gerontology is no guarantee that this expertise can be applied to one's own situation. A director of a senior center program commented on her inability to get her mother-in-law to participate in center activities:

I would try to shame her into going. She would say "I do not enjoy those old people—they have nothing to give me and I would prefer my TV and my reading and you and Roger and what goes on here. I never once got her to set foot in a senior center—she did not enjoy old people [#43—57-year-old daughter-in-law, who had been caring for her 81-year-old mother-in-law for 14 years].

Although their teenagers no longer need a baby sitter, one caregiving daughter remarked that when she and her husband go out we "now have to have a baby sitter for my mother . . . it is a burden" (#143—46-year-old daughter, who had been caring for her 72-year-old mother for about one year).

For many of these elders, the caregiver and caregiving family represent the total social life and, in some cases, the only human contact the elder has. This places a tremendous burden on these caregivers. A 38-year-old caregiver, who had been caring for her 64-year-old mother for just 6 months, when asked how much social support she provided for her mother, responded "About 110%" (#30).

Another responded that her mother feels that she could do more:

Mother feels that I should talk to her more and spend more time with her, read to her, and write more for her. She does not need me in the house all the time although she did when she first came here. Now, if we leave for a while, she is content and comfortable to have the whole house to herself. Part of my burden is that I really don't have the house to myself. My children are in college, but they live at home. We constantly have people in the house [#109—49-year-old daughter, who had been caring for her 80-year-old mother for nearly 13 years].

Most caregivers tried to set aside some private time to spend alone with the elder. This appeared to be very important for the elder:

I move a living room chair into the kitchen so that when I got home at night she could sit in the kitchen and talk to me while I got supper. She and I had an hour or so just to chitchat—while everyone else was still doing something. That was her social life [#143—46-year-old daughter, who had been caring for her 72-year-old mother for about one year].

I give her coffee in bed in the morning. She gets up for it. I bring her coffee before I go to work and we chat. If she complains, I try to listen to her and comfort her. Sometimes she starts crying and it is not all that easy [#2—54-year-old daughter, who had been caring for her 87-year-old mother for nearly 8 years].

This caregiver went on to discuss how pleased her mother was that the minister came, "She was in her glory because he came and visited." The daughter noted that "he came under sadder circumstances, my husband had just passed away."

This theme was evident in several other interviews—the caregiver is not able to grieve for the loss of a spouse or child because all of his or her energy must be devoted to keeping the elderly parent stable. These caregivers feared that if they showed any indication of grieving or emotional upset, this would be extremely detrimental to the emotional and physical health of the elderly parent. If this happened they would have to pay the price in terms of the additional care that would be required. For these caregivers, suppressing their own grief was the easiest path to take.

With all the best intentions, it was still not possible for the caregivers to meet all the demands and needs of their elderly parents. In a somewhat humorous vein, one caregiver said:

I could probably give more, emotionally, than I do. I could give more moral support than I do. A little devil inside of me keeps saying, "Don't do another thing, I've had it" [#110-111—55-year-old daughter, who had been caring for her 74-year-old mother for 55 years and 89-year-old great aunt for 5 years].

Unfortunately, when competing needs arose, such as another family member's illness or the need to provide temporary care of another kin, the elder interpreted this as a withdrawing of care, love, and support. For example, a three-month visit from the caregiver's granddaughter brought on bouts of jealousy from the elderly mother in one family.

[Debbie] stayed for three months until she got a job and her own apartment. Mother was jealous of her and made it miserable . . . She made her feel like an intruder . . . I didn't know what to do. Debbie was something nice in my life, it gave me a life [#31—58-year-old daughter, who had been caring for her 82-year-old mother for 2½ years].

Since providing emotional support to the elder was reported by over 95% of the sample, it is obvious that fulfilling this dependency need had a major impact on most of the caregivers and their families. Caregivers who provided high amounts of social/emotional support for the elderly experienced significantly greater amounts of dependency and total stress than did caregivers providing lower amounts of social/emotional tasks. No difference in scores were observed for the caregivers' use of CMT; however, elders who required higher levels of social/emotional support used significantly higher amounts of physical abuse, crying, and manipulation, than those elders who required lower amounts.

MENTAL HEALTH DEPENDENCY

Mental health dependency focused on the mental state of the elder and the behavior resulting from mental/emotional problems. This index contained such items as helping the elder with decision making as well as items that attempt to ascertain nonrational or explosive behavior.

Mental health tasks are provided for about 94% of the elders (see Figure 5.1). Some 85% of caregivers reported problems resulting from the elder's loss of memory. Over three-fourths of the caregivers stated that they had to assume at least some of the decision making; 30% reported that they helped with all decision making. In all, 55% of the caregivers reported explosive behaviors such as verbal or physical violence, and 41% reported nonrational behavior such as paranoia or uncontrolled imagination. Over half (52%) had to watch the elder, and one-third of the caregivers reported that the elder "got lost." This reflects the degree to which caregivers need to control the environment in order to protect the elder.

Total mental health dependency scores could range from zero (seven families obtained this score) to 28 points. No family reported the highest score; however, three families had scores of 24. The midpoint and mean of the total mental health dependency index were 7.5 and 9.17 respectively. Only 6% of the caregivers (n = 7) did not provide any mental health tasks.

Decision making. In a regressive developmental sense, the caregiver/ elder interaction resembles the way parents often attempt to help children make decisions at different developmental stages. Some caregivers considered it to be very important to encourage and even insisted that their elderly parent continue to make decisions regarding their responsibilities as long as possible. In a manner similar to parents telling adult children—"it's your decision, you have to live with it."

> Generally, when she is adamant about something, we tell her that it is her decision to make. She is an adult and we know that she is alert and in her right mind. It is her responsibility.

> Interviewer: It sounds like you let her make her own decisions.
> Caregiver: Yes, that is very important that in her stage she has something left [#103—43-year-old daughter-in-law, who had been caring for her 90-year-old mother-in-law for 7 years].

For other families, the decision-making process required only some guidance from the caregivers, reminiscent of the techniques parents use with older teens:

> We plant the seed of the decision and then step back. Then within an hour or sometimes in a couple of days they would have thought of a way to do it. Then they consider it to be their idea, not something that my husband or I suggested [#104/105—58-year-old daughter, who had been caring for her 88-year-old mother and 93-year-old father for 2½ years].

There were also caregivers who had to override the decision made by an elder because it was not in his or her best interest. In these circumstances making the decision, or changing the decision that an elder made is considered to be the lesser of the two evils.

> Sometimes I have to intervene when I think her decision is not good for her and is really going to be hard on me. Sometimes she doesn't realize how it will effect me. When she moved in with us, she really didn't want to.

However, I know that from her living alone for one month that it was going to be very hard on me. She was calling me up every day and I had a son, 6, and a daughter, 2, and I work all day, every day. She would forget to tell me this and that. We finally had to say, "It's not going to work living alone. I think you should live with us or my brother," and so she did [#137—30-year-old granddaughter, whose parents recently died, and, who had been caring for her 82-year-old grandmother for over 1 year].

The concern over denying parents their rights as individuals in an effort to protect them from harm, was raised in several interviews. At what point do we have the *right* to override another adult's wishes— even if we know we are right—"mother knows best"? At what point should we disregard the parent's feelings because, in *our* best judgment we feel we know what is best for this elder? Do we have the right to insist, and to obtain whatever "legal" backing is necessary to move an elder out of his or her home because the eyesight is failing or negotiating the steps is problematic, even though the elder's mind is fairly alert and he or she has adamantly insisted on staying in familiar surroundings? Finally, when are decisions being made on the basis of the adult child's best interest, to avoid feelings of guilt, rather than on the basis of the elderly adult's need to maintain his or her independence (even if some risks are involved)?

Finally, the day comes when caregivers recognize that they will probably be responsible for making all decisions regarding the care, maintenance, and handling of personal property for their parent:

It is difficult because I suddenly find myself having to make decisions for another person, decisions that will affect her life drastically. There are times, I realize, that it is necessary, but I feel it is almost unfair that I should have this burden . . . I now feel responsible for everything that happens to her. If she is unhappy in a nursing home, it is a decision I made . . . I question, "Am I doing the right thing?" [#5—52-year-old son caring for his 74-year-old mother for 1½ years].

I have reached the point and I have told the Pastor, my sisters, my children, my nieces, [and] . . . my father . . . I am not going to make an issue out of this . . . I am not going to make an issue out of her health problems. I'm not going to push her to go to see a doctor. I will wait, and when the time comes that she asks for help or finds herself in a position where she no longer controls things . . . where she can no longer say "I won't go," then I will take the necessary steps of getting medical attention for her. If she requests it, I will immediately take steps [#104/105—58-year-old daughter who has been caring for her 88-year-old mother and 93-year-old father for 2½ years].

Senility. Probably one of the more difficult aspects of caregiving occurs when the elder begins to show signs of senility. In some cases it is the forgetfulness of the elder that makes caregiving akin to caring for the "terrible two"—who has conquered mobility skills but lacks the cognitive capabilities to assure his or her safety.

While playpens and cribs are appropriate for confining a 2-year-old, tying an elder into bed or locking the elder in his or her room is considered to be inappropriate. Thus the senile but mobile elder must be watched 24 hours a day. This is further complicated by the catnapping in which sleep occurs in two- to three-hour segments around the clock. A full night's sleep for these elders, unless medicated, is unusual. Likewise, a full night's sleep for the caregiver is also unusual. The impact on the caregiver of this prolonged sleep deprivation is obvious:

> He has his own bedroom. I have a bedroom too, but I never get to sleep in it. If I sleep upstairs in my room, I'm afraid that he will fall and I won't hear him. Therefore, I sleep downstairs on the couch . . . I have [done this] ever since he has been here. I don't think I have slept in a bed a dozen times since he has been here. He does prowl a lot at night. He is up getting a drink of water and going to the bathroom and getting a little bit of cereal and back and forth. I've had to try and learn to block that noise out at night because it is just a constant thing. Up and down, up and down. He must get a drink a half dozen times at night . . . go to the bathroom. He sleeps so much during the day time . . . I guess this is what old people do as a result of sleeping all day or so much of the day. I guess I haven't really had a good night's sleep since he has been here [#95—66-year-old daughter, who had been caring for her 86-year-old father for 4 years].

The most difficult part of providing care for one respondent was

> not being able to sleep . . . Your whole routine, your whole life is upset. Your whole life is not your own is the best way to put it [#45/46—45-year-old daughter, who had been caring for her 80-year-old mother and 71-year-old mother-in-law both for 3 months].

The impact of being responsible for the 24-hour care of her 71-year-old mother-in-law who was suffering with severe bed sores was noted:

> The bed sores were out of this world. We had to change those dressings every hour. I don't mean when 11 o'clock came at night we didn't change them the rest of the night. It was continued through the night. Trying to get her to eat was also an hourly task [#45/46].

Forgetfulness, often with the threat of accident, such as wandering into the streets, turning on and forgetting the stove, smoking and forgetting where one left the lit cigarette, was a constant source of concern. Unfortunately, reminding the elder to do, or not do certain things produced anger.

I took her to the podiatrist once when she was here. She wouldn't tell the podiatrist how old she was. She got furious at the nurse for asking. "All you have to know is that I am over 60. You don't have to know anything else. The nurse kept saying, "Mrs. Brown, I need to know." Rationally there really was no reason why the woman needed to know how old she was. Mother had Medicare, she was a one-time visitor. What was the purpose except that it was a place on the form and the nurse always had people tell her how old they were. Well, the issue was that mother does not remember how old she is. Rather than say, I don't know how old I am, she got furious at the nurse for asking.

Interviewer: Do you feel that she must be watched or confined most of the time?
Caregiver: She must be protected [#6—40-year-old caregiver, who had been caring for her 68-year-old mother for 3 months].

One 93-year-old mother, after losing three of her children and seeing her grandson paralyzed while in the Marines, was rapidly becoming senile. The caregiving daughter related a frightening incident that occurred while everyone was in bed:

She wandered out of here—and it was cold—with nothing but bedroom shoes on. No coat or housecoat—no hat . . . so many times I had to call the police to find her . . . locking the doors didn't do any good [#98—58-year-old daughter, who had been caring for her 93-year-old mother for 8 years].

Imagining things or paranoia is another complaint frequently mentioned by caregivers. This aspect of the aging process not only causes distress for caregivers, but burdens social service and protective service agencies as they try to disentangle cases of actual abuse from the imagined threats "experienced" by elderly individuals with mental deterioration. Some examples provided by respondents are enlightening:

I have noticed that when I go out—which I seldom do, that there is always someone breaking in or trying to break in. No one ever breaks in while I'm home, and I think that he is afraid. I curtail my activities. It isn't worth the hassle [#95—66-year-old daughter, who had been caring for her 86-year-old father for 4 years].

One day she called us up and said that she had been shot. Several times, in the middle of the night she would come in our bedroom and she would want to know why or where her [dead] sister Helen was now. [#127—47-year-old daughter, who had been caring for her 84-year-old mother for 5 months].

She felt the cousin was taking her things . . . My mother lost her ring and she still thinks her cousin took it . . . She would put her name on everything [#11—60-year-old daughter, who had been caring for her 84-year-old mother for 3 years].

In other families, there are indications that this behavior is simply a continuation of earlier patterns of interaction complicated by the limitation imposed by a restricted social environment and the freedom to go where one wants and when one wants.

Interviewer: Do you sometimes feel that having your mother in the house gives you a sense of burden?

Caregiver: Yes, it does in different kind of way. She gave up her home, although that was something that happened long before she moved in with us. She can't pick up and go, she just can't. I feel bad that she has no way to get to anyone else, even though she resists that. She has always resisted friendships. She is very suspicious and paranoid. She always feels people are coming to get you. They are stealing things. They are walking on your property . . . it is not that she is so much work for me; not that kind of burden. More, the burden is that she needs more and I'm not capable of seeing to it that she gets it. Maybe I don't do enough for her [#7—36-year-old daughter, who had been caring for her 65-year-old mother for 2 years].

Caregivers categorized as providing high levels of mental health-related support experienced significantly greater amounts of family, dependency, and total stress than did caregivers who provided lower levels of support. A significantly greater number of the "high" group also reported feeling burdened by this responsibility, and were more likely to seek advice, to use verbal abuse, and to force the elder to eat or take medicine. Elders requiring more mental-health support used significantly greater amounts of pouting, refusing to eat or take medicine, physical abuse, crying, and manipulation. These elders appeared to be most disruptive and their caregivers were considerably more likely to experience stress and feelings of being burdened.

Summary

In summarizing the dependency levels of the elderly in this sample, one must remember that these are the levels at one point in time—a snapshot examination of family dynamics. However, as discussed in the previous chapter, the length of time an elder has been dependent on the caregiver in these generationally inverse families does not predict the level of dependency. Except for comparisons between the "youngest" elderly and those making up the "oldest" group, few differences were observed.

The total dependency scores, which was the sum of each of the six dependency scores, could range from zero to 164. No caregiver received a zero, the lowest score, however, a score of 14, was obtained by two caregivers. One caregiver received a score of 132, and 39% of the sample had scores of 82 or higher on a scale in which both the mean and midpoint were 70.

The total dependency score for each of the six categories was significantly correlated with the other five dependency measures and dependency stress. This is consistent with Reece et al. (1983) who noted that caregivers with the highest level of task involvement were more likely to report negative effects of caregiving on themselves and their families.

However, except for mental health dependency, no relationships appeared between the level of dependency and the elder's use of control maintenance techniques. Caregivers reporting high levels of mental health dependency used significantly greater amounts of levels of advice seeking and verbal and medical abuse. Elders in these families used significantly higher levels of pouting, refusing to eat or take medicine, crying, physical violence, and manipulation.

Of the 90 possible relationships between the dependencies and CMTs for caregivers and elders, only 17% (n = 15) differed significantly. It appears that being required to perform high levels of dependency tasks for the elder is not significantly related to the caregiver's use of verbal, psychological, or physical abuse. This finding is particularly interesting since caregivers who provided high levels of one category of dependency were significantly more likely to score high on other types of dependencies; and the elders in this group were significantly more likely to resort to physical abuse in an attempt to maintain control.

In the next chapter, it will be demonstrated that there are considerable differences between the level of task performance and the caregiver's perception of the stress resulting from this task performance. The level of dependency and the ability of the family to provide quality care must be balanced by the cost to the caregiver and caregiving family. The fragile nature of these caregiving arrangements is acknowledged in the following quote.

> I know that we may come to a point where I will feel that I am pretty much tied down here because of this, but I think it's a time in my life where I really owe it to her. If she really got to a point where I couldn't take care of her, then we would have to make other arrangements, but it would be a last resort [#3—56-year-old daughter, who had been caring for her 82-year-old mother for 3 years].

In the following chapter, we will examine the caregiver's perception of stress and burden. Caregivers who perceive performing dependency tasks or dealing with certain problems to be stressful will be compared to nonstressed caregivers, in order to examine differences in family and dependency stress, overall levels of dependency, and the control maintenance techniques used by caregivers and elders.

Note

1. Table 5.1 presents the probability levels for statistically significant differences between caregivers in high and low dependency categories. As in the previous chapter, the scores for specific variables can be found in Table C.2 in Appendix C.

6

IS IT WORTH THE EFFORT?
THE IMPACT OF STRESS ON
CAREGIVERS AND THEIR FAMILIES

DON'T DO IT, DON'T EVER, EVER DO IT! Do whatever you can.
You can give them so much more of yourself when you go to visit them if
they are not living with you. It is so easy to be loving and to carry them to
the doctor's office when they don't live with you . . . I could give her more
moral support and a lot more loving attention if I didn't have to physically
care for her . . . I could go get her and say "Oh your hair is so pretty and
let's go here and let's go there." I don't feel like taking her to Longwood
Gardens on Sunday when I've had her 6 days a week besides . . . I would
have a much better relationship, [if we were] separate. The way it is now,
all I want to do is to get away from her [#110/111—55-year-old daughter,
who had been living with her 74-year-old mother for 55 years and her
89-year-old great aunt for 5 years].

We tend to think that feelings such as those expressed by the above
caregiver are the result of the increased responsibilities and tasks that
one is required to perform when he or she assumes the care of an elderly
parent. We might also expect that the greater the number of tasks or the
longer a caregiver has been responsible for care, the greater the
likelihood that the caregiver will report being stressed by this role.

The analysis in this chapter suggests that often it is the "subjective"
perception of stress or feelings of burden resulting from performing
certain tasks, rather than the "objective" actual amount of tasks being
performed that negatively affects caregivers and their families. In some
families, caregivers can be providing a tremendous number of tasks for
an elderly parent, and have been doing so for a fairly long time, yet
report little stress and no feelings of burden. In other families, even
providing a limited amount of care for a few months is perceived to be so
stressful that it becomes necessary to find alternatives.

In this study, dependency stress was based on the question: "How
much stress did it cause (or how much did it bother you) to perform that

TABLE 6.1
Sources of Family Stress Experienced by Abusive
and Nonabusive Caregivers (in percentages)

Items	Nonabusive	Physically Abusive
Employed female	22	22
Single head	6	15
Teenagers	36	52
Small children	26	33
Financial problems	27	37
Emotional problems	24	26
Physical disability	13	18
Recent death	21	11
Alcohol	10	11
Other stress	35	30

task or deal with some issue related to caregiving?" Sources of stress were affiliated with the provision of specific instrumental caregiving tasks such as assistance with financial, health, or household tasks, and the expressive tasks such as providing a social life and easing loneliness (see Table 6.1). There were also tasks that were a combination of expressive and instrumental components, such as those required when caring for a senile but mobile elder or allocating space to enable each generation to maintain a sense of privacy.

Family stress that results from such factors as having to care for another family member who was sick, handicapped, alcoholic, or drug addicted; caring for small children or teens; heading a two career or single parent family; or a recent death in the family were also examined.

Relative stress, based on the caregiver's feeling that he or she should be doing more for the elderly parent, or the perception that the elderly parent or other family members thought that the caregiver should be doing more, is another source of stress that was analyzed.

In this chapter we will examine the relationship between the six dependency categories discussed in the previous chapter, the family stress and total dependency stress (which are a summary of the individual items), as well as the combined stress measure (family stress plus dependency stress). The relationship between the frequency with which a caregiver must provide each of these tasks and the amount of stress being experienced will be discussed.

Next, the 12 specific stress measures—measures based on the respondents' reports of how much stress that providing a task (or dealing with an elder's problem) caused them, are examined. The impact of stress resulting from the caregivers' feeling that they could do more as well as parents and kin who expressed these feelings, and family stress will be presented.

Dependency and Stress

The six dependency categories and their Pearsonian correlation with the measure of total dependency, family, and total stress measures provide interesting insights.[1]

HOUSEHOLD DEPENDENCY

Light housekeeping had small nonsignificant correlation to dependency stress, family stress, and total stress. This might reflect, however, the fact that light housekeeping is probably the most commonly performed task. By the time elders require that other tasks be performed for them, household tasks have probably also been provided, thus household tasks seem relatively innocuous.

Similar findings were observed for other seven items that constitute this index. In fact, only the item "run errands" was found to be significantly correlated ($r = .24$) with the total dependency stress measure, and none of the items were significantly correlated with family stress or total stress. The total household dependency score had a moderate ($r = .20$) and significant correlation with dependency stress, but weak, nonsignificant correlations with family and total stress. One interesting finding was the negative relationship between family stress and the household dependency score. Apparently, when there is a high level of family stress, it may not be possible to fulfill these household-related tasks—possibly they are delegated to others—or just aren't done as frequently as before.

This data suggests that neither the individual items in the household dependency scale nor the summary measure are significantly related to stress. Out of 27 possible relationships (eight individual items plus the total household dependency score) correlated with family, dependency, and total stress,[2] only two reached significance (see Table C.4 in Appendix C for the correlation matrix). Thus it appears that the *frequency* with which a caregiver reports performing household dependency tasks is not correlated with stress.

This should not be interpreted as meaning that these families did not experience any stress. It appears that mother-daughter conflicts often intensify when mother becomes a child to her daughter. One daughter suggested:

You can't run your house the way you did before—you have another person. When she first came, I would clean my bedroom. The next day she would have cleaned it again. I just made up my mind that since she liked to clean—let her do all the cleaning that she wanted to do. You have to compromise and not let things upset you [#136—56-year-old daughter, who had been caring for her 92-year-old mother for 9 years].

It appears that much in the way that we hold our breath and allow the 3-year-old, 10-year-old, or teenager to take on new tasks that we could perform more quickly, more efficiently, and with less mess, these caregivers were suffering the consequences of allowing their elderly parent an attempt at maintaining their independence by taking on tasks that the caregiver could more easily perform by him- or herself. One daughter noted how unsettling it was to see her mother attempt to feel needed:

I think that she is afraid that she will get so that she can't do anything and she just wants to help so badly with everything. On my days off when I am home, I try to run the vacuum and she says, "If only I could do that" or "I wish that I could do that." Those are the kind of things that get on my nerves. She just talks about it all the time so I try to let her do something [#148—46-year-old daughter, who had been caring for her 84-year-old mother for 2½ years].

It is clear that not only are these attempts to maintain some sense of worth, self-esteem, and sense of being needed, but in some instances, they also contain an element of competition with the message: "I am the mother and I will show you how it should be done!" It also becomes clear that when caregivers are asked how much it bothers or stresses them to perform these tasks (as compared to the researcher measuring the frequency of tasks and correlating it to measure of stress), caregivers do report being stressed.

However, in other families, it is not just a desire to maintain independence, but the belief that by virtue of being older, one is owed the right to have his or her own way. One elder, who spent every winter with her son and his family and took over the entire second floor while she was there, elicited the following response from her daughter-in-law:

When she was in better health, she used to rearrange everything. She ripped all of the spreads off of any beds that she was going to use. She doesn't believe in them because they get soiled. Then while I was at work, she would take down the draperies because she said there must be more light in the room. She does not like Venetian blinds, which are under the draperies, so she would haul them up to the top. She does not care for rugs ... they would be hauled off and put in the attic. The whole place would be transformed . . . She would make over the whole second floor and the kitchen to suit her, but you would never be allowed to do anything like that in her house . . . if you went to her house, you couldn't touch one single thing, borrow a single thing [#27—64-year-old daughter, who had been caring for her 90-year-old mother-in-law for 7 months during the winter for the past 18 years].

PERSONAL GROOMING/HEALTH DEPENDENCY

Although fewer caregivers performed personal grooming/health tasks, and the frequency with which they were performed was considerably less than household dependency tasks, personal grooming/ health tasks were more highly related to measures of stress. Only the items "hair care" and "other" failed to reach significance when correlated to the total dependency stress measure. Although none of the items comprising this scale were significantly correlated with the index measuring family stress, four of the seven items in this index (bathing, doctor's orders, medication, and bedding) were significantly correlated with the total stress measure (see Table C.4 in Appendix C).

The relationship between the total personal grooming/health score and dependency stress was strong and highly significant, but that between total personal grooming/health and family stress displayed no differences. The significant relationship between total stress (a combination of family and dependency stress) probably reflects the high relationship between dependency stress. However, out of the 24 possible relationships, less than half (42%) reached significance.

FINANCIAL DEPENDENCY

Contrary to what one might expect based on the interviews, "paying bills " (writing out checks) for the elder was the item in the financial dependency index that had the strongest relationship to the dependency stress index ($r = .37$; $p = .0001$). This was followed by the item "manage resources" suggesting that the decision making needed to manage the elder's resources, pay bills, and keep finances in order was considerably more likely to be related to stress measures than was having to pay for the elder's needs. This might reflect the additional bookkeeping required in order to maintain two separate accounts. If the caregiver is financially responsible for the elder, there is only one family account to be managed—the elder's expenses are all handled within a single account. However, when the elder has his or her own resources, then the caregiver is responsible for maintaining separate financial accounts and being certain that the elder's money is used in a judicious fashion. In fact, the item "pay for essentials" produced a small, nonsignificant correlation with dependency stress providing further support that the management of finances and the time it requires is more stressful for most caregivers than the actual financial support of the elder.

Although the costs associated with caring for a handicapped family member or one coping with substance abuse might be expected to be correlated with financial dependency, only "having teenager in the house" of the nine items in the family stress index was significantly correlated with financial dependency. However, there was a strong ($r = .35$) highly significant correlation between total dependency stress measure and the elder's financial dependency, and between total stress and financial responsibilities. Out of the possible 21 relationships, nearly half (48%) were significant.

Much of the financial strain reported by the caregivers resulted from the inability of the social service system to meet the needs of these elders. The frustration and anger experienced by one daughter when she attempted to get services for her mother was not unusual.

> I could get no help for my mother. I could not get Medicaid . . . I thought that I'd better be prepared because we were in no financial position to provide that care. I went to social security to put her on Medicaid. They said, "How much social security does she get?" I told them. They told me, "you know your mother has to pay her fair share." I said "What do you mean by that?" They said "Add up all your expenses. If your expenses are $1,200 a month and there are four people living in the house then you divide four into $1,200. Your mother must be giving $300 a month in order for her to be eligible for Medicaid." I said "Look, my mother doesn't get $300 a month, where is she going to get the other $140 a month to pay her fair share?" They determined that she was not eligible and told me that she could get food stamps. What good does that do? None.

> Interviewer: Did she have Blue Cross/Blue Shield?
> Caregiver: In order for her to get into a nursing home and for them to pick up that tab, she had to go directly from the hospital into a nursing home. . . . They wouldn't take her out of here to a nursing home. Nobody would put her in a hospital. The one time we had her in there they sent her home. . . . I called various agencies around trying to find help, but there wasn't any. It's a horror story, I'll tell you [#26—50-year-old daughter, who had been caring for her 87-year-old mother for nearly 15 years].

Similar disgust with the inadequacy of financial assistance for frail elderly with medical problems was reported by another caregiver:

Medicare would take care of it . . . if she was going to die in the next two or three weeks . . . Medicare wouldn't even help supplement the three nights of nursing care at $90 per night . . . I learned that you had to be a millionaire or you had to have absolutely positively nothing. The middle class people—forget it. [Social services] don't apply . . . for the middle class. United States is the only country in the world that I know of that could take their aging and put them some places. . . . In Europe they are [treated] like God. In this country if you are not young—forget it [#45/46—45-year-old daughter, who had been caring for her 80-year-old mother and 71-year-old mother-in-law, for 3 months).

Unfortunately, families in European and developing countries are facing trends similar to those experienced by American families, such as increasing life expectancy, increasing numbers of women entering the work force, increasing numbers of female-headed households, and smaller family size. The problem of who will care for the aging parent is being considered worldwide (see *The Gerontologist,* 1983, Vol. 23, p. 6, which was devoted to examining cross-cultural comparisons of care-giving in developed and developing societies).

Although the caregiver quoted next gives the appearance of accepting the burden of providing care, it should be noted that this is a relatively young caregiver, and she has been providing care for only two months.

It is hard to put into words. We think that we've reached a point where things are not so hard, and we thought we could get ahead. But then I realize that we are not going to get ahead. Sometimes it bothers me, but most of the time, I just accept it as God's will and He gives me strength [#101—46-year-old daughter, who had been caring for her 77-year-old mother for 2 months].

Possibly one of the most difficult aspects for caregivers to resolve occurs when the financial cost of caring for a parent comes into direct competition with the costs of providing for one's children's future. A 64-year-old son described his situation—a 90-year-old mother, who does not actually *need* the son to pay her expenses but *expects* him to do so, and the problems that he and his wife might face if they retire.

This didn't bother us until inflation came along . . . we have a daughter who had graduated from college and worked in hospital work. She is very, very good at it . . . but she needs an advanced degree for hospital administration. She decided last fall that she would like to go and get an M.B.A. in hospital administration. She got a $4,500 scholarship to go . . . they raised the [tuition] to something like $5,500. She has a family . . .

husband and child, but they still require her parents to send copies of their income tax forms to Princeton along with the rest of the papers for the application. Now both my husband and I will be retired in another year and we won't have hardly a nickel. It is going to be very hard on us if we have to help her with all that . . . You see, we are caught between the child and the parent [#27—64-year-old daughter-in-law, who had been caring for her 90-year-old mother-in-law for 7 months during the winter for the past 18 years].

MOBILITY DEPENDENCY

Moderate but statistically significant correlations were found between help in and out of chair or bed and help in walking and the dependency stress measures. The fact that the relationship between stairs and dependency stress was weak and nonsignificant may reflect accommodations made by caregivers to avoid steps, thus removing this obstacle as a source of stress.

The total mobility dependency score was strong and significantly correlated with the dependency, family, and total stress indices. Although relatively few caregivers provide more than moderate levels of help with mobility tasks, the impact on caregivers providing these tasks, as measured by the high correlation between total mobility and the three stress indices, appears to be heavy. However, out of a possible 12 relationships, only three (25%) were statistically significant (see Table C.4 in Appendix C). Perhaps providing occasional help with mobility related tasks is not perceived as stressful. When an individual requires consistent help with one of these tasks, they are likely to require help with several tasks, thus the total mobility related dependency is very stressful.

MENTAL HEALTH DEPENDENCY

The impact of mental health dependency on caregivers is considerable. All of the items in the mental health dependency index had extremely high, statistically significant correlation with dependency stress and the total stress index. However, only decision making and nonrational behavior were significantly correlated to family stress. Table C.4 in Appendix C reveals that overall, 18 of the 24 items (75%) were statistically significant, supporting the relatively strong impact that providing the elder with mental health support had on caregivers and their families. The following quote clearly illustrates the predicament faced by caregivers.

It is difficult because I suddenly find myself having to make decisions for another person, decisions that will affect her life drastically. There are times I realize that it is necessary, but I feel it is almost unfair that I should have this burden. One of the biggest burdens now is that I feel responsible for everything that happens to her. If she is unhappy in a nursing home, it is a decision I made. I think the question is, Am I doing the right thing? This keeps recurring [#4—60-year-old daughter, who had been caring for her 86-year-old mother for 4 months].

SOCIAL/EMOTIONAL DEPENDENCY

Emotional support, which taps such issues as elders' loneliness, privacy, and demands for attention, was highly correlated with dependency stress ($r = .47$, $p = .0001$). Two additional items, helping the elder make phone calls and make friends were also moderately correlated with dependency stress (.30 and .25, respectively).

The relationship between the measure of total social/emotional dependency and family stress was extremely small and nonsignificant, but the relationships between social/emotional tasks and dependency stress and total stress were fairly strong ($r = .31$ and .26 respectively) and highly significant. Contrary to the interviews in which social/emotional tasks were discussed in volatile, highly emotional ways, only one-third of the items that constitute the social/emotional index are significantly related to the stress measures.

In summarizing the findings, just over one-third (38%) of the possible 135 relationships between specific dependency tasks and family, dependency, and total stress were statistically significant. The above analysis correlated specific tasks with separate measures of stress. In the following section, we will examine the impact of stress when it is based on the caregiver's response as to how stressful it was to provide a particular task.

Perception of Stress: The Dependency Stress Index

In the previous section, the scores families received on each of six dependency tasks were correlated with measures of family stress, total dependency stress, and a total stress measure. In this section, analysis of the individual dependency stress items, based on the responses to "How stressful was it to have to perform tasks or deal with a specific problem?" are presented.

Caregivers were divided into two groups: those who perceived that a particular task or problem was stressful, and those who did not find that task or problem to be stressful. These stressed and nonstressed groups were then compared in four major areas: demographic variables, such as age, sex, race, length of caregiving; the six dependency categories (household, financial, personal grooming/health, mobility, mental, social/emotional dependency tasks); the stress measures (family stress, total dependency stress, total stress, burden, and relative stress); and the control maintenance techniques used by caregivers and elders.

Finally, the correlations between each of the 12 items and measures of family stress, total dependency stress, and total stress will be examined. (See Table C.3 in Appendix C for the specific scores and Table 6.1 in this chapter for a summary of the significant levels.)

STRESS RESULTING FROM PROVIDING HOUSEHOLD TASKS

Overall, 53% of the caregivers reported that providing household-related tasks for the elder was stressful (see Figure 6.1). Although families characterized by having high levels of household dependency stress tend to perform greater amounts of dependency tasks, such as household, financial, and social/emotional, these differences are not significant. The mean dependency scores, that is, the average amount of tasks being performed by caregivers who reported feeling stressed by providing household tasks for the elder, barely differed (22.44 versus 22.18) from those caregivers who did not report stress (see Table C.3 in Appendix C). This provides still further evidence that it is not how many tasks need to be provided nor the level at which these tasks and services need to be provided that produces the stress, but the subjective, individual perceptions of how much bother or stress is felt by the caregiver providing the task for the elder.

Often the stress resulting from having to provide a task or service for the elder is the product of a combination of factors, not just the specific item. In the next quote, the caregiver responds to the stress resulting from caring for a large two-story home, but it is evident that financial pressures that forced the caregiver into signing the home over to the elder as well as the elder's emotional problems contribute to the stress experienced by the caregiver.

> I don't think that the burden would be as great on me if we lived in a one story house. This house is the real burden. This house requires a great deal of maintenance, both cleaning and maintenance. I see things that need doing and I do not have the time . . . or the money for them. I think it is feasible that we move, but it is not to mother. She has it in her mind that she is going to die in this house, in that room. She will stay here come hell

Dependency Stress

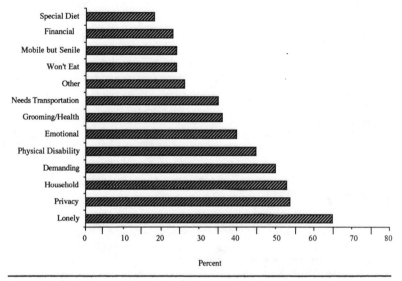

Figure 6.1   Stress resulting from dependency tasks, in percentages

or high water, and I'm afraid it's hell and high water. It's her house, she owns it. I signed it over to her. I need my head examined, but we decided that it [was best] for tax purposes, it was tax-free for her [#110/111—55-year-old daughter, who has been living with her 74-year-old mother for 55 years and her 89-year-old great aunt for 5 years].

Caregivers who were stressed by providing household tasks were not significantly different from nonstressed caregivers for any of the demographic variables. Of course, individual caregivers might experience considerable stress as the following exchange between the interviewer and a caregiver illustrates:

Caregiver: I don't drive right, I don't cook right, I don't clean right.
Interviewer: How much does that bother you?
Caregiver: Four! [always] It is the thoughtlessness on her part. I come home and after dinner I would like to just relax and pick up a book. She won't sit still. She has rested all day and she is ready to go [#3—56-year-old daughter, who had been caring for her 82-year-old mother for 3 years].

For one daughter-in-law, being required to maintain the home exactly as her mother-in-law had was considered to be extremely stressful:

> The house is decorated in the way his wife left it seven years ago. This includes the lace doilies and lace curtains . . . the general decorating, he doesn't want it touched. He wants everything left as it was. Somebody dies, and we just close the door to their room forever and never change it . . . I am basically pretty easygoing, but he has photographs of everybody all over the place . . . [his children's] high school graduation pictures and are all over 40 years . . . he does get extremely upset by any changes [#133—44-year-old daughter-in-law, who had been caring for her 68-year-old father-in-law for 1 year].

Another daughter noted how difficult it was to try to do chores while her mother attempted to help:

> I'm trying to cook dinner and she is right there washing dishes while I'm trying to cook . . . drives me buggy . . . She is always wishing that she could do more and if she'd just stay seated at the table, it would help me so much more. I do think that it is hard for two women to be in the same house and she used to have her own [#148—46-year-old daughter, who had been caring for her 84-year-old mother for 2½ years].

Caregivers who reported being stressed by having to provide household- dependency tasks also reported significantly greater family, dependency, and total stress, and feelings of burden. They also reported feeling that their siblings thought that the caregiver should do more. However these caregivers did not, themselves, feel that they *could* do more. Household-dependency stress was strongly, and significantly correlated with overall dependency stress, family stress, and the total stress: .58, .28, and .55, respectively (see the correlation matrix, Table C.4 in Appendix C).

As could be expected, families characterized by high levels of stress tended to use less talking and more yelling, threats, or medical or physical abuse to control the elder. In fact, one of the most consistent findings was the considerably higher levels of verbal and physical abuse used by caregivers who reported that providing tasks for the elder was stressful (see Table 6.2 for significance levels; actual scores are located in Appendix C table C.3). Those caregivers who reported being stressed had a mean score of 0.30 for physical abuse as compared with a mean score of 0.05 for nonstressed caregivers. Similar differences were observed for severe physical abuse and the total abuse measure. All differences were highly significant.

Although the sequence of events are not clearly ascertained, stressed caregivers reported that the their elder was more likely to pout, hit, refuse to eat or take medicine, and manipulate the caregiver. These elders were also significantly more likely to invade the caregivers' privacy. It is possible that these actions on the part of the elders contribute to the feelings of stress and burden experienced by caregivers.

STRESS RESULTING FROM PROVIDING PERSONAL GROOMING AND HEALTH CARE

In all, 36% of the caregivers reported that providing personal grooming and health-care-related tasks for the elder was stressful. These caregivers, as a group, were characterized as performing significantly higher amounts of all dependency tasks except for social/emotional ones. When caregivers replied that dealing with personal grooming/health-related activities was stressful, it appeared to be because this represented concrete evidence of the elder's inability to live up to former standards, and was further indication of deterioration in the elder's mental and physical health status. The mother's lack of concern over her appearance was particularly distressing for one daughter who described the mother's previous image:

> She is much more fashionable than I am and has always been. She has always looked perfect! [#6—40-year-old daughter, who had been caring for her 68-year-old mother for 3 months].

Bathing was a problem in some families because the intimacy was stressful. "My mother is an overly modest person" was the reason one daughter gave for the stressfulness of this task:

> We never had a close relationship like that. I would not feel embarrassed bathing my children, but I do feel funny with my mother. My relationship with my mother was of the old school where we dressed and undressed in the closet. If I had to bathe my husband or my 24-year-old son, I would not be embarrassed. However, bathing my mother bothers me [#101—46-year-old daughter, who had been caring for her 77-year-old mother for 2 months].

In other families, it was the time consuming nature of the task that was the most difficult part of caring for the elder.

TABLE 6.2
Stress Resulting from Provision of Dependency Tasks: Significance Levels

	Household	Grooming/ Health	Financial	Mobile but Senile	Social/ Emotional	Transpor- tation	Physical Disability	Elder's Loneliness	Not Eating	Special Diet	Elder's Demands	Privacy
Demographic												
elder's age	—	—	—	—	—	—	—	—	—	—	—	—
caregiver's age	—	—	—	—	—	—	—	—	—	—	—	—
length of caregiving	—	—	—	—	—	—	—	—	—	—	—	—
total illness	—	—	.01	—	—	—	—	—	—	.02	—	—
race	—	—	—	—	—	—	—	.03	—	—	—	—
relationship	—	—	—	—	—	.05	—	—	—	—	—	—
elder's sex	—	—	—	—	—	—	—	—	—	—	—	—
caregiver's sex	—	—	—	—	—	—	—	—	—	—	—	—
residence	—	—	—	—	—	.03	.02	—	—	—	—	—
Dependency												
household	—	.04	—	.02	.002	—	.03	—	—	—	—	—
grooming/health	—	.0001	—	.0006	.003	—	.009	.02	.02	—	—	—
financial	.02	.0008	.0004	—	—	—	.008	—	.02	—	.003	—
mobility	—	.0007	—	—	—	—	—	—	.01	—	—	—
mental health	—	.0001	—	.0001	.0001	.03	.02	—	.004	—	.03	—
social/emotional	—	—	—	.03	.0008	—	—	.001	.02	—	—	—
total dependency	—	.0001	.01	.0001	.0001	—	.004	—	.002	—	—	—
Family/Self Stressors												
extra kin	—	—	—	.05	—	—	—	—	—	—	—	—
parents—you do more	—	—	—	—	—	—	—	—	—	—	—	—

relatives–you do more	–	–	–	–	–	–	–	–	–	–	–	–
siblings–you do more	.02	–	–	–	–	–	–	–	–	–	–	–
you–you do more	–	–	–	–	–	–	–	–	–	.03	.03	–
family–related stress	–	.0001	.02	.02	–	.03	–	–	–	–	.0001	–
total dependency stress	.0001	–	.0001	.0001	.0001	.0001	.0001	.005	.0003	.009	.0001	.0001
total stress	.0001	.0001	.0001	.0001	.0001	.0001	.0001	.005	.007	.01	.0001	–
burden	.0001	.002	.0001	–	.03	.003	–	.0006	–	.01	.0009	.0006
Control Maintenance Techniques												
Caregiver												
talk	–	–	–	–	–	–	–	.04	–	–	–	–
advice	.02	.002	–	.004	.0002	–	.02	.002	–	–	.03	–
yell	.05	.05	–	.008	.001	–	.01	–	–	–	.03	–
ignore	–	–	–	–	–	–	–	–	–	–	–	–
medical abuse	–	.05	–	.04	.04	–	.02	–	–	–	–	–
threaten nursing home	–	–	–	–	.02	–	–	–	–	–	.03	–
physical abuse	.02	–	–	.04	.02	–	.01	–	–	–	.02	–
emotional abuse	–	–	–	–	.03	–	–	–	–	–	–	–
severe physical abuse	.007	–	–	–	.03	.04	.004	–	–	–	.04	–
total abuse	.009	.02	–	.004	.004	–	.001	–	–	–	.04	–
Elder												
yell	–	–	–	.05	–	–	–	.03	–	–	.0006	–
pout	–	–	–	.01	.03	.001	–	.008	–	–	.0001	–
refuse food or medicine	–	–	–	–	.001	–	–	–	.0001	–	–	–
hit	–	.02	–	.007	.0001	.04	–	–	.03	–	.02	.008
cry	–	–	.01	–	.003	.0001	–	–	–	–	.02	–
manipulate	–	–	.0004	–	.02	.0001	–	.001	–	.0004	.0001	.0001
call police	–	–	–	–	–	–	–	–	–	–	–	–
invades privacy	.007	–	.005	–	.01	.003	–	–	–	–	.0001	.002

Getting her ready for the day, up and washed, combed, and dressed, and fed. By that time it was noon. It was just like caring for an infant. Her constant demands all day . . . you just couldn't get anything done [#140/141—62-year-old daughter, who had been caring for her 83-year-old mother for one year and her 90-year-old mother-in-law for 18 years].

None of the demographic variables distinguished caregivers who reported being stressed by providing personal grooming/health dependency tasks from those who were not. Stressed caregivers reported significantly higher levels of family and total stress and feelings of burden. Stressed caregivers used significantly more yelling, medical abuse, and total abuse; the elders in this group used more physical abuse.

Correlations were computed between the measure of personal grooming/health stress and the family, dependency, and total stress indices. Dependency and total stress were highly and significantly correlated (.53 and .46, p = .0001) and family stress (.18) approached significance.

STRESS FROM PROVIDING ASSISTANCE WITH FINANCIAL TASKS

Only 23% of the caregivers reported that helping the elder with financial dependency tasks was stressful. Although caregivers who report being stressed from providing financial assistance to the elder tended to be providing somewhat greater levels of all dependency tasks, only financial dependency differed significantly.

Complicating the caregiving process is the lack of services and financial support for those families who have elected (or have no alternatives) to care for an elderly parent. As noted earlier, part of this problem results from eligibility requirements that consider the total family income, for example, son's, daughter-in-law's, as well as the elder's income. The income of the elder living alone probably falls within the income limits required for eligibility for many services and programs. However, when the elder moves in with an adult child, the total family income often exceeds the eligibility limits, and the elder can no longer receive subsidized medical visits, prescriptions, food, and other services, such as visiting nurses and home health aides. When these services are no longer subsidized, the costs become prohibitive to caregivers, and they must often forgo those not absolutely critical to the elder's well-being, such as home health aides or homemaker aides that might provide the caregiver with respite.

Noting the irony of a government that is glorifying family care of the elder, but refuses to help them in this endeavor, one caregiver stated:

The person taking care of their parent in their home gets no help whatsoever. . . . They wonder why more people don't take care of their elders in the home. More people would probably do so if they could get some help. Not necessarily financial . . . perhaps a lady to come in every day for a few hours. It would cost a lot less for the state than what it is costing them for nursing home care . . . [#44—51-year-old daughter, who had been caring for her 86-year-old mother for 7 years].

Unfortunately, for some caregivers, attempts to discuss the need for the elderly parent to help with the finances fell on deaf or rebellious ears. In one family (#130), after such a discussion, the 81-year-old mother reluctantly agreed to contribute about $20 every few weeks to help her 50-year-old daughter with household expenses. However, a similar discussion brought only a deepening sense of resentment from another daughter:

The thing that bothers me is the fact that she won't offer to [help financially]. She knows that nobody keeps me but me. I'm making a woman's salary and keeping a big house. That kind of irks me that she won't say, "Look here, I'll give you so much a month towards paying the bills." We have monstrous electric bills. . . . It's an obligation, which I think that she should partly assume. . . . She doesn't feel that way. I'm her daughter, she gave me life, she provided for me when I was young and couldn't do it for myself. This obligation is now on my shoulders. That is her reasoning [#31—58-year-old daughter, who had been caring for her 82 year mother for 2½ years].

Other caregivers noted that it was possible to perform the household-dependency tasks *or* the personal grooming/health tasks, but providing both became extremely stressful. These respondents felt that additional money would have lessened their burden because it would have enabled them to purchase services.

It was hard starting to care for someone at 8 or 9 o'clock in the morning. It takes hours and hours. She would be up for a few hours and then I'd put her back in bed for a nap . . . I found myself not doing what I should do . . . such as cleaning the house. I would run out and shop. During that time had I been able to afford it, I could have had someone do those things. It would have been great [#26—50-year-old daughter, who had been caring for her 87-year-old mother for 15 years].

The only demographic variable to distinguish those caregivers stressed by assistance with financial matters from those reporting no stress was total illness. Not only are the expenses related to caregiving greater when the elder is ill, but the elder's resources are likely to be depleted much sooner. Elders who had resources and sources of income, yet refused to contribute to the household expenses, were a special frustration to caregivers, especially women with small salaries or fixed incomes. It does seems apparent that in some instances these elders are simply continuing patterns of behavior developed earlier in life.

> Father could never do anything right, yet he was the sole picture of patience. He didn't know how wealthy he was when he died. She was the boss. She has done this with me. She directed all financial things. He [the father] was a giver and she was a taker. I'm the giver, and she is the taker. Us givers, we don't end up with much. The takers all seem to [#31—58-year-old daughter, who had been caring for her 82 year mother for 2½ years].

Family, dependency, and total stress scores were significantly higher among caregivers who reported that providing financial tasks was stressful. This group was also more likely to report feeling burdened. The control maintenance techniques were quite similar between the two groups of caregivers, however, elders in the stressed group used significantly greater amounts of crying, manipulation, and invading the caregivers privacy. The correlations between financial dependency stress and dependency, family, and total stress indices were strong and highly significant.

STRESS FROM CARING FOR A SENILE BUT MOBILE ELDER

Slightly under one-fourth of the sample (24.4%) felt that caring for an elder who was mobile but senile was stressful (see Figure 6.1). It should be noted, however, that only a relatively small proportion of caregivers had experienced this problem. However, almost all caregivers who experienced this situation found it to be stressful. In all, 58 caregivers reported that their elder needed to be watched, and 27 caregivers reported that their elderly parent or kin "got lost." Since 29 of the caregivers reported that caring for a senile but mobile parent was stressful, approximately 60% of those whose had to watch their parent and all who reported that their parent "got lost" found this experience to be stressful (55% reported that it was "almost always" or "always" stressful, the two highest levels of stress). A daughter, who had been caring for her 88-year-old mother for about 20 years noted:

> She does not remember who I am. I have my two granddaughters here and she thinks that they are my daughters . . . Just a couple of weeks ago . . . I

had gone upstairs to bed and I came out of my room and she wanted to know who I was. "Mother, I'm your daughter, I live here." She said, "I've never seen you before." Mentally she is very, very bad . . . physically she does alright . . . she has to be watched. I have seen her go to the freezer and take out something that's frozen . . . she just didn't realize that it wasn't cooked [#49—66-year-old daughter, who had been caring for her 88-year-old mother for 20 years].

Another daughter noted:

When I take her shopping, I don't leave her. If I walk down the isle and come back, I will see her walking around like she's lost . . . As she gets older, she gets a little confused [#22—60-year-old daughter, who had been caring for her 80-year-old mother for 14 years].

Concern over potential harm intensified the need for one caregiver to constantly watch her 82-year-old father. As an example, she related the time that she and her husband were working in their garden:

I had to constantly keep watching . . . to make sure that he was still sitting in the back yard . . . the other day, when I came back, he told me he was going to sit there in the yard at the table. I looked over from the garden and he was wandering out to the road and I had to run all the way back . . . the rest of the folks were busy and they did not realize that he was taking off [#102—48-year-old daughter, who had been caring for her 82-year-old father for 3 years].

The daughter of a mother suffering from Alzheimer's disease noted the stress that resulted from having to be always conscious of her mother's needs:

The constant knowledge that unless everyone kept her organized, that you couldn't fall back. There was no way you could build it in to her. What you did today was totally forgotten tomorrow. You didn't build up that much ability. You built up more time in which she is conscious, but you didn't ever build up skills [#6—40-year-old daughter, who had been caring for her 68-year-old mother for 3 months].

The cyclical relationship of stress and nonrational behavior involving both the elder and caregiver is apparent in the following description of the impact of stress on an elder suffering from Alzheimer's disease.

Interviewer: Does she exhibit nonrational behavior?

Caregiver: Yes, not all the time, but a considerable amount of time. As long as there is no stress, she is perfectly rational, but any time there is stress in which she has to have an opinion or make a decision, then she is nonrational.

Interviewer: Does she ever have verbally or physically explosive behavior?

Caregiver: Verbal, temper tantrums . . . fierce verbal abuse. In the hospital it was quite a problem because the nurses . . . tend to be confrontational and challenging and . . . you can't work with an older person like that [#6—40- year-old daughter, who had been caring for her 68-year-old mother for 3 months].

The preceding discussion indicates how the mother's experience resulted in her behaving in a nonrational, verbally explosive manner, which in turn was extremely stressful for the caregiver. The caregiver experiences the additional stress resulting from the need to ensure a stress-free environment for the elder. The detriment to the caregiver's health is obvious. One caregiver reported:

I have high blood pressure and I'm going through the change. I don't sleep all night. I listen for her to see if she calls or turns over [#44—51-year-old daughter, who had been caring for her 86-year-old mother for 7 years].

Caregivers who reported being stressed by caring for a senile but mobile elder provided greater amounts of all other dependency tasks. Except for financial and mobility dependency, the differences were significant. None of the demographic variable differed significantly between the two groups. The stressed group had significantly higher family, dependency, and total stress scores. As might be expected, caregivers who reported that they had other kin who could help with caregiving reported significantly lower stress scores.

Stressed caregivers used significantly higher levels of verbal, medical, and physical abuse. Their total abuse scores were also significantly higher. Elders used significantly greater amounts of yelling, pouting, and physical abuse. All correlations between stress resulting from caring for a mobile but senile elder and dependency, family, and total stress were strong and highly significant.

STRESS ASSOCIATED WITH SOCIAL/EMOTIONAL ASSISTANCE TO ELDER

Based on the in-depth interviews, providing for the social/emotional needs of one's elderly parents is considered to be most stressful. However, only 40% of the sample of caregivers reported feeling stress from meeting the social/emotional needs of the elder. It is possible that

for these caregivers, this experience is extremely potent and is dispro-
portionately reported, at length, to the interviewers. The data provide
some support for this position. Of those caregivers reporting stress, over
half (56%) experienced this stress "always" or "almost always." Often it
is an overattachment to one family member that makes it difficult for
this member and others to continue to function in the family, in their
social life, and at work. When the family member must leave for work or
business trips, the caregiving family is left to deal with temper tantrums,
crying spells, and refusal to eat or take medicine as "punishment"
because the "favored" family member has left. This is illustrated by the
following quote:

> I think that she has a lot of emotional dependency particularly on her son.
> She leans on the whole family because we are all there, but she gets very
> upset when her son goes way from home for a while, even if he is sent away
> on a business trip. This is something that bothers me [#123—53-year-old
> daughter-in-law, who had been caring for her 92-year-old mother-in-law
> for 8 years].

Feelings of guilt based on the perception that the caregiver should do
more, or that parents, relatives, or siblings thought that the caregiver
should do more was frequently reported by caregivers. One caregiver
noted that she felt that:

> No matter what I did, I wasn't doing enough. I'm sure I would have felt
> that way even if I had her living with me permanently.

> Interviewer: Did she make you feel this way or did you make yourself feel
> this way?
> Caregiver: I think in a way she did by saying things like "I was always
> willing to have taken my mother" . . . (which she never had to
> do) . . . and I felt that there was a moral judgment placed on the
> difference. She was good and I was bad. A lot of it was in my
> own head, but I think some of it came from her [#37—50-year-
> old daughter, who had been caring for her 72-year-old mother
> for 8 years].

Another caregiver responded that she provided emotional support
and her mother's social life "to the detriment of my own . . . all the time."
When asked to elaborate she commented:

> I have very little social life of my own and I have to include her in all my
> plans unless my brother is free on a particular night. I will ask him in

advance if he and his wife will do something with her. They have done that on occasion. They did it once around Thanksgiving and again last Saturday night. That's the only time I have ever been away from her. Wherever I go, I take her . . . She says she is too old to stay alone and will not stay alone except during the day when I work . . . She isn't antisocial, she is very sweet . . . Our likes and dislikes are very different and we have really nothing in common. We don't like the same things at all, which means that I have to do all the giving. I'm from the old school where your mother and father are right and children are bad [#31—58-year-old daughter, who had been caring for her 82-year-old mother for 2½ years].

Another noted:

You always feel that you could do more. Given any situation, you could always do more. I cannot afford to let that play on my mind. I did as much as I could under the circumstances. Yes, I did feel that I could do more [#138—42-year-old daughter, who had been caring for her 69-year-old mother for 8 years].

Caregivers reporting that they were stressed by having to provide for the social/emotional needs of the elder provided significantly more personal grooming/health, mental health and social/emotional tasks, and significantly fewer mobility dependency tasks. None of the demographic variables significantly differentiated the two groups. The mean scores were quite similar between the stressed and nonstressed caregivers for family stress. However, stressed caregivers had significantly higher dependence and total stress scores and were significantly more likely to report feelings of being burdened.

Stressed caregivers consistently used significantly greater amounts of the negative control maintenance techniques: verbal, medical, psychological abuse, and the physical abuse measures than did nonstressed caregivers (see Table 6.2). It is possible that the elder's use of control maintenance techniques contributed further to the stress being experienced by caregivers. Except for verbal abuse and calling the police, elders being cared for by stressed caregivers used significantly greater amounts of all control maintenance techniques.

Since caregiver-elder interaction is ongoing, the caregivers' stress from providing social/emotional tasks no doubt contributes to the forms of interaction chosen by the elder. In a cyclical fashion, the caregiver perceives that the elder is *demanding* and responds less quickly to what the elder perceives to be "requests." When these requests are not met, the elder cries, yells, pouts, or hits the caregiver. This behavior intensifies the stress the caregiver is experiencing and reduces his or her ability to engage in positive nonconflictual (nonresentful) interaction.

Social/emotional stress was highly and significantly correlated with dependency stress and total stress indices (.66 and .54, respectively, p = .0001 for both), but weak and nonsignificant for family stress.

STRESS ASSOCIATED WITH PROVIDING TRANSPORTATION

Stress resulting from providing transportation was experienced by just over one-third of the sample (35%). However, these caregivers rarely elaborated on this aspect of caregiving, and they were virtually indistinguishable, as a group, from caregivers who did not find providing transportation to be stressful.

Two demographic variables, residence and sex of elder, differed significantly between stressed and nonstressed caregivers. Female caregivers were significantly more likely to be stressed than male caregivers (16% versus 39%). This might reflect males providing a secondary role more often (even when they identified themselves as the caregiver).

Considerably fewer small town and rural caregivers reported that providing transportation was stressful. Whereas caregivers who resided in the city and suburbs were about evenly divided into stressed and nonstressed categories, only about one-fourth to one-fifth of those living in small towns, or rural caregivers reported being stressed.

A possible explanation might be related to the lack of public transportation in small towns and rural areas. Caregivers living in these areas might be used to driving fairly great distances for shopping, and medical services, and so on, therefore, providing transportation for the elder required less adjustment in one's daily patterns.

However, public transportation is also virtually nonexistent in suburban Delaware. If the above was based on previous transportation patterns, one would have expected suburban caregivers to resemble more closely those living in small towns or rural areas than those living in the city.

Stressed caregivers reported significantly higher dependency and total stress scores and feelings of burden, but similar control maintenance techniques. In fact, only the higher use of severe physical abuse among the stressed groups was significantly different between the two groups.

One wonders about the impact of isolation on the use of physical abuse. Since both the spouse- and child-abuse literature link isolation and abuse, perhaps the elder's need for transportation indicates not only a stressor for the caregiver (who has to interrupt his or her activities to transport the elder), but it may also be an indication that alternative transportation or a means for the elder to interact with others is lacking. Elders in the group characterized by transportation dependency stress were significantly more likely to pout, use physical abuse, cry, manipulate, and invade the caregiver's privacy.

All correlations between the stress resulting from providing transportation and family, dependency, and total stress indices were strong and significant.

STRESS ASSOCIATED WITH THE ELDER'S PHYSICAL DISABILITY

As indicated in Figure 6.1, 45% of the caregivers reported that having to deal with the elder's physical disability was stressful. In some families the stress resulted from very specific disabilities suffered by the elder.

It is very frustrating when you talk to someone and they don't hear a word that you are saying. We already have tried a hearing aid and it didn't work [#112—44-year-old daughter, who had been caring for 77-year-old mother for 6 years].

I just don't feel free; it feels like all I'm doing is taking care of her. I know it's going to get worse if she gets bedridden. I had a taste of it when she came home from the hospital, but I managed to get through it, so I guess I can continue if my health stays up [#108—61-year-old daughter, who had been caring for her 93-year-old mother for 14 years].

We were scared to let her live alone. We have a two story house and I have her in a back bedroom on the first floor. We remodeled the kitchen and made a laundry room so I put her in our bedroom downstairs. She got sick so we put our bed into the laundry room and made it a bedroom . . . so I could hear her when she got sick and it just was more convenient. We aren't afraid of her falling, but it's her breathing. We just stay there. I do have an intercom, but it is just more convenient to hear her and be close by [#108—61-year-old daughter, who had been caring for her 93-year-old mother for 14 years].

Caregivers who reported that they were stressed by the elder's physical disability also reported that they provided significantly greater amounts of all but household and social/emotional tasks. Residential area was the only demographic variable to differ significantly between caregivers who experienced stress from coping with the elder's physical disability and those who did not. Caregivers who resided in the city were significantly more likely to report stress (73%) than caregivers residing in small towns (29%). In the sample, 38% of caregivers in rural areas and 47% of those in suburban areas reported being stressed by the physical disabilities of the elderly they cared for. Stressed caregivers reported significantly greater dependency and total stress scores, and used significantly greater amounts of verbal, medical, and physical abuse. The stress produced by having to cope with an elder's physical disability was highly correlated with dependency and total stress (.56 and .45 respectively, $p = .0001$ for both), social/emotional dependency stress was not, however, correlated with family stress.

STRESS RESULTING FROM ELDER'S LONELINESS

Nearly two-thirds of the sample (65%) reported that they experienced stress because the elder was lonely. Furthermore, 42% of this group noted that they found the elder's loneliness to be "always" or "almost always" stressful.

Recognizing the elder's loneliness and being unable to resolve this problem adequately because of competing demands on their time and energy further intensified caregivers' feelings of burden and distress. The following portion of an interview with a caregiving daughter illustrates these dynamics. When asked if her mother was lonely, the daughter replied:

She is terribly lonely, but she'd never own up to it.

Interviewer: Does it bother you?
Daughter: Yes, It bothers me a lot. She has always been a private person and I have always been gregarious. That was our initial difference—a big difference. Her being alone bothers me more than it bothers her.
Interviewer: How much would you say it bothers you?
Daughter: All the time because there is no one else in her life but my husband and myself. Therefore, we [and our children] are her total existence and it is smothering [#7—36-year-old daughter, who had been caring for her 65-year-old mother for 2 years].

In most of these caregiving situations, the elder has been moved from his or her community, friends, neighbors, and own home. Therefore, it is easy to see how they might become lonely and overburden the caregiver and family in their search to fill this loneliness. One caregiver related that her Dad has a strong yearning to go back to Norway. There is virtually no one left in Norway as far as family is concerned. His whole town is different. I don't think that he has been back since 1920. We try to tell him that it's more fun to remember the way it was than to see what progress has done to it. . . . He does become weepy at times over this and feels that he doesn't have any family. . . . It is the Norwegian heart that he is missing. I play the Norwegian National Anthem for him and he just bursts into tears [#104/105-58-year-old daughter, who had been caring for her 88-year-old mother and 93-year-old father for 3 years].

Another daughter tried to encourage her father to become more involved outside the home:

I try to get him to go to the senior center, but he doesn't want to go. He complains that he is the loneliest man in the world. We try to get him to go out. He does go to see his girlfriend, who he had known before he came here to live [#125—46-year-old daughter, who had been caring for her 70-year-old father for 6 months].

One of the problems faced by caregivers is that although it is possible, in most cases, to provide for the elder's physical, medical, and basic social needs, it is not always possible for the caregiver to alleviate the elder's loneliness and make the elder happy. One son, described his futile attempt to create a "perfect" existence for his mother:

I do deeply love her and I want her to have a happy life and I want to please her and make her as happy as possible. I feel a sense of burden because I don't feel that I am really being that successful. . . . She has all the material things, she is well taken care of, she is warm, she has food, but she is not having a complete life and I have not been able to get her involved in a social life or interested in something productive, which I think would be essential to her well being [#5—52-year-old son, who had been caring for his 74-year-old mother for 18 months].

Later in the interview when this caregiving son was asked if his mother's loneliness bother him, he responded:

Not so much that she's lonely, it bothers me all the time that she feels insecure at being alone. She is afraid of being alone. She's afraid of dying by herself. That bothers me all the time. It bothers all of us all the time [#5].

Outliving friends and family, and especially one's child, can produce extreme feelings of loneliness and a sense of futility. Caregivers found this to be especially difficult to handle. When an elder lost her own daughter, this loss deeply affected the elder and resulted in the granddaughter not only mourning the loss of her own mother, but attempting to care for her grieving grandmother.

> It's been very hard for us since my mother died. It was her only child. I am trying to help her cope with her daughter's death . . . more in helping her not feel sorry for herself. . . . She tends to do that a lot and when she does that she doesn't want to do anything else . . . she won't eat . . . She will say "I don't have anything left to live for." At one point she would say "You don't really know what it is like to be old." She tries to put on a guilt trip . . . she did it with mother and it worked [#137—30-year-old granddaughter, who had been caring for her 82-year-old grandmother for 15 months].

Caregivers reporting stress as a result of the elder's loneliness performed slightly higher amounts of all dependency tasks, however, only the higher levels of financial and social/emotional dependency differed significantly (see table 6.1). The only demographic variable to differ significantly was race—black caregivers were less likely to experience stress as a result of the elder being lonely. We cannot ascertain, from the data, whether black elders were more likely to be living in the same community as when they lived independently, or whether they more easily adjusted to new environs and thus experienced less loneliness, or whether the black elder was just as lonely as his or her white counterpart but that the caregiving child did not find this aspect of caregiving to be particularly stressful. Furthermore, because of the small number of black families any statistical analysis and explanation is speculative.

Caregivers who reported feeling stressed as a result of their elder's loneliness experienced significantly higher levels of dependency and total stress and feelings of burden. Stressed caregivers made significantly greater use of talking and seeking advice, the elders in these families used greater amounts of verbal abuse, pouting, and attempts to manipulate the caregiver (see Table 6.2). Finally, correlations between being stressed by the elder's loneliness and family, dependency, and total stress were all found to be moderately strong and significant (see Table C.4 in Appendix C).

STRESS RESULTING FROM ELDER NOT EATING

Almost one fourth of the caregivers (24%) reported that they found the elder's eating habits to be stressful. In some cases the lack of interest in food can be related to decreased sensitivity of the taste buds, medicine, and lack of activity. In other cases, elders decide that they will eat only certain food cooked in a particular way.

> It is not a matter that she won't eat, she likes certain kinds of food. She is picky. That bothers me, usually [#17—59-year-old daughter, who had been caring for her 84-year-old mother for 6 years].

When the elder ate out of sequence with the family, this was very stressful. One daughter noted the following self-imposed pattern demanded by one elder.

> In the beginning, she wanted to eat six times a day. She wanted it at a particular time, eight, ten, twelve, three, six, and nine at night. It was like having a baby in the house [#33—56-year-old daughter, who had been caring for her 83-year-old mother for over 3 years].

Research on eating disorders, especially anorexia, has found that this is often the way young women (the predominant victims) attempt to regain control over their environment, or the way a young child attempts to get more attention. In some families, the elder also uses this approach, possibly the only remaining way that he or she could exercise some control. It is interesting to note that "not eating" appears to be a mechanism used primarily by women. Some 29% of the female elders, but no male elder, used this method. A typical response is provided by a 54-year-old caregiving daughter, who had cared for her 87-year-old mother for nearly 8 years, who noted, "Once she [her mother] gets upset, she will refrain from eating and go to her room (#2)." Another daughter observed that her mother would refuse to eat if

> I have leaned on her too much or given her too many orders. She is beginning to feel . . . that she ought to assert her independence, and I can't blame her [#4—60-year-old daughter, who had been caring for her 86-year-old mother for 4 months].

In other families, loss of appetite was related to other sources of stress, such as grieving over a lost relative. This was a particular concern to caregivers when the elder was diabetic and carefully balanced meals were necessary to keep the diabetes under control.

> Yes, it bothers me all the time. It bothers my wife all the time because that's when we do have to check on her. We have to be sure she eats because she will refuse to eat, and with her diabetes that's extremely

important . . . we think that has caused some of the problems so we are watching that more carefully now [#5—52-year-old son, who had been caring for his 74 year old mother for 18 months].

When meals were not critical, caregivers tended to take a more relaxed approach, as one caregiver noted:

It sounds terrible, but sometimes there is no way to force people. Some elderly people can refuse to eat to a point. After having four children, I figured, if they are hungry, they are going to eat, and if they are not . . . forget it [#102—48-year-old daughter, who had been caring for her 82-year-old mother for 3 years].

The difficulty with this approach is knowing when intervention by means of intravenous or tube feeding is necessary to prevent malnutrition. Caregivers are often faced with having to make the difficult decision of when to ignore a (rational) elder's wish if it is not, from the caregiver's perspective, in the elder's best interest. This is an unfortunate position, one that further deprives the elder of personhood and the ability to make personal choices. Yet it is necessary if the caregiver wishes to follow legal dictates and provide the elder with the socially expected protection from life-threatening circumstances such as malnutrition or medical complications resulting from improper diet or refusal to take medicine.

Stressed caregivers tended to have slightly higher levels on all dependency indices and, except for household dependency, the difference between stressed and nonstressed caregivers was significant. No demographic variables differed significantly between the two groups. Stressed caregivers reported significantly higher levels of dependency and total stress, but no trends appeared for the other stress variables or CMTs. Elders in these families were significantly more likely to refuse to eat or take medicine, and use significantly greater amounts of physical abuse.

STRESS RESULTING FROM
AN ELDER NEEDING A SPECIAL DIET

Only 18% of the caregivers reported that providing for special dietary needs of the elder was stressful. As noted earlier, stress was often generated when a caregiver was following medically ordered diets, which the elder resented. One caregiver, recognizing the elder's right to make decisions regarding personal choices, explained:

I used to tell her, years back, that something was not good for her. She would say "at this point in my life, I am not going anywhere, so what difference does it make if I have that candy today? I have only got today." I said, "You made your point. How many pounds do you want?" When she told me she wanted something, I got it for her. I didn't care what it was she wanted. She made me realize that all she had was today and a little bit of pleasure today meant more to her than maybe an extra day, week, or month [#143—46-year-old daughter-in-law, who had been caring for her 72-year-old mother-in-law for a year].

Unfortunately, the relatives of caregivers who make these choices often interpret this attempt to allow the elder a modicum of control over his or her environment, as neglect. The caregiver quoted above later reported that she got into a real quarrel with her brother-in-law over the candy.

He has assumed no responsibility . . . has come to see her [his mother] three times in 14 years . . . but when she wanted taffy at Rehobeth and I went and got it for her . . . he criticized me [#143].

Although this caregiver's motives are honorable and she should be applauded for recognizing that it is vitally important that the elderly be encouraged to make independent judgments as much as possible, one can easily understand how a visiting nurse, social worker, or doctor might have reported the caregiver's behavior as neglectful and potentially life-threatening to the elder.

Forgetting what had been previously consumed, a problem for those on restricted diets caused concern for another caregiver:

She'll say, "I don't know whether I ate my bread for breakfast or shall I just save it for dinner." Or if she ate toast at breakfast, I'll have to tell her at dinner that she already has had her quota of bread . . . when she was first here . . . she would stuff her pockets with cookies and eat them in the basement. She was pulling little tricks like that until I found out and I had to say "You are eating cookies at the washing machine, I found the crumbs." She said "I only ate a couple." I said, "I'm going to have to take it off of your sugar allotment. Your quota is going to be overdone by the end of the day" [#22—60-year-old daughter, who had been caring for her 80-year-old mother for 14 years].

Special diets often necessitated the preparation of separate meals. A bout with infectious hepatitis when she was about 40, resulted in the need for special food preparation for an elderly mother. Her daughter described a fairly elaborate procedure:

She has special dietary needs. . . . It is practically a zero fat diet and comparatively limited sugar diet. Her digestion has been getting increasingly irritable over the years, which is partly a result of the hepatitis. She eats bland cereals and toast for breakfast. She eats beef, chicken, and turkey, and would probably eat lamb or veal if we could afford it. It has to be defatted and then boiled twice in two different waters to remove any of the residual fat . . . However, she can eat salt.

Interviewer: Does this present a problem working this diet around your own family schedule?

Caregiver: It just means cooking another set of meals most of the time . . . My husband has a special diet, which is different from mine too, so I am an old hand at this. It is no strain, just an effort to remember . . . You have to cook it [meat] ahead and have it for her. It is not what I would call a big hassle. I think my brother's wife finds it to be a pain in the neck [#32—56-year-old daughter, who had been caring for her 79-year-old mother for 1 year].

However, in other instances, this self-imposed diet is an attempt to place the caregiver in the role of a surrogate servant—an obvious attempt to maintain control. A school teacher whose mother-in-law has spent 7 months a year with the family during the winter for the last 18 years describes the ritual required by the mother-in-law.

You know that when you get home from school and you're tired, she is sitting in her chair with her toddy and she's looking at you and expecting the meal just as ordered. For dinner, she must have two fresh vegetables, not frozen or canned, and a piece of meat, which is either roast lamb or roast beef. She does not like hamburger because in the summertime that's what she gets for herself when she is alone and she says she would rather not eat that [hamburger] when she's with us. Every week, alternating, we have to buy rib roasts of beef or leg of lamb. She is very fond of cold meat that has been baked like that. That's the way her diet goes . . . The thing that bothers me is that it takes so long to prepare these things. Now the ordinary person coming home from work, if it has been a busy day and they were tired, may get out some frozen vegetables and hamburger and call it quits. This you cannot do. You must have this whole procedure. Her tea is a regular ritual. First, you must pour hot water into the teapot. She has a special little teapot. Then, you must put the hot water into a measuring cup, up to a certain point. We finally had to put a piece of adhesive tape on the line. Then the water must go in and then the tea bag and then the cover on. It must steep for a certain amount of time before she has her tea . . . exactly 10 minutes. It must be exactly right [#27—a

64-year-old daughter-in-law, who had been caring for her 90-year-old
mother-in-law for 7 months during the winter for the past 18 years].

This caregiver reported that she had returned to teaching school in
order to get away from the stress of caring for this demanding,
inconsiderate mother-in-law.

A comparison of caregivers who reported being stressed from the
elder's special diet with caregivers who reported no stress revealed only
one significantly different demographic variable: stressed caregivers
were caring for elders with significantly more illnesses. Inconsistent with
the other stress variables examined in this chapter, stressed caregivers
did not perform significantly greater amounts of any of the six
dependency categories, and were significantly more likely to feel that
they could be doing more for the elder. They also experienced
significantly greater levels of dependency and total stress, and were
more likely to feel burdened. No differences were observed between the
two groups of caregivers in their use of CMTs. However, the elders in
these families were significantly more likely to attempt to manipulate
the caregivers.

The correlations between the stress associated with meeting the
special dietary needs of the elder and dependency and total stress indices
were moderate and significant; for family stress they were not significant.

STRESS RESULTING FROM ELDERS' DEMANDS

Exactly half of the sample reported that complying with (or
attempting to ignore) an elder's demands was stressful. Further, the
stress levels were extremely high. Among those caregiver's reporting
stress, nearly half (49.2%) reported that they "always" or "almost
always" experienced stress from the elder's demands. Nagging, com-
plaining, demanding attention "immediately" were complaints commonly expressed by caregivers.

> She makes everything so difficult . . . Even an outing can turn sour on us.
> If you make the effort, she still may find something to complain about.
> The car isn't right, or the weather isn't right. This makes me want to do
> less with her . . . she may not find something [clothes] she likes that is
> ready made, if I try to make it, it never turns out to her liking [#2—54-
> year-old daughter, who had been caring for 87-year-old mother for 8
> years].

The most difficult part of caring for my mother-in-law was getting her ready for the day, up, washed, combed, dressed, and fed. By that time it was noontime. It was just like caring for an infant. Her constant demands all day. You couldn't get anything done [#140/ 141—62-year-old daughter, who had been caring for her 90-year-old mother-in-law for 18 years and her 83-year-old mother for 2 years].

Caregivers who reported being stressed by the elder's demands tended to perform slightly more dependency tasks than did nonstressed caregivers, but only financial dependency differed significantly. Stressed caregivers were significantly more likely to feel that they could do more, and to experience higher levels of family, dependency, and total stress, and to report feeling burdened. None of the demographic variables, however, differentiated the two groups.

Caregivers who were stressed by the elder's demands used significantly higher levels of threats and verbal and physical abuse. As could be expected, elders who were perceived as constantly demanding attention were dramatically higher in their use of all of the control maintenance techniques. Only refusing to eat or take medicine and calling the police failed to reach significance (see Tables 6.1 in this chapter, and Table C.3 in Appendix C). One can wonder if perhaps this explains why caregivers found meeting the demands of the elders to be so stressful. These data suggest that perhaps the personality of the elder is important in understanding caregiver stress in these generationally inverse families. It appears that some elders are simply more demanding and *any* caregiver providing care to this individual might find the job to be stressful.

The correlation between the stress that caregivers experienced as a result of an elder's demands and the three stress indices were extremely strong and highly significant: r = .65, .43, .66 for dependency, family, and total stress, respectively, and all were significant at the p = .0001 level.

STRESS RESULTING FROM LACK OF PRIVACY

In all, 53% of the caregivers reported that privacy issues were stressful. Among the stressed group 50% noted that it was sometimes stressful, 28% stated that it was almost always stressful, and 17% found it to be *always* stressful. In some families the lack of privacy became an invasion of one's intimate moments. A daughter-in-law describes the feelings expressed by many respondents:

The lack of privacy bothered me all the time. Our house is very openly designed and it didn't seem that there was any place in the house that my husband and I could talk that it wasn't possible that she might hear us.

That disturbed me. It disturbed me to know that she was right across the hall from our bedroom, and I'm sure that every child still has hang ups about their parents knowing that they are actually engaging in sex. . . . That bothered me. I figured that there was nothing that I could do about it, so it didn't prevent our marital intimacies, but it was always on my mind. My husband felt the same way that I did. We realized that it was temporary . . . and necessary [#38—54-year-old daughter, who had been caring for her 90-year-old mother for 11 years].

This temporary situation has, however, existed for 11 years. Other caregivers reported that the elder's actions very deliberately invaded other family members' privacy. When asked about privacy issues, another caregiver noted:

She will ask about my phone calls . . . One thing that really bothers me is with my own children. I can't have any privacy. I can't go and see my daughter in Pennsylvania. I have to take my mother along and she just thinks that that is the way it is supposed to be. . . . There are times when we [my daughter and I] like to talk together. That isn't allowed. She intrudes into my private affairs all the time. In fact, I have no private affairs, she knows everything [#31—58-year-old daughter, who had been caring for her 82-year-old mother for 2½ years].

It is clear that in many families this unwillingness to respect the privacy of adult (caretaking) offspring is based on a lack of filial maturity, that is, the elder's refusal to recognize the child's adult status. Many caregivers reported that the elder, especially if it was their mother, felt perfectly comfortable entering the caregiver's and spouse's bedroom at any time, putting clothes away in their drawers and cleaning up. This behavior, quite appropriate when the elder was the head of the house and her motherly concern and household responsibilities overruled the child's need for absolute privacy, is now inappropriate and greatly resented by the adult child.

These elders not only feel that their children should not keep secrets from them and have no need for "private" areas, such as the master bedroom, but also insist on adhering to a dictum from an earlier era—that their own room is off limits. Whether this represents patterns of behavior learned earlier and difficult to change, or whether these are direct attempts on the part of the elder to maintain some semblance of power and control is not clear. What is clear is that this behavior is extremely disruptive. The impact of the elder's disruptive behavior on feelings of burden is demonstrated by a Poulshock and Deimling (1984) study in which path analysis revealed that the greatest direct effect on a caregiver's perception of feelings of burden was the elder's disruptive behavior.

Caregivers and their families often make considerable concessions in order to provide the elder with the best accommodation. In some instances the caregiver was forced to sleep on the living room couch after relinquishing the only bedroom to the elder. In other instances, a child had to give up or share his or her bedroom with an elder. In still other families, the guest bedroom was converted to a den so that the elder parent would have someplace other than his or her bedroom in which to spend time and entertain friends. For one family, the entire second floor was taken over by the mother-in-law during her annual seven month sojourn, a pattern that had existed for 18 years. Finally, some families did extensive renovations in order to create special living quarters for the elder.

There appeared to be a conscious effort on the part of caregivers to provide for the privacy of the elder, perhaps out of respect for the parent status, often to the detriment of providing for their own privacy needs.

I think it bothered my husband more than it did me. It bothered him "almost always," it bothered me "sometimes" . . . We gave them the extra bedroom. They had their own bath. It was not to keep them away from us, but we felt that possibly if they wanted to get away from the kids they wouldn't have to sit in their bedroom, they had the den. Occasionally, if we have friends over, it sometimes bothered me because we couldn't visit with them. Mom and Dad enjoyed them too. Occasionally it bothered me. You just want to be with your friends once in a while [#18/158—41-year-old daughter, who had been caring for her 59-year-old mother and 61-year-old father for 6 years].

For some families, lack of privacy is synonymous with lack of freedom. Having completed their child rearing responsibilities, many caregivers expected some time to spend on themselves.

The lack of privacy bothers me. My attitude towards the whole thing has changed. I am getting weary of the responsibility . . . I thought that I would be free of this. All my children are gone and [I thought that] I would be more pampered than before [when they were young] . . . The lack of freedom bothers me a lot, all the time, and the lack of privacy [#132—52-year-old daughter, who had been caring for her 74-year-old mother for 27 years].

The lack of privacy sometimes bothers me. It is taking me a little time to get used to the idea that "this is my father." I have been divorced for about

10 years and have had to answer to no one and it has been hard to get used to "Where have you been," etc. . . . He makes me feel like a child [#125—58-year-old daughter, who had been caring for her 70-year-old father for 8 years]

Not all elders are unaware of the need for their adult children to have privacy. Possibly because they experienced the lack of privacy when they were newly married and starting a family, some elders are extremely careful not to intrude on the privacy of their children. This extreme sensitivity to privacy issues was itself stressful:

She is delighted to be living here, and it has worked out beautifully for us, but whenever my husband comes home, she becomes scarce and stays out of the way. She doesn't want to interfere in our lives in any way, to the point where it is almost too much, really. The minute my husband drives in the driveway, if we are sitting here having tea or talking or whatever, she scoots into her little sitting room and shuts the door. This is the one thing that we notice. My husband wonders, you know, what's the matter. . . . Every time he comes in, she's off. But then, she will come and have dinner with us and sit around the fire and watch television and she's fine. She sort of carries that a little to far . . . she overdoes the privacy.

Interviewer: Do you think that she doesn't want to feel that she is intruding?
Caregiver: Yes, definitely [#3—56-year-old daughter, who had been caring for her 82-year-old mother for 3 years].

A comparison of caregivers who reported being stressed by the lack of privacy with those who experienced no stress, revealed no discernible patterns or significant differences between the two groups in the performance of dependency tasks or demographic variables. However, total dependency stress, and burden were significantly higher among stressed caregivers. The use of control maintenance techniques was quite similar for the two groups, but elders in families reporting stress used significantly more physical abuse, manipulation, and invasion of the privacy of the caregiver. The latter finding suggests that it might not be only the caregiver's perception that their elderly parent did not respect their privacy. Perhaps these elders did invade the caregiver's privacy to a greater extent.

OTHER FACTORS PRODUCING STRESS

Approximately one-fourth of the sample (26.1%) reported other aspects of caregiving that they found particularly stressful. For example, caregivers felt that having the total responsibility for the elder was a considerable stress. One elder had lived with her daughter for eight years until the daughter was no longer able to cope. At this point the mother moved in with her son and 53-year-old daughter-in-law. This daughter-in-law noted, "We are at eight years and no end is in sight (#123)."

A caregiver who has had that responsibility for a 74-year-old mother noted that the largest source of stress and burden was:

> The total responsibility. I can't even go out to lunch without checking out the situation at home first. A major problem is that she just can't accept [her infirmity and aging]. I took her to her to my brother's in North Carolina while we went on vacation. It was a disaster [#132—52-year-old daughter, who had been caring for her 74-year-old mother for 27 years].

The above caregiver, who is employed and has had cancer for the past five years, later noted that her 26-year-old son is a source of moral support.

> He is pretty frank with mother. He is not bothered by grandma's tears. It helps her see sometimes what she is doing to me [132].

> I guess you would call it cabin fever, just in here all the time together, and I can't live my life and I have to try and live his life for him and I just feel that it's an infringement on me, I really do. If this is selfish then it's selfish. That is how I feel. He has lived his life. I should have a chance to live mine. I worked 45 years of my life and I would like to have a little time to live before I die [#95—66-year-old daughter, who had been caring for her 86-year-old father for 4 years].

ADDITIONAL SOURCES OF STRESS AND OUTCOME

Family stress. In earlier studies (O'Malley, 1979) it was suggested that nearly three-fourths of the families were experiencing some additional form of stress, such as alcoholism, drug addiction, medical problems, or long-term financial problems. However, it was also noted that the elderly victim was a source of stress to the abuser primarily because of the physical, emotional, or financial care required.

In this study, 86% of the families were experiencing family situations that have been found to be stress producing. Some 89% of those who were abusive experienced family stress, compared to 85% of the nonabusive caregivers. When the percentages of the individual items comprising the family-related stress index were compared for violent and nonviolent caregivers, the greatest differences were found for items that reflected evidence of role conflicts: caring for one's children (small children and teenagers) versus caring for one's mother. Likewise, single headed families were less likely to have someone to share the burden of care (see Table 6.1). Furthermore the mean family stress scores were higher for abusive than nonabusive caregivers (7.89 versus 5.70).

Although these differences may not appear to be dramatic, family stress is an additional source of stress that can exacerbate an already difficult situation.

Consequences. In some families, the stress reached such high levels that the caregivers became ill, or divorced, or experienced suicidal feelings when alternative arrangements were not possible. One daughter noted that she was discussing her problems with the insurance man because he had had a similar experience. The insurance man said that "unless somebody has gone through this they have no idea what it is like. My mother almost drove us crazy. As a result of her being there, my wife left me. She did come back, and then as a result [of the caregiving responsibility] she got sick and was in the hospital" (reported by #95—a 66-year-old daughter, who had been caring for her 86-year-old father for 4 years).

Later in the interview, this caregiver described her own feelings:

There are times when it crops up . . . when I feel so guilty about feeling like I do that I just think I must be no good to anybody . . . there are times when I think, if I could die and get out of the whole stinking mess . . . without having to live with it day in and day out. The thing goes on and on. There is no end [#95].

When asked how she coped with this high level of stress she responded:

I have left here sometimes at 8:00 in the morning and walked the streets until 3 or 4 o'clock in the afternoon. I guess just to let off steam. That's the only way I can explain it [#95].

In a similar vein, another caregiver reported:

I was so tired. When I thought about sleep, I had the most peaceful feeling come over me and I wished that I never had to wake up again. When I thought about this it frightened me. This came to me one time. Getting away from it all comes to me many times, wishing I could get away. This created a lot of guilt feelings [#135—56-year-old daughter-in-law, who had been caring for her 79-year-old mother-in-law for 8 months].

A more philosophical approach was offered by a daughter, who had been caring for her mother for 14 years.

> There are times when I wish I could have the day off, but then I always say to myself there will be another day. It isn't going to last forever. You just have to cope with it. I try to cope with it. It worked out all right [#22—60-year-old daughter, who had been caring for her 80-year-old mother for 14 years].

> You just have to take it a day at a time or an hour at a time. And that at the time you are going through it, you just think that there will never be an end [#45/46—45-year-old daughter, who had been caring for her 80-year-old mother and 71-year-old mother-in-law for 3 months].

The extreme frustration and feeling of inadequacy and hopelessness are evident in the responses of a son who was caring for a 92-year-old mother and a 90-year-old mother-in-law. He noted that he and his wife had always hoped that their parents would die at home. He noted that his mother was

> totally out of it, she had no relationship to reality at all, yet, somehow her heart kept beating. We just wished for a coronary and it didn't come. It was hard to see her put in the hospital and watch her go downhill after that. It was so slow and very hard [#23/24—61-year-old son, who had been caring for his 90-year-old mother-in-law for 9 years and his 92-year-old mother for over 15 years].

Feelings of guilt and inadequacy often place additional stress on the caregiver. It is clear that conflicting expectations between the caregiver and elder, between the caregiver and medical and social service personnel, and between the caregiver and other family members was burdensome. In the following quote, the caregiver expresses frustration over her inability to perform the caregiving role according to some preconceived standard.

> I would say that sometimes it gets to me and sometimes I would just like to be able to go out and throw a rock at a train or something. That's the frustration on my part because I feel inadequate to really handle it [#5—52-year-old man, who had been caring for his 74-year-old mother for 18 months].

Although most of this chapter has focused on the stresses experienced by caregivers, we should not overlook the fact that most parents work extremely hard in order to be able to provide the best for their children. Their aim in life is to enable their children to live a good life and to be able to leave them at least a small inheritance. The realization that they have become an emotional, physical, and financial strain on their children is not to be taken lightly. This is most poignantly expressed by the 66-year-old caregiver, who has cared for her 86-year-old father for four years:

> I told my daughter-in-law this morning... "I want you to promise me that when I get like this that you will please put me someplace." She said that "she couldn't do that." I said, "I want you to do it because I don't want to wreck peoples lives. Please put me someplace. Let me maintain my sense of dignity. I don't want to be in somebody's home, and I don't want to feel that I am a burden, because that is what it is, a burden [#95—66-year-old daughter, who had been caring for her 86-year-old father for 4 years].

Summary

An analysis of the correlations between performing the tasks that make up the six dependency categories, and measures of family stress, dependency stress, and total stress reveals that only about 35% (n = 41) of the 118 relationships for specific tasks (the "other" category scores were not included for this analysis) were significantly correlated. However, when the correlations between the caregiver's response that performing a task was stressful and family, dependency, and total stress were analyzed, out of 36 relationships 86% (n = 31) were significant. This provides further substantiation that the number and frequency of tasks that a caregiver performs is not necessarily related to the stress experienced. Rather it is the caregiver's perception of the stressfulness of having to perform these tasks. When caregivers reported stress associated with the provision of dependency tasks, about 40% (n = 29) of the possible 72 relationships with dependency stress differed significantly; 6% of the possible 108 pairs of demographic variables differed significantly; and about 7% of the family-relationship items (e.g., feeling that you, your parents, your siblings, or other relatives thought that you could do more) differed significantly.

There were no differences between stressed and nonstressed caregivers in the use of control maintenance techniques for five of the stress-producing categories: financial, transportation, not eating, special diets, and privacy. However, among the remaining seven categories, higher levels of verbal abuse, medical abuse, psychological abuse, physical, and

total abuse characterized stressed caregivers. It appears that instrumental tasks, household, financial, transportation, getting the elder to
eat (adequately) and special diets are, in general, less likely to produce
abusive caregiving than are the expressive tasks, such as dealing with a
mobile but senile elder, their demands, or providing social/emotional
support.

   In conclusion, although an individual's perception of stress and
burden is not related to family and social structural factors, caregivers
who perceive that caregiving is stressful and a burden are more likely to
use negative forms of control maintenance techniques. A fuller exploration of the use of all techniques by elders and caregivers in attempts to
gain or maintain control will be examined in the following chapter.

Notes

   1. See Appendix C, Table C.3 for the mean scores of each dependency stress item;
table C.4 for a correlation matrix. Figure 6.1, the frequency with which each dependency
stress item is experienced, and Table 6.2, a summary of the significance levels for these
items, are included in this chapter.
   2. The correlations for each of the six categories being discussed in this section of the
chapter are based on the individual items in the dependency category, the total
dependency score for that category, family stress, dependency stress, and total stress
indices.

ELDER ABUSE:
VICTIMS AND PERPETRATORS

Interviewer: Did you ever have to resort to yelling and screaming?
Caregiver: Yes, sure. She'd scream right back at me.
Interviewer: Did you ever have to use physical restraint?
Caregiver: Yes ... she threw something at me one time when I was forcing
               her to eat.
Interviewer: How often did you have to force her to eat?
Caregiver: Every day, literally, she had to be fed. If I left her alone the
               food would sit there [#26—50-year-old daughter, who had
               been caring for her 87-year-old mother for 15 years].

Elder Abuse: A New Social Problem?

This book represents one of the first studies on elder abuse to focus
exclusively on abuse occurring within the family setting; to gather the
data from the caregivers, not third party professionals; and to use
face-to-face, in-depth interviews. Therefore, comparisons of these
findings with those conducted primarily by mail surveys of professionals,
interviews with abused elders, or data collected from social service or
law enforcement agencies are tenuous. These earlier studies do,
however, provide insights into characteristics of abusers and victims and
the settings in which the abuse occurs.

In one of the first studies of elder abuse, a mail survey of over a
thousand medical personnel, social service professionals, and paraprofessionals, only 183 reports of elder abuse were received (O'Malley et
al., 1979). It is likely that this relatively low number of cases is probably
a result of the lack of attention given to the topic at that time. When a
phenomenon does not have an identifying label, a set of characteristics
describing it, and a specific mechanism for recording the incident, then
the likelihood of the event being identified, much less remembered, is
quite small.

An example of this is provided by comparing the reported cases of elder abuse after passage of the Connecticut Elderly Protective Service Law. During the first six months (June 1978-January 1979), 87 cases of physical abuse, 314 cases of neglect, 65 cases of exploitation, and 8 cases of abandonment were reported (Block, 1980). Within three months, there was a 91% increase in neglect cases; a 107% increase in physical abuse cases; a 95% increase in cases of exploitation; and an unbelievable 300% increase in abandonment. It is most unlikely that these tremendous increases in such a relatively short period of time reflect actual increased incidents of elder abuse. It is more likely that the additional publicity regarding the law, heightened sensitivity regarding abusive behaviors, and additional training for professionals combined to create an atmosphere in which previously occurring behaviors were now being identified, labeled, and reported as elder abuse.

Although these studies suggest relatively limited cases of identified and labeled elder abuse, the characteristics of those being abused and their abusers suggest that family members figure prominently in the victimization of the elderly. In the O'Malley et al. study (1979) discussed earlier, 75% of the reported victims lived with the abuser, and in over 80% of the reports, the abuser was a relative. In this present study, 23% of the caregivers used some form of physical abuse (hitting/slapping, restraining, threat of physical abuse, forcing food or medicine). Of this group only 22% reported that it happened "almost never," which can be interpreted as perhaps a few times. The largest single group, 44%, reported that they used some form of physical abuse "sometimes" and 22% noted that they "always" used some form of physical abuse to control the elder when there was a problem. As has been noted frequently abuse, like charity, begins at home.[1]

The forms of abuse examined in this book are not limited to physical abuse. In this study we have measures of psychological abuse and verbal abuse, as well as pro-social interactions, such as talking and seeking advice. The information solicited is not identical with behaviors considered abuse under most adult protective statutes, which include self abuse, self-neglect, abandonment, sexual abuse, and financial exploitation. Although we did not request specific information on neglect, caregivers' descriptions of how certain tasks or problems were handled might be construed as indication of neglect if this behavior occurred frequently or even sporadically over a long period of time. Likewise, caregivers' discussions of financial problems and handling of the elders' resources provided information on resource mismanagement. It was obvious that self-abuse and neglect or the concern that such abuse was imminent, often precipitated the move to the caregiver's home.

The goal of each of the chapters in this book has been to start with the simplest form of analysis, the frequency of occurrence, and then proceed to provide a more in-depth analysis, that is, the characteristics of caregivers or elders who select specific control maintenance techniques.

ELDER OR CAREGIVER ABUSE?

One of the confounding aspects of abuse of elders by adult children is that it is not always possible to separate the victims from the perpetrators. The meshing of personalities combined with a long history of intimate interaction often obliterates clear-cut distinctions between the abused and the abuser—victim or perpetrator. This is illustrated in the following quote from a daughter regarding the care of her mother who noted that "the actual work didn't bother her, it was getting mother to accept it from me" that was extremely stressful—so stressful that

> I ripped her dress off when she refused to get ready to go out. I was sorry right after to think that I let her get to me, but she just refused to get ready [#37—a 50-year-old daughter, who had been caring for her 72-year-old mother for 8 years].

This caregiving daughter, who feels sorrow that she has allowed her mother to provoke her to this level of aggression, not sorrow for what she had done to the mother, clearly sees herself as the victim.

In the following section, the actions taken by caregivers in their attempts to control the elder are discussed separately from those actions selected by elders in their attempt to maintain control. It must be recognized, however, that these are reciprocal interactions—elders often deliberately "aggravate" the caregivers and the caregivers often deliberately "aggravate" the elders. This excuses neither elders or caregivers from their actions, but is noted in this section because, with few exceptions, these were adults, fully aware of their behaviors and often continuing patterns of behavior begun early in life.

One final point needs to be strongly reiterated. The caregivers interviewed for this research were not the adult children stealing social security checks, beating mother into submission, or locking father in his room, described in lurid detail in the media. These were caring, thoughtful, loving children who were duty bound to provide the best possible care for their elderly parent.

The overwrought, exhausted, and stressed adult child who does use psychological, verbal, physical, or medical means to maintain control often does so with the best intentions.

Control maintenance techniques. A different approach has been taken for measuring interpersonal conflict resolution interactions in this study. Earlier studies of domestic violence adapted the CTS scales (Straus, Gelles, and Steinmetz, 1980) for measuring the behaviors of all individuals being studied. There were several reasons for not employing these measures.

First, we believed that the adult/child caregiver would use quite different methods, because of his or her better physical and emotional health, greater resources, and the ability to seek alternatives, than would the vulnerable elder. In fact, conditions such as limited mobility or senility could result in completely different tactics being deployed by an elder.

Second, since this was a study of adults, terms such as discipline seemed grossly inappropriate. Third, many of the situations that might have resulted in a caregiver's attempt to maintain control were not necessarily conscious disagreements or conflicts, for example, the elder forgetting to take medicine or wandering off. Likewise, techniques employed, such as using guilt or sympathy to obtain a favor, were very definitely attempts to maintain, gain, or regain control, not necessarily, however, to resolve a conflict.

Thus the methods measured were ones that reflected elders' and caregivers' attempts to resolve issues over control, and, in many ways reflected patterns of interaction that were developed throughout a lifetime. They were not limited to behaviors that would be analogous to disciplinary techniques, although some, for example, hitting and yelling, are certainly abusive "disciplinary" techniques found in child- and spouse-abuse studies.

Many of the techniques used by elders paralleled those used by the caregivers. This is not surprising since the evidence suggests that these caregivers learned these ways of interacting during their own childhood. Elders and caregivers both yelled and hit. Caregivers "ignored" the elder as a way of maintaining control, and elders, "pouted," usually in the form of staying in their rooms, or leaving the area where the rest of the family had gathered—a method quite similar to "ignoring." Elders refused to eat or take medication; caregivers forced food or medication. Elders called the police or others in authority for some real or imagined problem or as an attempt to control; caregivers sought advice on control issues, for example, how to get mother to eat or to listen to them and take their advice.

ELDER'S USE OF CONTROL MAINTENANCE TECHNIQUES

Elders used a variety of forms of manipulation, especially guilt and attempting to use their disability or old age, to gain sympathy. If one does not have the ability to carry out threats (as caregivers did), then one uses more subtle, manipulative forms that play on others' weakness and vulnerability, instead of challenging their strength and power.

Elders also used physical force—hitting, slapping, throwing things. The difficulties in adjusting to the new responsibilities, obligations, and constriction on one's independence and privacy faced by both the caregivers and the elder were acknowledged by a daughter-in-law, who was caring for her father-in-law.

> There is no opinion about anything except his. It has just occurred to me that . . . I am describing a very domineering man who is very resistant to change. But on the other hand he has done a lot of it and it certainly has not been easy for him with the [grand] kids around [#133—44-year-old daughter-in-law, who had been caring for her 68-year-old father-in-law for 3 years].

Verbal abuse. One of the ways that an elder attempts to gain or maintain control is through yelling. Over 34% of the caregivers reported that their elderly parent or kin yelled in an attempt to get their way or show displeasure. When asked whether her father-in-law ever exhibited explosive behavior, the respondent stated:

> Yes, especially at times towards my husband. He would have spells of, not shouting, but if things didn't go his way, he wasn't too willing at times to accept changes [#16—52-year-old daughter, who had been caring for her 89-year-old father for 14 years].

Another caregiver discovered that her father was interacting in a manner that was quite similar to her adolescent-aged son.

> He is a very verbal, loud person. It is interesting at times. . . During the last year we have decided that my son, who is at that horrible age in the development, [and my father] both operate on the same level. He is inclined to temper tantrums. He exhibits a lot of the same behavior as an adolescent does [#133—44-year-old daughter-in-law, who had been caring for her 68-year-old father-in-law for 3 years].

> She got mad at me over nothing and I was not in the right mood either. We didn't see eye to eye for quite a while . . . She did get really angry and loud and verbally lashed out at me. I finally made the offer to straighten things out. We could not live like this for very long. Our biggest problem, I think, is that she is living in our house but still she isn't a member [#126—58-

year-old daughter-in-law, who had been caring for her 82-year-old mother-in-law for 8 years].

Elders who were verbally abusive were living in families characterized by significantly greater levels of family dependency and total stress. The caregivers provided significantly more household tasks, but did not differ on any of the other dependency categories. Elderly males were significantly more likely to be verbally abusive than were females, and younger elders were more likely to be verbally abusive and to direct this abuse to younger caregivers.

Crying. Approximately 37% of the elderly cried as a way to gain sympathy or control. With some elders, changes in personality, such as an increased use of verbal or physical aggression or extreme emotions, are directly related to illness such as a stroke or hypertension, as illustrated by the following quote:

Since she had her stroke, she cries easily. She is more aggressive in that occasionally she has hit me if we have been having a disagreement. She is more aggressive in her behavior since she had the stroke. She is also much more affectionate since the stroke. She is quite apt to hug or kiss almost anyone [#17—59-year-old daughter, who had been caring for her 84-year-old mother for 6½ years].

Other elders, however, are simply continuing to use behavior that has worked throughout his or her lifetime.

She will have a temper tantrum if she wants to get her own way. I can't stand to see her cry and she knows it, she is a little character [#31—58-year-old daughter, who had been caring for her 82-year-old mother for 2½ years].

Cry, on occasion, yes. One time my sister came in and he started crying. You would have thought that someone had beaten him half to death. He can do that real well. If he finds out that he is not going to get his own way or something, he turns on the tears [#95—66-year-old daughter, who had been caring for her 86-year-old father for 4 years].

Although these relationships are most likely reciprocal, elders who cried lived with caregivers who experienced significantly higher levels of dependency and total stress and performed significantly higher levels of financial, mental health, and social/emotional dependency tasks. They did not differ significantly on the other characteristics examined.

Pouting. Pouting, often described as the elder wanting to be left alone, or, as a 39-year-old daughter-in-law described her 84-year-old father-in-law's actions, "Just being stubborn, closing his ears, ignoring" (#12/13). Pouting was reported to be used by over 60% of the elders. One mother, residing with her daughter for 26 years, had learned that determination, being stubborn, and ignoring the pleas of her daughter was an excellent way to maintain control.

> She could be very definite. You didn't win her over all the time. She had very strong convictions. That is one of the reasons that kept her going, She really has a determined spirit [#92—60-year-old daughter, who had been caring for her 92-year-old mother for 26 years].

Elders who pouted were significantly more likely to live in families in which the caregiver reported significantly higher levels of family, dependency, and total stress and were performing higher levels of mental health dependency tasks.

Manipulate. Attempts to manipulate the caregiver by the use of guilt, or to gain sympathy because of one's illness or frailty, or by playing one family member against another were used by 63% of the elders. When asked if the elder manipulated family members to get her own way, one caregiver responded:

> Well, mother is very generous and she likes to give things to my children. She knows I won't approve of it so she does it anyway. It is out of generosity. She is not trying to prove anything or get her own way. She just likes to give things to people [#15—65-year-old daughter, who had been caring for her 87-year-old mother for 15 years].

Although the true intentions of mother's behavior appear to the caregiver as innocent gifts, other caregivers acknowledged the deliberate attempts of elders to control the caregiver and caregiving family. A daughter who is responsible for her severely ill 74-year-old mother and fairly healthy 89-year-old aunt, related one way that her mother attempted to control the family:

> Mother is an actress. It was recognized by the people in the hospital. She has had four or five deathbed scenes where she told everybody that she was dying and she has the family called in to say goodbye. We've been through that several times and I told her that was never happening again. That when she dies she is going to die alone holding my hand and that's it. I'm not calling the family in again [#110/111—55-year-old daughter, who

had been living with her mother for 55 years and her 89-year-old great aunt for 5 years].

Another component of the variable *manipulate* is the use of guilt. The following quotes suggest that many elders, especially mothers, have perfected the art of inducing guilt through a lifetime of practice.

> My mother called me the other day and said, "this is the last time you will hear my voice." I said, "What?" She said, " Well, I keep calling you and you don't call me so I'm not calling you so I figure it will be the last time you will hear my voice." I called her the next day and invited her for dinner. She said, "Guilty conscience" [#18/119—39-year-old daughter, who had been caring for her 59-year-old mother and 61-year-old father for 5 years].

> Her inability to relate to other family members was a big stress on me because then I was the go-between . . . her strong use of guilt to create a situation to absolve herself of things. She was never able to resolve having to give up her home to come and live with us . . . She pouts and sighs and says she has pains in the chest and states, "This is too much pressure to live under" [#138—42-year-old son, who had been caring for his 69-year-old mother for 8 years].

Only significantly higher levels of dependency and total stress experienced by caregivers differentiated elders who used manipulation from those who did not use this method. It is possible that individual personality differences account for the methods chosen by elder— methods, which appear to be used in other situations. For example, one daughter, whose 93-year-old mother is extremely difficult to control, noted that she has placed her mother in a foster home but "she didn't fit in." She later had placed her in a mental hospital:

> The police took her down there. She had gotten on my nerves so bad that I thought maybe they could help [#98—58-year-old daughter, who had been caring for her 93-year-old mother for 8 years].

However, this caregiver faced another problem, one that results when the elder lives to an advanced age, outliving not only their own brothers and sisters, but also their own children:

> When my sister was alive . . . she used to come and get her and take her home with her for a couple of months and that was enjoyment to her.

Then . . . she used to go down south [to my brother's home] and stay down there for a while. . . now she's found out that she doesn't have these places to go anymore and she gets depressed [#98].

Invading privacy. By invading other's privacy, elders demonstrate that they still had the right to attend to their children's business. It is recognized, of course, that loneliness and a need to be a part of the ongoing activities motivated this type of behavior. Nevertheless, 40% of the adult offspring in the generationally inverse families studied reported this problem and considered it to be most disturbing. Furthermore, 25% of the sample found privacy issues to be stressful "sometimes," and 22% found this behavior to be "almost always" or "always stressful."

Caregivers stressed by lack of privacy reported significantly higher family, dependency, and total stress scores and were more likely to feel burdened. They were providing significantly more personal grooming/health dependency tasks and social/emotional support than nonstressed caregivers. When the last three variables: manipulation, pouting, and invading privacy were combined into a variable labeled *emotional abuse,* nearly 75% of the elders used at least one of these methods in an attempt to control the caregiver.

Calling the police. Approximately 6% of the elders called the police or others in authority for a real or imagined concern. In some instances, the action is an attempt to show the family, or perhaps to prove to themselves, that they still have the ability and authority to exercise some control. The description of the activities of a 91-year-old father in the care of his 53-year-old daughter for 31 years are of interest. This is especially revealing when it is realized that the daughter and her family were forced to rent out their own home and move into the father's home when he was no longer able to care for himself, yet refused to give up his home.

Three generations in the house is just too much. . . . He has called the police to report a car parked in front of the house for no reason . . . Stated "you wish I were dead." He doesn't respect privacy . . . because this is *his* home [#116—53-year-old daughter, who had been caring for her 91-year-old father for 31 years].

Elders who called the police were significantly younger, required more mental health dependency tasks provided for them, and had caregivers who reported significantly higher levels of total stress.

Refusing food or medicine. Another mechanism for maintaining control over one's environment is through the refusal of food or medicine. In some instances, this is the result of diminished sensitivity of the taste buds and difficulty in swallowing. However, in other instances a loss of appetite and lack of interest in eating are to blame. In still others, senility and confusion result in elders forgetting to eat or take medicine or fearing that it is poisoned.

> She wouldn't take her medicine at all. I had to put her in the hospital, my mother is like that . . . The first time my mother ever went to a hospital was when she broke her hip. We had to stay with her night and day because she was so upset, because she had never been in one . . . she never liked doctors. Taking her medicine, NO! She would not take her medicine. I had to force her to take her medicine . . . I have to force it in before she would throw it in the garbage cans . . . hold it in her mouth. The doctor said to try to get it in her coffee. I put a capsule in her coffee and it didn't dissolve and she drank her coffee and it was still there. She sneaked out of here, got on a bus and called my sister and said that I was trying to put poison in her coffee [#98—58-year-old daughter, who had been caring for her 93-year-old mother for 8 years].

Just under one-fourth of the sample of elders refused to eat or take medicine. These elders were significantly younger, and their caregivers experienced significantly higher levels of dependency and total stress and performed more mental health dependency tasks.

Physical violence. When one thinks about the use of physical violence between elder and caregiver, we tend to picture the caregiver as the perpetrator and the elder as the victim. We should not be surprised to find that a considerable number of elders use violence and that they tend to use it frequently. Based on studies of other forms of family violence, we know that individuals tend to resort to violence when all else fails (Gelles, 1974; Steinmetz, 1977; Straus et al., 1980).

The elderly, especially those who have given up most of their independence and must resort to being cared for by their adult children have few other ways to maintain control. In our society, the elderly are not accorded respect based on their age, they do not have high status, they have often lost possession of their homes, furniture, cars. They have limited money and financial resources and often can barely call a bedroom their own. When the caregiver is unwilling (or unable) to meet the elder's demand, the only method the elder perceives to be left, in an attempt to enforce that demand, is physical violence. The time-worn pattern "I told you once—I told you twice———smack" used during childhood, is dusted off and used again. In this study, 18% of the elders used physical violence, and of those using violence, greater than half (57%) were reported to use violence "sometimes."

In some families the violence appeared to be a recent phenomenon, possibly attributed to a stroke or senility. A caregiving daughter reported the doctor's description of her mother as "senile... the mind is all confused and she doesn't know what's happening." She noted that her mother would

maul me up the side of the head. She would say you're my child, I'm not your child, and I'm you mother and then maul me [#98—58-year-old daughter, who had been caring for her 93-year-old mother for 8 years].

Another caregiver reported:

One time when my aunt was here, she [mother] went upstairs and I tried to talk to her and she kicked and was really not herself at all [#148—46-year-old daughter, who had been caring for her 84-year-old mother for 2½ years].

Other elders were quite violent, and their behavior appeared to be a continuation of life-long patterns of violent interaction between parent and child, such as the 90-year-old grandmother who broke her glasses by hitting her 10-year-old grandson (#134), or the 91-year-old father whose 53-year-old daughter reported:

He would cry, scream, yell all the time he was being bathed. He hated fresh air. He threatened to kill me, one time at the dinner table and another time on the cellar steps. One time he threw a sled at me. He had a bad temper and he constantly said, "If you don't like it here, then move somewhere else." I would say that "I would like to"... we have lived here because he would not move into our house... we still have ours down the street that we rented out. But then he was sorry for saying it [#116—53-year-old daughter, who had been caring for her 91-year-old father for 31 years].

She would just as soon pick up something and throw it.... During the last six weeks, generally towards the end, she only made a swipe at me once. She never really threw anything in those last six weeks. She was always a very physical person [#26—50-year-old daughter, who had been caring for her 87-year-old mother for nearly 15 years].

Elders who used physical violence as a way to gain control required significantly more personal grooming/health, financial, mental health, and social/emotional tasks performed for them, which provides support for the use of resource theory to explain an elder's use of violence. The caregivers in these families reported significantly higher levels of family, dependency, and total stress.

CONTROL MAINTENANCE TECHNIQUES USED BY CAREGIVERS

The techniques used by caregivers can be grouped into four categories:

Discussion, such as talking or seeking advice;
Verbal aggression;
Psychological abuse, ignoring requests (or demands), threats; and
Physical abuse, forcing food or medicine as a form of control, hitting, slapping, use of restraints, and the use or the threat of physical abuse.

Two component measures of physical abuse are used in this chapter. One, referred to as physical violence or physical abuse in the preceding chapters, measures the actual use of physical force as well as the threat of physical violence. A second measure, severe physical abuse, which is used only in this chapter and the next, has the threat component removed.

The rationale for having "threat of physical violence" in the physical abuse measure is quite understandable when one considers such factors as the tone of voice, body stance, and actual fear arousal, which are evident when someone is threatening to use physical violence, especially when the threatener is considerably stronger and healthier than the victim. It has also been included in measures of physical violence in a number of other studies (Steinmetz, 1977, 1978, 1981, 1983; Straus et al., 1980).

However, an equally cogent argument can be made for limiting the measure to actual use of physical violence. Therefore, both measures were used in this chapter, which has as a goal: teasing out the relationships between the control maintenance techniques used by caregivers and elders and demographic variables, levels of dependency, and stress experienced by caregivers. Although hitting or shaking may not seem like "severe" acts, when the recipient is a frail, elderly person, the potential for physical injury and emotional trauma is severe.

Discussion. As could be expected, most caregivers (82%), attempted to talk to the elder in order to resolve problems. A careful examination of the transcripts suggests that the 18% (n = 22) of caregivers who did not report "talking" to resolve problems in many cases had no problem or had the type of problem that could not be discussed, or it would not be understood by the elder or would have been misunderstood and create still more problems.

Control Maintenance Techniques

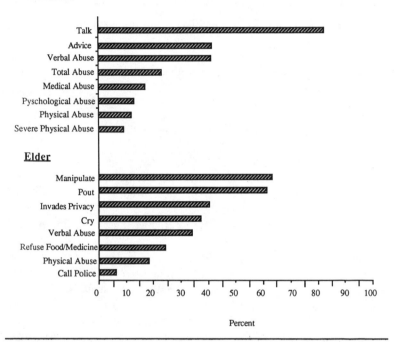

Figure 7.1 Control maintenance techniques used by caregivers and elders, in percentages.

In all, 69% of the caregivers reported that they sought advice for problems in caring for the elder (see Figure 7.1). Most advice tended to be from medical doctors or counselors and was for information on specific issues. One daughter and her husband had taken the mother to a local family counseling center because

> she was very angry with my husband, and I thought that maybe if she had an opportunity to talk to disinterested parties and vent her feelings that she would feel better and also maybe put things in the proper perspective ... unfortunately, she did not approve of the persons who were qualified in social work [#2—54-year-old daughter, who had been caring for her 87-year-old mother for 8 years].

Do caregivers who discussed problems with the elder or sought advice differ in any significant way from those caregivers who did not report discussing problems with the elder? Only providing significantly more social/emotional support differentiated caregivers who talked with the elders in an attempt to maintain control and those who did not. Caregivers who sought advice tended to be caring for mother, have significantly higher dependency and total stress scores, and were significantly more likely to report feeling burdened and to provide significantly higher amounts of mental health tasks.

Verbal aggression. Whereas many caregivers reported talking in "loud voices" or "argumentative tones," 41% reported that they did yell at the elder during a conflict (see Figure 7.1). It appears that controlling violence may have more to do with the relative health, strength, or mental state of the parent rather than some moral precept about the social undesirability of using violence on family members. The next quotes demonstrate that many families believed that fights and lower levels of violence were necessary and normal. Much in the same vein as catharsis-theory proponents such as Bach and Wyden (1968), these families believe that normal "lower-level" acceptable fights relieve tension thus clearing the air and preventing more destructive, "higher-levels" of violence. As one daughter suggested:

My mother and I have a good fight now and then. Well, everybody does. You can't have a good relationship unless you have a good fight [#18/119—39-year-old daughter, who had been caring for her 59-year-old mother and 61-year-old father for 5 years].

Later, this respondent reported:

If she said something to hurt me, I would come back with something just as bad. That's a normal reaction. If they hurt your feelings, you want them to hurt as bad as you do. I never can think of what to say until about two hours later [#18/119].

Another caregiver noted that:

I had to yell at her sometimes. If you just talked to her, she wouldn't listen. She would take advantage of me [#98—58-year-old daughter, who had been caring for her 93-year-old mother for 8 years].

About 80% of caregivers residing in a large city in this sample were verbally abusive as compared with 37% of suburban caregivers, 39% of small town caregivers, and 40% of rural caregivers. Verbally abusive caregivers are significantly younger, provide significantly more mental health dependency tasks, and experience more stress over the elder's physical disability. They also report higher levels of dependency stress and have significantly higher total stress scores.

Psychological abuse. There are two categories classified under psychological abuse: threats and ignoring the elder. As shown on Figure 7.1, only about 5% of the caregivers reported ignoring the elder. It appears that these caregivers were simply not responding as quickly to the elder's demands as they might have, rather than ignoring them.

In one small way, these caregivers are attempting to exert at least minimal control over their action. They may recognize that being thirsty is uncomfortable; that mother wants a drink and can't get the drink herself; and that as the caregiving daughter it is her responsibility to get the drink for mother. However, they also recognize that no harm will come to mother if she waits five more minutes, and since this is the fourth time they have stopped eating their lunch, doing dishes, or folding laundry in the last half hour to answer mother's demands, she will just have to wait.

Caregivers often recognize that one of the methods elders use for testing their control over the caregiver is to see how quickly each of their demands are met. The next quote illustrates the bind that caregivers find themselves in—wanting to be good children—yet needing to have some control over their own needs.

> It's not that we don't want to do it; it is just that we are under stress to do it. She still wants to be independent, yet she still wants people to stop everything and do things for her "right now"[#109—49-year-old daughter, who had been caring for her 80-year-old mother for 13 years].

Ignoring the elder was measured by two components—confining the elder to a room, chair, or bed and withholding food, which, based on the transcripts, was most often ignoring requests for forbidden food or drinks. This measure of ignoring the elder is in terms of ignoring the elder's demands or not providing them with the desired attention. It is more a passive form of abuse than that noted by a caregiver who assumed the care of her father-in-law after his alcoholic daughter abused him:

> I highly resented Doug's [alcoholic] sister because I feel that she contributed to this illness by personal and emotional neglect. She abused him in that she didn't feed him and didn't take care of him and left him alone and took everything she could get from him as far as financial support, and gave nothing. She would lock her door against him. He was 89 years old and had had two cataract operations. He would walk to the store to get himself some soup or something. She didn't do his laundry,

change his bed, anything . . . As it turned out, the courts decided she wasn't fit to be his guardian, but on the other hand, I was only a daughter-in-law, so they awarded the bank with custody. After that happened, he only lived three weeks . . . I think it began to alter his view of his daughter. He realized that she was not all that he thought she was [#15—65-year-old daughter, who had been caring for her 87-year-old mother for 15 years].

Threat, the second component of the psychological abuse measure, consisted of two variables: threaten with physical aggression, and threaten to send to a nursing home. Just over 10% of the caregivers used threats to obtain control. In some instances the objectives are noble even though the means to the end are emotionally distressful to the elder. In desperation, one caregiver reported:

I couldn't get her to allow me to care for her and I threatened to take her someplace where they would make her do these things [#37—59-year-old daughter, who had been caring for her 72-year-old mother for 8 years].

In other cases, the elder is the one actually threatening to leave, although it is clear in these instances that they are probably voicing this view, because it has been implied in other conversations:

He talks about it. He will get upset with something and say, "Well, I guess that I will have to go someplace and find my own place to live" [#102—48-year-old daughter caring her 82-year-old father for 3 years].

In still other instances, previous actions possibly speak louder than words. When caring for her 93-year-old mother became too difficult the daughter who had been providing care for eight years reported that she had put her mother

in a foster home because maybe she would do better. Sometimes older people would do more for someone else than for their own. Therefore, I tried a foster home. She didn't fit in there. She quit eating and would not take her medicine. So I had to take her back to the hospital and they had to feed her through IV. [#98—58-year-old daughter, who had been caring for her 93-year-old mother for 8 years].

Over 13% of the caregivers reported that they used some form of psychological abuse. None of the demographic variables differed significantly between caregivers who were psychologically abusive and those who did not use this method of gaining or maintaining control.

However, psychologically abusive caregivers had been caring for an elder more than twice as long as had nonabusive caregivers. They also provided significantly higher amounts of all dependency tasks except social/emotional dependency, and reported higher levels of dependency and total stress scores than did nonabusing caregivers. Abusive caregivers tended to report higher levels of all dependency stress items, however, only social/emotional and physical disability and elder's demands differed significantly.

Medical abuse. The medical abuse index is composed of the variables "forcing the elder to take medicine" or "forcing the elder to eat." Medical abuse was used by 17% of the sample. Of this group, the largest percentage, 15%, used medication as a controlling mechanism. Caregivers were quite articulate in explaining the need for such medication, often noting that the doctor ordered the medication, and it was in the patient's best interest. One 66-year-old daughter noted that she gave her 97-year-old mother "medication to calm her down."

> I have given her tranquilizers. First, I have told her what they are, how long they will last, and what to expect from them. She has needed them and she has wanted them. They were not forced [on her] [#90—66-year-old daughter, who had been caring for her 97-year-old mother for 11 years].

Caregivers who used medical abuse were significantly more likely to reside in the city or suburbs, about 30%, as compared with 6% of caregivers who live in rural areas and 14% of caregivers residing in small towns. No other demographic variables differed significantly. These caregivers perform significantly more personal grooming/health, financial, mental health tasks, had significantly higher dependency scores, and experienced considerably more dependency stress and total stress (see Table C.7 in Appendix C and Table 7.1).

Physical abuse. The physical abuse measure contains the components: use of restraints, threat of physical abuse, and actual acts of physical abuse. The threat of physical abuse was reported by just under 4.5% of the caregivers, and hitting or slapping was reported by just over 2.5% of the sample. Just over 7.5% of the caregivers reported that they restrained the elder. When the above three measures, restraint, threat, and actually hitting or slapping were combined, about 12% of the caregivers reported that they used at least one of these methods (see Figure 7.1).

In some instances physical abuse takes place with the best of motives. For example, parents who slap their 2-year-old's fingers for playing with an electric outlet are certainly showing care and concern for the toddler. Likewise, the adult child caregiver who restrains an elder does so with the goal of protecting him or her from harm. Unfortunately, in both the toddler and elder example, these good intentions can result in physical abuse.

The need to use restraints, was a signal to some caregiving families that institutionalization of the elder was no longer unavoidable. As one son described:

> We sought hospitalization when we could no longer keep her in bed. We had a hospital bed and all the hospital paraphernalia, wheelchair, and the rest of it. It got to the point where she wouldn't stay in bed or even in a chair, but would stand up and fall down . . . She was unwell and unable to walk, but she kept trying. She'd get out of bed and fall flat on her face. We'd find her on the floor in the morning . . . When she had to be restrained in bed and in the chair, we felt that we couldn't do that. You can't tie your own mother to a bed [#23/24—61-year-old son, who had been caring for his 92-year-old mother for 15 years and his 90-year-old mother-in-law for 9 years].

When asked about the need to use restraints to control the elder, another caregiver responded that she had a burglar alarm.

> I would put the alarm on to keep her from going out . . . she used to sneak out at night. . . . Once she opened the door, the alarm would go off and we knew she was trying to get out [#98—58-year-old daughter, who had been caring for her 93-year-old mother for 8 years].

The interviewer later asked the caregiver if she ever had to tie her mother down. The caregiver's response clearly indicates that caregiving children who are required to provide 24 hour care do so with far fewer aids than do nursing facilities and hospitals:

> No, I never tied her down. When she was in the hospital, they had to tie her in bed to keep her in bed. She would try to get out of there [#98].

The quote above and the one opening this chapter clearly document the dilemma caregivers face. Without adequate training and the availability of support personnel, a caregiver attempts to force an elder to eat, recognizing the necessity to do so in order to prevent malnutrition. The screaming and yelling, forcing of food, and physical force needed to carry out this feeding ordeal are, however, clearly abusive. Likewise, the

TABLE 7.1
Control Maintenance Techniques Used by Caregivers and Elders: Significance Levels

	Verbal Abuse	Psychological Abuse	Physical Abuse	Severe Physical Abuse	Medical Abuse	Total Violence
Demographic						
elder's age	–	–	–	–	–	–
caregiver's age	.01	–	–	–	–	–
length of caregiving	–	–	–	–	–	–
total illness	–	–	–	–	–	–
race	–	–	–	–	–	–
relationship	–	–	–	.04	–	–
elder's sex	–	–	–	–	–	–
caregiver's sex	–	–	–	–	–	–
residence	.02	–	–	–	.03	–
Dependency						
household	–	.0008	–	–	–	.002
personal groom/health	–	.04	–	.04	.004	.01
financial	–	.03	–	.003	.008	.03
mobility	–	.001	.0002	.05	–	.03
mental health	.0001	.02	.0002	.0001	.001	.0001
social/emotional	–	–	–	–	–	–
total dependency	–	.004	–	–	.004	.0001
Dependency Stress						
household	–	–	.001	.0001	.03	.008

grooming/health	–	–	–	.05	.002	.001
financial	–	–	–	–	–	–
mobile/senile	.0002	–	.005	.0002	.005	.0001
social/emotional	.02	.01	.0001	.0001	.003	.0001
transportation	–	–	–	.02	.02	.04
physical disability	.01	.04	.03	.002	.006	.0002
elder's loneliness	–	–	–	–	–	–
not eating	–	–	–	–	–	–
special diet	–	–	–	–	–	–
elder's demands	.03	.03	.01	.02	–	.03
lack of privacy	–	–	–	–	–	–
Stress and Burden						
family-related	–	–	–	.001	–	.04
total dependency	.002	.008	.0001	.0001	.0001	.0001
total stress	.003	.01	.0001	.0001	.02	.0001
burden	–	–	–	.04	–	–
Elder's CMT						
yell	.0001	–	–	–	.03	.0005
pout	.001	.0004	.006	.02	–	–
refuse food or medicine	.05	.04	–	–	–	–
elder hit	.001	.008	.005	.0001	.03	.005
elder cry	.04	–	–	–	–	–
manipulate	.01	–	–	–	–	–
call police	–	–	–	–	.02	.02
ignores privacy	.006	–	–	–	–	–

hospital, with round-the-clock staff, used restraints to keep the senile, but mobile patient in bed. The caregiver with total responsibility for 24-hour care attempted to provide the same level of protection, but did so by being constantly on guard, instead of using restraints.

In some families the violence resulting from the stress of caregiving was not directed toward the elder, but displaced toward another person or object. This is similar to hitting the wall instead of one's spouse. It did, in one family, dramatically indicate how distressing the elder's behavior was.

> When my mother first came in, she used to lock all the doors all the time because, as I said, she is afraid that people are going to get us. One day, he [my husband] just smashed down the garage door when she locked him out when he went to the mailbox. He literally broke the door. He never said beans to her. She has never locked a door on us again. I think he made his point. That's the only thing he has ever done to show her that things bother him [#7—36-year-old daughter, who had been caring for her 65-year-old mother for 2 years].

When the sample was divided into those who used physical abuse and those who did not use physically abusive methods, none of the demographic variables differed significantly. However, abusive caregivers had provided care for considerably longer periods of time (14.3 versus 8.8 years), and mothers were most often the victim of the abuse, a finding that approached significance (.06). Although physically abusive caregivers reported higher levels of task performance than nonabusive caregivers, mental health dependency was the only category to differ significantly.

Comparing the levels of dependency with the stress perceived from providing these tasks reveal some interesting trends. Abusive caregivers did not differ from their nonabusive counterparts in the level of household tasks provided, but their perception of stress for the measures of "household" tasks, was significantly higher. Household dependency for abusers and nonabusers was 25.00 and 21.96; the household dependency stress was 2.29 and 1.08.

Although the amount of social/emotional tasks performed by the two groups barely differed (15.57 versus 14.21, abusers and nonabusers, respectively), abusers perceived these tasks to be significantly more stressful (2.71 versus 0.94). Of course, some variables were significant in both the dependency category and the stress produced by performing this task. For example, the dependency category of mental health differed significantly as did the stress measure specifically related to caring for a mobile but senile elder, which was one component in the mental health category (2.00 versus 0.49). Other dependency categories, such as financial dependency and personal grooming/health, did not differ significantly, and were more or less equal in the stress associated with performing these tasks.

Severe physical violence. This measure contains the items hitting or slapping, and the physical restraint measure. The item, threaten with physical abuse, had been removed from the index. Just over 9% of the caregivers reported that they used physical violence on the elder to gain or maintain control. The characteristics defining caregivers who use severe physical abuse on their elders' were similar to those discussed above for physical abuse. Two things are noticeably different. First, caregivers using severe abuse perform significantly more dependency-tasks. Although mental health dependency was the only category in which abusers had significantly higher scores among those using physical abuse, only household and social/emotional dependency were not significantly higher among caregivers using severe physical abuse.

Second, family stress and burden as well as the dependency stress and total stress were all significantly higher among caregivers who used severe physical abuse. It appears that caregivers characterized as having a high potential for severe physical abuse are those not only providing more dependency tasks, but they also experience significantly higher levels of dependency stress, feelings of burden, and family, dependency, and total stress.

Total violence. Total violence, the combined measure of physical abuse and medical abuse, acts that have the potential to produce severe injury, were reported by 23% of the caregivers or nearly one-fourth of the sample. Those caregivers who used any form of physical abuse performed a greater number of all dependency tasks, and all but household and social/emotional differed significantly. Abusers were also characterized by experiencing considerably greater amounts of dependency stresses, 7 out of 12 differed significantly. Family, dependency, and total stress were all significantly higher among abusing caregivers.

Summary

Although not all of the findings were statistically significant, consistent trends were noted that need to be examined on larger, representative samples. Elders and caregivers both used a variety of positive and negative methods in their attempt to gain or maintain control. Over one-third of the elders used verbally abusive methods (34%) and cried (37%) in attempts to maintain control. Possibly the method used most frequently by elders was to pout. Overall, 70% of the elders attempted to get their way by this method, and 63% of the elders used some form of manipulation usually through inducing guilt or sympathy. Calling the police or other authority was used by 6% of the elders. Just under one-quarter of the sample of elders refused to eat or take medicine, and 18% used physically violent means such as hitting or throwing things at the caregiver to gain control.

Some 82% of the caregivers talked over problems with the elder and 69% sought the advice of another. When these measures were combined every caregiver had used some positive form of problem solving. A total of 41% of caregivers were verbally abusive, and both the caregivers and elders in these families were significantly younger.

In all, 5% of the caregivers ignored and 10% used threats, and when these measures were combined to provide a total measure of psychological abuse, over 13% of the caregivers resorted to some form of emotionally or psychologically abusive methods. Caregivers who used psychological abuse performed significantly greater amounts of all but social/emotional tasks than did nonabusive caregivers. Stress from caring for a mobile but senile elder, a family member with a disability, or a demanding elder characterized psychological abusive caregivers.

Approximately 17% of the caregivers reported that they had used force to get the elder to eat or take medicine. The threat or actual use of physical abuse was reported by just under 12% of the caregivers. When the item "threaten with physical violence" was removed from the index, over 9% of the caregivers actually used physically violent means of control. This group was significantly more likely to report being burdened by the caregiving, and they were performing significantly greater amounts of personal grooming/health, financial, mobility, and mental health tasks. (Only mental health tasks differed significantly for the physical abuse measure). Caregivers using severe physical violence also appeared to be experiencing significantly higher levels of family and dependency stress than did caregivers who did not use severe physical violence as a control mechanism.

It is clear from an examination of the methods used by elders and caregivers in their attempts to grasp the reins of control or to hold on to them, that consistent trends emerge. Families in which more negative forms of interactions occur tend also to be experiencing somewhat more stress and performing more dependency tasks. Longer periods of caregiving also tend to be associated with many abusive adult child-elderly parent interactions. Abusive caregivers and elders did not differ on most demographic variables. Since so few demographic variables differed significantly between the two groups, biases that might have resulted from the nonrepresentative sampling techniques are not obvious. However, these findings cannot be generalized to other populations without considerable caution.

It appears, based on an in-depth analysis of the transcripts, that individual personalities and the interrelation of interaction of the participants must be considered when attempting to predict abusive behaviors. As the following quote suggests, not only are some elders easier to care for (because of health or personality), but some caregivers have personalities better suited to caring. One respondent described her feelings of burden as a result of providing care for her mother for five months:

> I didn't [feel burdened] in the beginning at all. I welcomed my mother. The last two months have been bad [#127—47-year-old daughter, who had been caring for her 84-year-old mother for 5 months].

Although these abusive methods might not produce emotional trauma or physical harm on a younger adult, the vulnerability of the elder causes even minor incidents to have the potential of producing severe physical abuse or emotional trauma. It should also be noted that these families, in spite of their use of abusive interaction, felt duty bound to provide almost heroic care for their elders. We can only wonder about the level of care provided by caregivers devoid of this love and concern.

In the final chapter we will examine present models for predicting elder abuse, examine family patterns of abuse and, using a symbolic-interaction theoretical framework, analyze the impact of perception of stress and burden on the caregiver role.

Note

1. See Figure 7.1 for percentages of elders and caregivers using each control maintenance technique; Table 7.1 for a summary of the levels of significance, and, in Appendix C, Table C.7 for the individual mean scores, and Tables C.5 and C.6 for correlations.

8

PATTERNS, PERCEPTIONS, AND PREDICTIONS

I can count on one hand the times I saw my mother cry. She would just as soon pick up something and throw it. During the last six weeks, generally towards the end, she only made a swipe at me once. She never really threw anything in those last six weeks. She was always a very physical person when I was younger. My father never spanked me, she did. When she was mad at me she would let me know . . . always vocally, and I'm just like her [#26—50-year-old daughter, who had been caring for her 87-year-old mother for 15 years].

My wife's mother took care of her own. They moved to their parents' home and stayed with them for a period of time. My mother took in her elderly aunt and brought her up. My mother's . . . mother died in childbirth, her father died at sea, and an aunt brought her up. Later she took that aunt in. Following that she took in another lady that had taken care of my aunt. So she had two elderly people that she took care of until they died. I guess I hadn't thought of that before [#23/24—61-year-old son, who had been caring for his 92-year-old mother for over 15 years and 90-year-old mother-in-law for 9 years].

The goal of this chapter is not only to describe the amount of violence being perpetrated on the elder and the characteristics that differentiate abusive from nonabusive caregivers, but also to develop models that can explain the relative contribution of each variable to abusive behaviors. Drawing on symbolic-interaction theory, and specifically the impact that one's perception of the events has on defining and responding to behavior, a flow diagram, developed from the apparent relationship between variables, will be presented.

Based on a combination of theory and previous analysis, path analysis will be used to order the relationship between variables and to provide insights into the sequence of events that lead to elder abuse. Since this research is not based on experimental design, true causality cannot be ascertained. However, the path model presented has a strong theoretical basis and is further substantiated by the testimony provided by the respondents interviewed for this research. The goal is to provide further insights useful for building predictive models based on this particular sample. Generalizations beyond this study, with a nonrandom sample are, however, problematic.

Finally, the findings will be grounded in a symbolic-interaction framework, demonstrating the importance of the definition of the situation in influencing abusive behaviors. In fact, the findings clearly indicate that an individual's perception of the stressfulness of providing a service or task for the elder contributes to elder abuse to a far greater degree than do specific tasks.

Predicting Elder Abuse

In order to begin to develop models that might predict elder abuse in this sample of caregiving adult offspring, five sets of regression analyses were conducted in order to eliminate variables that did not contribute significantly to predicting the likelihood of a caregiver being abusive toward their elder. The dependent variables were verbal abuse, psychological abuse, physical abuse, severe physical abuse, medical abuse, and total abuse.

The stepwise regression program in SAS will accommodate only 14 independent variables, so the regression analysis used the variables by groups that have been used for analysis throughout the book. The independent variables for the first set of analyses were the demographic variables that included age and sex of caregiver and elder, length of caregiving, race, where they lived, total number of illnesses, and marital status. The second group of variables entered into the regression equation were the family stress variables (small children, teens, two career family, single parent household, financial problems, recent death, alcohol or drug abuse, physical disability of a family member, family member with emotional problems, other family-related source of stress). The third set of variables were relative stress variables (parents, siblings, relatives, and you feel that you could do more) and burden as independent variables. The six dependency categories, plus the variable total illness, were the independent variables in the fourth set of analyses. The dependency task-related stress variables comprised the final set of independent variables entered into the regression model. Those variables from the five groups above that contributed significantly to each type of violence (verbal, psychological, medical, physical, severe physical, and total abuse) were then combined as a final set of independent variables.

Since there is abundant evidence suggesting that abusive interaction does not exist in a void but reflects a family unit in which abuse has become a part of the family's problem-solving repertoire, the control maintenance techniques used by the elder were added to each of the six violence models in order to examine their contribution to predicting elder abuse.

Because of the nonrepresentativeness of the sample and the relatively small size of the sample, several analyses were conducted to examine the impact of linearity, colinearity, and stability on the findings. First, in addition to running the variable using the stepwise program, which enables one to assess the increase of each added variable, the analyses were also run using the SAS Simple Regression Program with the standardized beta option and the Grand Linear Model Program with the options for upper and lower 95% confidence levels measures of colinearity. The values were within the confidence levels and first-order autocorrelation values were extremely low. The Durbin-Watson D values were also within the expected range.

In order to examine the data for systematic error, the predicted values and residuals were plotted and the scattergrams examined for evidence of linearity. Although these values were all within appropriate ranges, the relatively small occurrence of some types of abuse, less than 20%, could have distorted the data. Regression analysis on samples with this type of skewed distribution run the risk of producing Type I error, rejecting a true hypothesis or underestimating the actual power of the variable. However, since this means that we would be underestimating or producing a conservative estimate of the predictive ability of the model, this error is not considered to be serious for the purposes of this study.

Correction procedures, which would have the effect of increasing the R squares, were not used because the sample limitations and exploratory nature of the study argues for erring on the side of conservatism.

Verbal abuse. Three demographic variables were entered into the final model: caregiver's age, where they lived, and how long the respondent had cared for the elder. Three family stress variables: employed spouse, family financial problems, and other sources of family stress were entered. Two dependency variables: total illness and mental health dependency; and two dependency stress variables: senile but mobile and needs transportation completed the list of variables entered. No relative stress variables, for example, parents and siblings thought you could do more or burden, were entered.

TABLE 8.1
Regression Analysis for Verbal Abuse

Step	Variable	R^2	F	Prob > F
1	total mental health dependency	.199	29.00	.0001
2	employed spouse	.279	22.41	.0001
3	total health	.322	18.27	.0001
4	age of caregiver	.346	15.07	.0001
5	where resided	.383	14.01	.0001
6	mobile but senile	.400	12.45	.0001
7	other stress	.415	11.26	.0001
8	length of caregiving	.430	10.36	.0001

Regression Analysis when Elders' CMTs Are Entered

Step	Variable	R^2	F	Prob > F
1	total mental health dependency	.199	29.00	.0001
2	elder's verbal abuse	.336	29.40	.0001
3	employed spouse	.383	23.80	.0001
4	total illness	.419	20.57	.0001
5	where resided	.436	17.46	.0001
6	caregiver's age	.456	15.64	.0001
7	other stress	.471	14.11	.0001
8	financial problems	.485	12.97	.0001
9	length of caregiving	.496	11.92	.0001

As can be seen on the top half of Table 8.1, eight variables accounted for 43% of the variation. Nearly half of this, 20%, was accounted for by the variable mental health; and 8% was directly related to spouses who were employed (mostly women), thus carrying multiple responsibilities. A study of 41 noninstitutionalized frail elders by Reece, Walz, and Hagenboeck (1983) noted that although 36% of the women worked full-time, no significant relationship was found between caregivers' employment and levels of task involvement. Thus these employed caregivers are actually fulfilling two or three major (full-time) roles. As a result, one might expect the stress experienced from these multiple roles could produce more negative interaction with the elder. Total illness accounted for 4% and the remaining, 2%-3% each, by caregiver's age, length of caregiving, caring for a mobile but senile elder, where they live, and other family-related stress.

When the elder's CMTs were entered into the regression, elder's use of verbal abuse, the only elder CMT to be significant, and mental health accounted for 34% of the variance, providing a final model in which

TABLE 8.2
Regression Analysis for Psychological Abuse

Step	Variable	R^2	F	Prob > F
1	emotional dependency	.064	8.01	.0001
2	caregiver is married	.118	7.80	.0001
3	emotional problem	.161	7.35	.0001
4	small child	.181	6.29	.0001

Regression Analysis when Elders' CMTs Are Entered

Step	Variable	R^2	F	Prob > F
1	elder pouts	.143	19.55	.0001
2	caregiver is married	.179	12.69	.0001
3	emotional dependency	.219	10.76	.0001
4	emotional problem	.236	8.83	.0001

TABLE 8.3
Regression Analysis for Medical Abuse

Step	Variable	R^2	F	Prob > F
1	mental health dependency	.168	23.57	.0001
2	mobility dependency	.213	15.71	.0001
3	senile but mobile	.240	12.12	.0001
4	total illness	.261	10.06	.0001

Regression Analysis when Elders' CMTs Are Entered

Step	Variable	R^2	F	Prob > F
1	mental health dependency	.168	23.57	.0001
2	elder calls police	.239	18.20	.0001
3	mobility dependency	.291	15.74	.0001
4	elder refuse food/medicine	.320	13.44	.0001
5	total illness	.340	11.75	.0001

approximately 50% of the variance is accounted for by 9 variables listed.

Psychological abuse. Psychological abuse is a variable made up of the components: threatening the elder and ignoring the elder's demands. The demographic variable, married; the family stress variables, small child and family member has emotional problem; the dependency variable, financial dependency; and the dependency stress variable, social/emotional support were entered into the model. Four variables

TABLE 8.4
Regression Analysis for Physical Abuse

Step	Variable	R^2	F	Prob > F
1	social/emotional dependency stress	.118	15.69	.0001
2	emotional problems	.194	13.97	.0001
3	small child	.231	11.57	.0001
4	mobility dependency	.256	9.82	.0001
5	financial dependency stress	.278	8.69	.0001
6	household dependency stress	.295	7.80	.0001

Regression Analysis when Elders' CMTs Are Entered

Step	Variable	R^2	F	Prob > F
1	social/emotional dependency stress	.118	15.69	.0001
2	emotional problems	.194	13.97	.0001
3	elder yells	.242	12.26	.0001
4	recent death	.278	10.97	.0001
5	financial problems	.301	9.75	.0001
6	elder pouts	.319	8.75	.0001
7	financial dependency stress	.334	7.96	.0001
8	household dependency stress	.349	7.38	.0001

accounted for 18% of the variance. When the elder's CMTs were entered into the equation, the final model, in which elders' pouting replaced the small children variable, accounted for about 24% of the variance (see Table 8.2).

Medical abuse. No demographic variables or family stress variable contributed significantly to predicting medical abuse, that is: forcing medicine or food on the elder. Burden; two dependency variables: mental health and mobility dependency; two dependency stress variables: mobile but senile, elder won't eat and total illness were significant.

These six variables were entered into the regression model and four of these, mental health, mobility dependency, mobile but senile, and total illness accounted for 26% of the variance. With the addition of the elder's CMTs 34% of the variance was accounted for. In this final model, calling the police and refusing to eat or take medicine entered the model, but the variable, mobile but senile was no longer significant (see Table 8.3).

Physical abuse. None of the demographic or relative stress variables significantly predicted caregivers' use of physical abuse. Four family stress variables were significant: a family member experiencing an emotional problem, recent death, financial problems, and small children in the home. Two dependency variables: mental health and mobility dependency were significant, and five dependency stress variables: emotional stress, demanding, mobile but senile, financial dependency, and household tasks entered into this regression model.

Six variables: social/emotional and mobility dependency, emotional problems, small child, financial problems, and household dependency stress accounted for nearly 39% of the variance (see Table 8.4). The addition of the elder's CMTs provided two significant variables: yelling and pouting. The variable: small child was replaced with the variable: recent death, producing a final model that accounted for 35% of the variance with these eight variables.

Severe physical abuse. Since a small percentage of the sample, just over 9%, engage in severe physical abuse, this represents a very skewed distribution. Therefore, the amount of variance accounted for in this regression model will be somewhat underestimated. None of the demographic variables were significant, and thus were not entered into this model. Burden and five family stress variables: emotional problem, recent death, single parent household, spouse employed, and physical disability of another family member were entered. It is interesting to note that both single-parent and spouse-employed households face the same problem—no one at home to provide full-time care for the elder. Two dependency variables: mental health and mobility, and four dependency stress variables: social/emotional support, household, physical disability, and financial dependency were also entered into the model. Out of these 12 variables, eight accounted for 34% of the variance (see Table 8.5).

Since this is the most severe physically abusive measure in the study, caregivers who are engaging in these behaviors are placing the elder at considerable risk. The variables that predict this behavior are, except for mobility, the stress indices: family stress (recent death, single parent, and family member with emotional problems or physical disability) and dependency stress (social/emotional, household, and financial dependency). The addition of the elder's CMTs to the final model increased the variance accounted for from 34% to 40%. In this new model the variables: family member's emotional problems and recent death were eliminated, and employed spouse, elder's physical violence, manipulation, and pouting entered the model.

Total abuse. The total abuse variable is the combination of the physical abuse and medical abuse variables. None of the demographic variables were significant, but two family stress variables: family financial problem and teenager in the home and the variable burden

TABLE 8.5
Regression Analysis for Severe Physical Abuse

Step	Variable	R^2	F	Prob > F
1	social/emotional dependency stress	.124	16.52	.0001
2	household dependency stress	.186	13.25	.0001
3	single parent	.228	11.32	.0001
4	mobility dependency	.257	9.86	.0001
5	financial dependency stress	.289	9.19	.0001
6	emotional problems	.306	8.24	.0001
7	physical dependency stress	.323	7.57	.0001
8	recent death	.338	7.03	.0001

Regression Analysis when Elders' CMTs Are Entered

Step	Variable	R^2	F	Prob > F
1	social/emotional dependency stress	.124	16.52	.0001
2	household dependency stress	.186	13.25	.0001
3	single parent	.228	11.32	.0001
4	mobility dependency	.257	9.86	.0001
5	financial dependency stress	.289	9.19	.0001
6	elder uses physical abuse	.313	8.52	.0001
7	employed spouse	.333	7.93	.0001
8	elder manipulates	.351	7.44	.0001
9	elder pouts	.389	7.70	.0001
10	physical dependency stress	.405	7.35	.0001

were entered. Three dependency categories: mental health, mobility and social/emotional, and five dependency task-related stress variables: mobile but senile, physical disability, household tasks, invades privacy, and social/emotional stress were entered into the equation. Of these 11 variables, only mobility dependency, stress from caring for a mobile but senile elder and stress from providing social/emotional support were significant. However, they accounted for over 34% of the variance. When the elder's CMTs were entered into the equation, the above three variables along with, elder's verbal abuse, refusal to eat or take medicine, invading privacy and elder calling police accounted for over 45% of the variance.

It is clear from these models that caregivers who report being stressed by caring for a mobile but senile elder, by having to provide social/emotional support for the elder, and dealing with a lack of privacy are at risk of using abusive means to control the elder. This risk is intensified if the elder displays disruptive behavior, such as being verbally abusive, refusing to eat or take medicine and calling the police.[1]

TABLE 8.6
Regression Analysis for Total Abuse

Step	Variable	R^2	F	Prob > F
1	senile but mobile stress	.220	32.92	.0001
2	mobility dependency	.318	27.06	.0001
3	social/emotional dependency stress	.344	20.12	.0001

Regression Analysis when Elders' CMTs Are Entered

Step	Variable	R^2	F	Prob > F
1	senile but mobile stress	.220	32.92	.0001
2	mobility dependency	.318	27.06	.0001
3	elders' verbal abuse	.385	24.01	.0001
4	social/emotional dependency	.402	19.13	.0001
5	elder refuses food/medicine	.416	16.10	.0001
6	elder calls police	.439	14.60	.0001
7	lack of privacy stress	.456	13.28	.0001

Like Mother Like Daughter: Family Patterns of Abuse

We would probably like to ignore the above adage, especially since we live in a "disposable" society that prides itself on discarding the old and outdated for the new—the traditional for the innovative. However, the evidence in this study, both the qualitative data based on quotes from the respondents, and the quantitative data based on the questionnaires, does not permit us to do so. In this next section, we will explore the intergenerational transmission of behaviors used to resolve problems or gain or maintain control. Caregivers will be compared to elders in their use of the control maintenance techniques. For example, are elders who "yell" being cared for by their adult offspring who also yell? The specific scores for the next items can be found in Table C.7 in Appendix C.

Caregivers who used verbal abuse did so in families in which the elder also used verbal abuse. In addition these elders used significantly higher amounts of pouting, refusal to eat or take medicine, crying, manipulation, and physical abuse. The use of emotional abuse by caregivers characterized families in which the elder pouted, refused food or medicine, cried, and used physical abuse. When the medical abuse component (forced or withheld food or medicine) was examined elders in families in which caregivers used some form of medical abuse used significantly greater amounts of verbal physical abuse.

Caregivers who used physical abuse were more likely to be caring for elders who pouted and used physical abuse. Caregivers using severe physical abuse did so in families in which the elder yelled, pouted, and used physical abuse. The overall measure of abuse—total abuse—provides further support for the intergenerational transmission of behaviors. Caregivers who used each of the above abuse measures did so in families in which the elders were characterized as being physically violent. A similar pattern was observed for the total abuse measure. Elders in families in which the caregiver used abusive forms of interaction were found to use verbal abuse, refused to eat or take medicine, called the police and used physical abuse in their interactions with caregivers.

Further substantiation of the high correlation between caregivers' abusive CMTs and elders' use of physical violence can be found by examining the correlations matrix (Table C.8, Appendix C). Although relatively few of the correlations between elders' and caregivers' use of control maintenance techniques reached significance, two patterns emerge. First, caregivers' use of verbal abuse is significantly correlated with all of elders' CMTs, except crying. Thus, verbally abusive caregivers are interacting with elders displaying significantly higher amounts of a range of disruptive behaviors. Second, all of the abusive techniques used by caregivers were highly and significantly correlated with elders' use of physical violence.

FLOW DIAGRAM OF ELDER ABUSE

The flow diagram (Figure 8.1) was used to guide the analysis in previous chapters and helps to clarify the ordering of variables in the path analysis. The demographic variables (Box A) formed the basis of the analysis in chapter four. As can be observed on the tables that summarize the significant relationships in each chapter (Table 4.1, 5.1, and 6.1), few of the relationships between the demographic variables and family stress, dependency tasks, dependency stress, or the control maintenance techniques used by caregivers were significant. Similar patterns were observed between family stress and dependency, dependency stress, and CMTs. Although, many of the variables in the family stress index provided demographic background information on the family, such as small children or teenagers, single headed household, or employed women, this information was provided by the caregiver only if it contributed to stress. Other variables in this index, for example, a family member with a substance abuse, emotional problem, or a physical disability are unique circumstances that characterize each family situation.

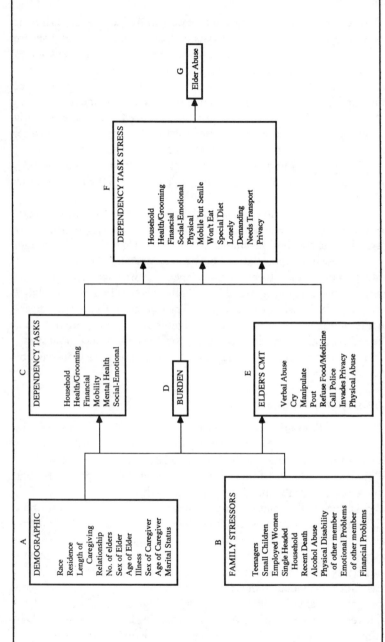

Figure 8.1 Flow diagram of relationship of variables affecting elder abuse.

Since they are problems characterizing other members of the family, not the elder, we are considering these to be conditions that are unrelated to the elder, most likely existing before the elder moved in, and simply compounding the problems faced by the caregiver, which explains the order noted in the flow diagram.

In Chapter 5 the relationship between the frequency with which tasks were performed and elder abuse was also tenuous. However, the relationship between dependency stress and elder abuse appeared to be much stronger. As suggested by Figure 8.1, demographic and family stressor variables may have some indirect influence on burden, dependency tasks, and the elder's CMT (Boxes C, E), but their direct influence on elder abuse was not observed. Although it might appear that the greater the number of tasks a person has to perform (Box C), the more likely they are to feel burdened (Box D) and to be abusive (Box E), these relationships, as discussed in chapter 5 were not strong and few were significant.

It did appear as if these variables might increase the dependency stress that caregivers' experience (Box F), and that the direct relationship is between dependency and elder abuse. In Chapter 6, it was demonstrated that strong, and often significant, relationships were observed between many of the dependency stress items and burden, family stress, and the physically abusive control maintenance techniques used by caregivers.

The elder's control maintenance techniques might be viewed in a reciprocal rather than a unidirectional fashion, since we know that the family is an on-going interacting unit. However, in the flow diagram these variables are shown as contributing to the impact of dependency stress and are an indirect precursor to elder abuse. This decision was based on several assumptions.

First, the family is an interacting unit, and the quotes from the respondents clearly indicate that they were describing patterns of behavior that characterized a life-time of interaction. As one respondent with the responsibility for a frail, mentally deteriorating elder noted:

> You see your mother getting no better and you know that she is getting worse. If you fix dinner for her she would refuse to eat. It really got on my nerves and I would sit and cry . . . I tried to fix her everything that I knew that she liked and tried to make everything comfortable for her. I couldn't understand why she didn't accept this . . . why she didn't appreciate what I was doing for her. It seemed like she never appreciated anything that I did for her. But my other sister, the one that is a big drinker, anything she did for mamma, she'd appreciated it. [My sister] would get so drunk that she lay her [mamma] out—it didn't bother mamma. I don't know if it was

because she was the baby child or what. Whatever I did, she was right
down my throat . . . Nothing I did seemed to please her [#98—58-year-old
daughter, who had been caring for her 93-year-old mother for 8 years].

Second, in addition to life-time patterns of interaction, time ordering
of these variables has been based on the assumption that parents'
treatment of their children predates the children's caregiving treatment
of their parents. Furthermore, the accumulated knowledge of other
forms of family violence clearly documents the relationship between
violent parents and violent children who become violent adults (Gayford, 1975; Bryant, 1963; Helfer and Kempe, 1974; Oliver and Taylor,
1971; Wasserman, 1967; Steinmetz, 1977; Straus et al., 1980). This
pattern of parenting, as well as the additional stress placed on the
caregivers when they do not feel appreciated, is illustrated by the
following quote:

I would say that if a parent has been a very loving parent and caring parent
then a child could handle that, but when you know that they haven't been,
it is very difficult to handle, very difficult. It's said that you have to forget
what is in the past. Honey, you don't forget these things. Even an old dog,
if you have beaten him, will cringe when he sees you. Even he doesn't
forget. He either cringes or bites you [#95—66-year-old daughter, who
had been caring for her 86-year-old father for 4 years.]

This respondent's comment at the end of the interview provides still
further insights:

The thing that irks me so is that when I was little and needed him, he was
never there. *He didn't take care of me* . . . I've never heard him say
thank-you [#95].

Therefore, elders' CMTs preceded dependency stress and elder abuse
in the flow diagram. The analysis in the preceding chapters provides
support for the ordering of the flow diagram. The analysis used in
Chapters 4-7 primarily relied on mechanical control of the variables,
that is, dividing the sample into males versus females, or high score
versus low score for a particular variable. The regression analyses
presented earlier in this chapter focused on the explanatory power of
different variables for explaining the variance in models of verbal,
psychological, and physical abuse, and was not concerned with "causal"
sequence.

Path analysis provides a method for presenting the best estimate
possible of a linear relationship approximating causality when the

research design does not allow for the measurement of change through experimental procedures or longitudinal design.

A Path Model of Elder Abuse

This path model (Figure 8.2) is an elaboration of the flow diagram described earlier. The variable "total abuse," which is the combined measure of physical and medical abuse, was selected to represent the dependent variable "elder abuse." The independent variables were the summary measures of family stress, total dependency, total dependency stress, the individual demographic variable, and the elder's CMT. Since a general model was desired, the overall measure of dependency, rather than a specific dependency was used. Likewise, the total family and dependency stress measures, rather than specific items that might have been statistically significant in earlier analysis, were used. The ordering of the individual variables was tested by comparing the total effects based on the standardized regression coefficients and the r^2 for the paths when the time ordering was not clear.

For example, it was obvious that the family stress index, after comparing the coefficients, was an independent variable that affected the elder's use of emotional abuse, not an intervening variable between demographic variables and dependency stress. Theoretical considerations, and earlier analysis serving as the foundation for the flow diagram, support this decision.

The first regression analysis identified seven significant paths: those between elder abuse and total dependency stress, total dependency, crying and emotional abuse, elder's age and illness, and caregiver's age (see Table 8.7 for the intercorrelation matrix and Figure 8.2 for path diagram). Following the hypothesized time-ordered sequence, which was supported by total dependency stress obtaining the highest standardized estimate (beta), the remaining six variables were regressed against total dependency stress, producing five variables with significant path coefficients: total dependency, burden, elder's use of physical violence (hit), and refusal to eat or take medicine.

The remaining seven variables were then regressed against the nonsignificant variables from the first regression and the remaining significant variables in the following sequence: total dependency tasks regressed against the remaining six variables; cry, emotional abuse, and physical violence were each regressed against the remaining three variables; and the final three variables, elder's age, illness, and caregiver's age were regressed against those variables that were not significant in the first regression analysis.

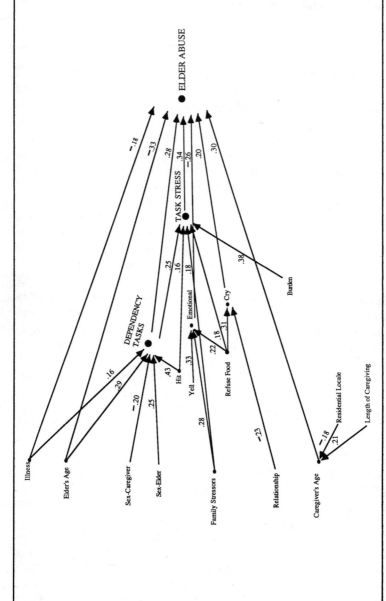

Figure 8.2 Path analysis of relationship between variables resulting in elder abuse.

TABLE 8.7
Intercorrelation Matrix of Variables Used in Path Analysis

	Total Dependency	Family Stress	Burden	Total Illness	Resp. Age	Resp. Sex	Elder Age	Elder Sex	Resident	Reside	No. of Elder	Resp. Race	Married	Elder Hit	Elder Cry	Elder Emotion	Elder Police	Elder Refuse	Elder Yell	Elder Relation	Total Abuse
Depend. stress	0.455*	0.417*	0.527*	0.149	-0.065	-0.007	-0.011	0.114	-0.087	-0.006	-0.144	0.082	-0.104	0.477*	0.290*	0.570*	0.356*	0.408*	0.366*	-0.005	0.447*
Total dependency		0.047	0.203*	0.247*	0.304	-0.044	0.341	0.286	-0.074	0.158	-0.153	0.037	0.053	0.352*	0.162	0.090	0.126	0.190	0.038	-0.066	0.361*
Family stress			0.240*	0.199*	-0.085	0.081	-0.106	-0.015	-0.142	-0.001	0.043	-0.092	0.027	0.215*	0.107	0.414*	0.131	0.140	0.262*	0.149	0.224*
Burden				0.109	-0.006	-0.21	0.016	-0.001	-0.096	0.076	-0.156	0.073	-0.147	0.096	0.050	0.221*	0.080	0.009	0.083	-0.138	0.199*
Total illness					0.120	0.032	0.023	0.095	-0.030	0.093	0.012	-0.135	-0.040	0.031	0.012	-0.004	0.014	0.084	-0.043	-0.102	-0.044
Resp. age						0.021	0.636*	0.214	-0.147	0.291*	-0.134	-0.024	0.227*	-0.131	-0.076	-0.061	-0.025	-0.028	-0.196	-0.302*	0.002
Resp. sex							0.108	0.048	0.051	0.015	0.273	-0.098	0.008	0.117	-0.070	-0.030	0.058	0.039	-0.175	0.004	0.011
Elder age								0.090	-0.099	0.148	-0.058	-0.009	-0.058	-0.022	-0.013	-0.074	-0.086	-0.024	-0.178	0.033	-0.083
Elder sex									0.075	0.082	-0.169	-0.023	0.003	-0.050	0.060	0.083	-0.012	-0.034	-0.098	-0.131	0.080
Resident										-0.079	-0.077	-0.014	-0.073	-0.117	0.001	-0.089	-0.107	-0.021	-0.083	-0.041	-0.071
Reside											-0.037	-0.030	0.227*	0.074	0.036	0.047	0.053	-0.011	0.020	-0.124	0.057
No. of elder												-0.121	0.058	-0.020	-0.105	-0.124	0.009	-0.041	0.064	0.116	0.058
Resp. race													0.215*	0.332*	0.013	-0.010	0.330*	0.211*	0.011	0.101	0.064
Married														0.079	-0.062	0.079	0.099	0.093	-0.001	-0.002	0.028
Elder hit															0.226*	0.334*	0.360*	0.405*	0.330*	0.122	0.348*
Elder cry																0.502*	0.119	0.312*	0.152	-0.120	0.158
Elder emotion																	0.217*	0.328*	0.473*	0.002	0.184*
Elder police																		0.483*	0.356*	-0.071	0.312
Elder refuse																			0.234*	0.064	0.104
Elder yell																				0.093	0.365*
Elder relation																					0.048

*Significant at 0.05.

217

The path diagram clearly indicates the improvement over mechanical control and provides support for the original proposed diagram. Several paths are of interest. First, although the coefficient for total dependency stress was .34, when the indirect effect of total dependency (.25) was added the total effect increased to .43. Likewise, the direct effect standardized coefficient for total dependency stress, .34, when combined with the indirect effect from the variable burden, .38, increased to .47.

Possibly the most interesting path, however, because it supports the cycle of violence theory—that is, violence is learned behavior that is passed from generation to generation—is the relationship between the elder's use of physical violence and elder abuse. Elder's use of physical violence ("hit" on the path diagram), had an indirect effect on two variables: total dependency and total dependency stress.

The improvement for the relationship between dependency tasks and elder abuse when combined with the indirect effect of "hit" increased the direct effect of .28 to a total effect of .40. The path between total dependency stress and elder abuse was increased from the direct effect coefficient of .34 to the total effect of .39. Only the path between burden, which has no direct effect on elder abuse, and dependency stress (.38) increased the direct effect of the task stress on elder abuse to a greater degree with a total effect of .47.[2]

Path analysis provides considerable strength for the thesis of this book, that is, that an individual's perception of the stress and feeling of burden— subjective measures—are far stronger predictors of elder abuse than the more objective measures, such as demographic variables and amount of tasks that are required in order to care for the elder. It is recognized that an individual's definition of the situation influences the terms selected when describing how much task performance is required, and it is possible that those who find the tasks to be burdensome are likely to perceive and report that they do more. However, only limited support was found for this position.

As noted in Chapter 5 (see Table 5.1), those who "reported" that they performed more dependency tasks also reported higher levels of dependency stress. However, only in one-third of the dependency categories (household and mental health dependency) did a significantly higher number of caregivers report feelings of burden. In Chapter 6 (see Table 6.1) only 42% of caregivers who reported experiencing dependency stress reported performing significantly higher amounts of dependency tasks. However 75% of the groups characterized by high levels of dependency stress were also characterized by burden. Thus the subjective measure—dependency stress—was more than twice as likely to predict feelings of burden as was the level of dependency (33% versus

75%). Poulshock and Deimling (1984) report an extremely low correlation between the elder-caregiver relationship (their measures of burden) and activities of daily living (r = .05), but an extremely strong correlation between the caregiver-elder relationship and the elder's disruptive (and stressful) behaviors (r = .63), thus suggesting that perceptions of stress and burden are more strongly correlated than are objective measures of task performance and burden. The impact of caregivers' perceptions, that is, the definition of the situation, will be further examined by using illustrative materials from the transcripts.

Perceptions

Perhaps the most dramatic way to demonstrate the impact of providing care for an elder on the caregiver and caregiving family is to present brief sections from some transcripts. The caregiver's discussion on a variety of topics clearly illustrates the tremendous amount of effort required to provide care for an elderly parent who is experiencing physical and mental disabilities.

The family quoted below consists of an 84-year-old mother, her 60-year-old daughter, and the daughter's husband, who had had open-heart surgery soon after mother moved in with them. She recently placed her mother in a nursing home after providing care for three years. Throughout the interview, the caregiver insisted that everything had been under control, that she understood her mother's problem with senility (probably undiagnosed Alzheimer's disease), that she was doing fine without help, and that her mother was not a burden. However, as the interview progressed, it became clear that this daughter had experienced considerable stress and was probably at the breaking point when she had her mother admitted to a nursing home. The excerpts from the interview demonstrate the degree to which caregivers feel duty bound to provide the best care, and blame themselves when this is not possible. This caregiver (#11), provides the following response to the question "Why did your mother come to live with you?"

My mother shared an apartment with a relative . . . a cousin. [This cousin] could no longer manage. [Mother] had reached the point where she was suspicious of this person who had been a truly good friend. She thought that she was taking her things. The cousin understood perfectly that this was not her responsibility to help care for my mother when she reached this stage in her life.

Interviewer: Is her senility a problem?

Caregiver: She was incapable of following any kind of directions whether they were written or not. We might just have had breakfast and she was sitting comfortably. I would say, "I'm going to take the dogs around the block and I'll be right back." By the time I got back, she would have turned the stove on and tried to boil water to make coffee. The burner would be glowing red. I just felt very uncomfortable.

Interviewer: Is she incontinent?

Caregiver: We came to a point before she went to the nursing home, I didn't realize it for a long time, but I think she would get up in the night, that's when it usually happened; maybe she didn't get up soon enough or forgot where to go. I suddenly noticed her slippers were wet and beside her bed was wet. Sometimes the bed. She didn't seem to have so much trouble during the day. I don't remember her clothes ever being wet. This happened many times at night. I don't know why, but I just didn't realize what was happening for a few weeks.

Interviewer: Does she ever cry or act depressed?

Caregiver: She would not really discuss anything. She would cry for hours and there was nothing I could say or do to comfort her. As a matter of fact, she would tell me to get out when I said "Mom, what's wrong" or "Can I help?" She would say, "You know what's wrong, get out of here." There wasn't anything new or different that had happened. I think my mother still has moments of rationality. It is so frustrating and upsetting to someone who had been so able to do everything. She wasn't the kind of woman that my father did everything for. She handled business and that sort of thing, so it was awful for her to have to have somebody do that for her.

Interviewer: Are there any relatives who can help?

Caregiver: No, I am an only child. I did have a great deal of support and help. My husband's parents are equally as old. They are both living and they are very helpful . . . They would stay with mother so that we could go away for a few days. However, we had reached the stage where they wanted to help but I realized that it was not a good thing because my mother-in-law, for instance, couldn't sleep at night because she was listening to my mother walking around. It worried her, and I felt this was not a fair thing to do. This was too much to ask of them.

Interviewer: Was she ever violent?

Caregiver: Well she threw the furniture . . . She might throw something on the floor in the kitchen if it was out. I don't mean open the box, just put the whole thing on the floor.

Interviewer: Why did you place your mother in a nursing home?

Caregiver: She had deteriorated quite a lot . . . In June, she wanted to stay in her car all night. There was no way we could persuade her or trick her to come back into the house. . . . She fell asleep. My husband went out and said "We're back home again, let's go in," thinking she'd think that we had been to the shore again and had arrived home. It didn't work . . . I called the doctor the next day and talked to him about it. He prescribed a mild tranquilizer for her so that she would not be so belligerent. She really did seem to continue to go downhill . . . In August, we were spending some time at the shore. We were staying at a place where she had been many, many times. During the night she would apparently become frustrated. She would get up and was disoriented. Even though we had tried to leave the lights on and explain before she went to bed how everything was. She took a 45-page printout of the speech my husband was going to make and wadded it up into little balls and threw it under the bed. She didn't do it to be mean, she didn't even know she was doing it. She was apparently just frustrated.

Interviewer: Was this her way of dealing with the situation?

Caregiver: Yes, I guess that she could not find her way back to her room. She would turn off the lights. She was not cooperative. We would say "Mom, we will leave the lights on so you won't have problems getting back if you get up." She would say "Yes," then get up and turn them off and then not know where she was . . . She was belligerent enough that she would take things away and do whatever she wanted to. This was, of course, after a personality change.

Interviewer: Does she impose guilt?

Caregiver: She imposes guilt by telling me that my father wouldn't approve of what I was doing. This is in relation to her living in the nursing home. How can I do this to her? What did she ever do to me? How could I be so mean? This sort of thing.

Interviewer: Do you consider this caregiving to be a burden?

Caregiver: It's distressing. I would not describe it as a burden, I don't consider my mother to be a burden. I would be glad to continue to care for her if she was not unpredictable and I could. This is the selfish part . . . I want to do some of the things I like to do because I'm not very young anymore either. This is what happens when you have elderly children taking care of the elderly . . . If I had continued caring for my mother, I think that I would have become almost resentful. I don't know how else to say it . . . If my mother were not financially able to take care of herself, I guess we would have to manage. This is what happens to poor people, isn't it? They don't have the choices we do [#11—60-year-old daughter, who had been caring for her 84-year-old mother for 3 years].

With just this glimpse of the caregiver's three-year experience, it would be difficult to not consider this a burden. Yet this caregiver, like others quoted in this chapter, has redefined the situation into one that more closely fitted her perception of a "caring" daughter. If she considered her mother a burden, then she would have to consider the possibility that she had placed mother in a nursing home because she was a burden, not because she needed more medical care than was possible at home. During the interviews caregivers present the impression that the decision to place a parent in a nursing home is made for "medical" reasons. Yet this position was not supported in the following statistical analysis.

Four variables located in different sections of the questionnaire provided a measure of caregiver's consideration of finding, or actual decisions to find, alternative care for the elder: seeking alternatives to caring at home, sought admission to a nursing home, threatened with nursing home placement, and placed in a nursing home. Likewise there were four measures that provided an indication of physical illness: the total illness measure, physical functioning, physical disability, and the personal grooming/health dependency index. The intercorrelation between the four illness measures and the four alternatives to caring at home measures were extremely low; many were negative relationships and none reached significance (see Table 8.8).

Next, correlations between the above four measures of alternative care and a measure of the elder's use of emotional control techniques (a combination of pout, manipulation, and invades privacy); two dependency stress measures: mobile but senile and emotional dependency stress; and the total mental health dependency measure were also computed.

Strong, positive, statistically significant correlations between "sought alternative care" and "threatened to send to nursing home" (two of the caregivers' CMTs) and all measures of the elders' emotional status were found. This provides support that it is the emotional aspects of caring, not the elders' physical health status that precipitates seeking alternatives. Furthermore, "placed in an institution" was significantly correlated with three of the measures of elder's emotional status. However, these correlations were negative. This suggests that the actual placement in an institution, as well as seeking this alternative, may be negatively related to the elders' emotional/mental health status. What differentiates these variables from others that are significant is the elders' use of emotional CMTs. It appears that when elders use such methods as pouting, manipulation, and invading privacy, caregivers resort to

TABLE 8.8

Correlations Between Seeking Alternative Care and Measures of
Elder's Physical Health Status Versus Elder's Emotional/Mental Status

	Sought Alternative Care	Sought Institution	Placed in Institution	Threatened Nursing Home
Health/grooming dependency	.06	−.14	−.18	.07
Total illness	−.09	.10	.00	.02
Diminished physical function	−.12	−.11	.11	−.15
Physical disability	.16	−.13	−.17	−.06
	Sought Alternative Care	Sought Institution	Placed in Institution	Threatened Nursing Home
Mobile/senile	.31*	−.18	−.23*	.20*
Total mental health dependency	.29*	−.23*	−.24*	.19*
Emotional dependency stress	.28*	−.08	−.24*	.27*
Elders' emotional CMTs	.22*	.00	−.08	.24*

*Significant at 0.05.

seeking alternatives or threatening to do so. However, when elders do not resort to these behaviors, then the likelihood of being placed in an institution, regardless of their emotional status, is smaller.

Overall, 75% of the relationships between the elders' emotional and mental health status and caregivers' stress resulting from providing emotional/mental health tasks and measures of alternative care were statistically significant. However, none of the correlations between variables that indicate extensive medical problems and measures of alternative care were significant and many were negative relationships.

Caregivers also redefine violence, perhaps in order to make it more acceptable and easier to deal with. The following excerpts are from the transcript of a fairly young couple with two small children who are caring for a 62-year-old mother and 64-year-old father (#19/20). Both parents have serious medical problems. The daughter describes fairly explosive, violent interaction between her and her mother, yet sees this as a normal interaction.

Dad is a diabetic, but that is under control. My mom has heart problems, cancer, diabetes, arthritis . . . she has had both breasts removed because of cancer. She has had 60% of her stomach removed because of ulcers. She has had four or five major heart attacks. They put a strainer, they call it an umbrella, into her blood veins to strain the clots and prevent heart attacks. She has had bowel troubles and just about everything . . . I got pregnant right after we were married. I worked right up until the baby was born. My mother had her heart attack the day I stopped work and the baby was born the next day. They both came out of the hospital together. My son and my mother have been together ever since. Mom went into the hospital. I went in to have a baby, and she's there with a heart attack.

Interviewer: Do you have conflicts over housework?—the laundry?

Caregiver: That's a fight. My mother does it when she is feeling good. If not, I do it . . . Yes, I like it nice and neat, and she just does it any old way. She is not supposed to do it. She says "I feel better when I do it." We get into fights about that.

Interviewer: Does she make excessive demands, complain if you don't do things she wants done?

Caregiver: I don't take care of the kids the way she thinks they should be taken care of. I'll get mad and scream at the kids and she'll say, "I never did that when you were growing up."

Interviewer: How much does that bother you?

Caregiver: Two (sometimes). It doesn't bother me to any extent. My husband will correct them [the children]. He grew up in a big family. He will hit my son and my father will step in and say "you shouldn't do that. He's smaller than you." My father has actually turned my husband upside down because he has done something to my son.

Interviewer: Does that upset you?

Caregiver: No, I more or less stay out of the picture with the kids. I get mad at them and Mom will say "I didn't do that to you." I'll say, "Yes, but when your three older children were younger, you told me that you weren't as patient with them as you were with my sister and I." We have a little conflict there . . .

Interviewer: Do these fights escalate into violence. Does she ever exhibit explosive behavior, physically or verbally aggressive, temper tantrums or crying?

Caregiver: Yes, she has. It's hard to explain. She has had so many medical problems like losing a breast and then losing the other, which is something you just can't take. About four and a half years ago when she had her first heart attack, right after that she got very violent. I know I get on her nerves. I speak the truth. If I want to say something, I'll say it. She'll do the same thing. She and I clash more than anybody else in the house.

Interviewer: When you say she got really violent, what did she do?

Caregiver: I said something to her, and she reached for me and grabbed my neck to strangle me. I turned out, and said "Go ahead and kill me," and she dropped her hands then. She was just so mad at me at that time. It was the first time she had ever done anything like that.

Interviewer: Did she ever do that when you were growing up?

Caregiver: No. I was just married, just had a baby, I had everything on top of me. I was trying to straighten out my life and hers. Other than that, we have not had any real violence . . . she has screamed and yelled at me . . .

Interviewer: Does she ever slap you or throw things at you when she is mad?

Caregiver: She has thrown things at me a couple of times. And then she will say, "I didn't mean to hit you. She will throw a pillow or a shoe. She threw a shoe at me one day and just missed me. She wasn't that mad at me; she was slightly irritated [#19/20—27-year-old daughter, who had been caring for her 62-year-old mother and 64-year-old father for 6 years].

It is clear in this family that the daughter has chosen to close her eyes to the conflict and chaos resulting from caring for her parents. The mechanism for dealing with the violence is to note that there are no difficulties, yet it is obvious that the grandparents disapprove of the physical violence that the parents use on their children, and the elder mother has been, and still is, extremely violent toward her daughter. One can speculate: At what point will the daughter's verbal "clashes" with the mother become physically violent ones?

Based on the path diagram this caregiver certainly has the potential to become abusive. The family consists of a very ill mother and her daughter living in a family characterized by other members having physical problems, small children, financial problems, and an employed wife. Earlier analysis suggested that younger caregiver/parent combinations are likely to be more difficult because of lack of filial maturity and a shorter period of adjusting to caregiving. The path diagram suggests a direct, negative relationship between the caregiver's age and elder abuse (−.33) and an indirect one between length of caregiving and elder abuse (.21 × .30 + .30 = .36).

Torn loyalties, noted in a variety of ways, is another problem faced by these families. In the following quote, the power plays used by family members in an attempt to maintain or obtain control are extremely distressing. Does one side with one's parents or one's spouse? Either way there are feelings of disloyalty and resentment.

If David and my parents will have a disagreement, who are you supposed to be loyal to? I must say, there were several times when I was really torn. It really got to me. I just wanted to walk out that time. You're torn two ways, it was very difficult [#18/158—39-year-old daughter, who had been caring for her 59-year-old mother and 61-year-old father for 5 years].

Competing demands between one's offspring and one's parents also present problems:

Our youngest was 12 or 13 when mother came. There were things that my husband and I wanted to do with this child which mother really was incapable of doing with us, but she didn't realize this. So she was very annoyed or hurt. It's not that Grandma was a real bother, but you had to go at her pace. She didn't understand that she couldn't sit in the sun in an open boat and fish all day long. But this was the main interest of the younger child. This presented problems [#11—60-year-old daughter, who had been caring for her 84-year-old mother for 3 years].

Conclusion

A major focus of this book has been to measure and describe family interactions in terms of the tasks that dependent elders need their children to provide and the stress and conflict that arises in these families. However, we have also attempted to elucidate the factors that are seen as operating to increase the likelihood of a caregiver abusing an elderly "parent." A symbolic interaction perspective has provided a framework for interpreting the findings from the perception of the caregivers and their definition of the situation.

Support for the importance of the definition of the situation for understanding elder abuse can be found by examining the relationships between dependency stress and burden, which exhibited considerably stronger relationships to elder abuse than did the demographic variables, family stressors, or levels of dependency.

Overall, 23% of the caregivers admitted to using physically abusive methods to control the elder. Stepwise regression analysis identified seven variables (stress resulting from caring for a mobile but senile elder, stress from providing emotional dependency, total mobility dependency, elders' who used verbal abuse, refused to eat or take medicine, called the police, and invaded the caregiver's privacy) that accounted for 46% of the variance in explaining elder abuse.

Path analysis provided a model of a "causal" sequencing that demonstrated the impact that variables, such as the sex and age of elders and caregivers, the caregiver-elder relationship, elder's illness, and family stressor, had on dependency, burden, and, to a lesser degree, on the elder's use of control maintenance techniques. These later variables (dependency tasks, burden and elder's CMT) although in some instances directly effecting elder abuse, operated as intervening variables through dependency stress.

Finally, the cycle-of-violence theory gained additional support through an examination of the impact of elder-adult child interaction, thus extending the cycle into an additional generation. Elders' use of physical violence, the variable "hit" on the path diagram, increased the total effect of both dependency and dependency stress to elder abuse. Since no variables in the model appeared to "cause" elders to use physical violence (note that in Figure 8.2 there are no variables shown by an arrow to lead to the variable "hit"), this suggests that perhaps it is part of a well established on-going repertoire of behavior, a position consistent with many of the respondent's quotes. It also provides support for considering the elder's violence as preestablished, rather than as a reaction to their caregiver's behavior toward him or her.

THE FUTURE

The number of frail elderly increase daily. We can expect the problem of elder abuse to become epidemic without societal intervention. We can also expect to see public pressure for better quality, less expensive alternatives to providing care in one's home. In fact, given the growing number of women in the work force (who are likely to continue working until 70 unless they are experiencing serious medical problems), we need to ask: "Who will care for these elderly parents"? Furthermore, many adult children, after the experience of providing care, have made it clear to their own children that they want alternative solutions.

"I don't have anyone to go to . . . I was so deeply depressed." She told me she didn't want to go into a home. What can I do? I told my son, "If I get disabled I don't want you to hesitate. I don't want to be a burden on you. Put me in a home, I won't mind it. I've been through it. I know what it is" [#98—58-year-old daughter, who had been caring for her 93-year-old mother for 8 years].

"I want you to promise me that when I get like this that you will please put me someplace." She said "I couldn't do that." I said, "I want you to do it because I don't want to wreck someone's life, and that is exactly what it is . . . Please put me someplace, Let me maintain my sense of dignity. I don't want to be in somebody's home and I don't want to feel that I am a

burden—that's what it is a burden"[#95—66-year-old daughter, who had
been caring for her 86-year-old father for 4 years].

In spite of a somewhat dismal picture there is a ray of hope. Child
abuse and spouse abuse, as a result of 10 years of programs in public
awareness, education, and services, declined dramatically. The second
national survey of family violence found a 47% decrease in child abuse
and a 21% decrease in wife abuse (Straus and Gelles, 1986).

The question to be posed is: Will we as a society be willing to spend
the needed resources on a population defined as no longer economically
productive? Will we as a society be willing to use our scarce resources to
ensure that those who were once productive members of our society are
provided a healthy, dignified environment in which to spend the final
years? Will we, on the pinnacle of the mountain, look with hope and
happiness toward the parental generation looking up at us, as well as
with pride and feelings of accomplishment at the legacy embodied in our
children still reaching for the pinnacle? Will we as a society acknowledge,
with words and actions, the debt owed to this older generation as well as
that owed to the middle generation, duty bound to provide family care
for their elders?

Notes

1. It might appear that the elder's were calling authorities *because* of the maltreatment
they were receiving, however, an inspection of the transcripts revealed that these calls were
for matters totally unrelated to the family, such as calling the police because a car is parked
in front of the house, or the elder imagined that someone stole something from him or her.
These calls represent one more task, dealing with the police, that the caregivers have to
perform.

2. To compute the total effect, multiply the regression coefficients between the two
paths: (independent variable to intervening variable) × (intervening variable to dependent
variable) and add this product to the coefficient for the direct effect. In the example of the
effect of burden on elder abuse, just discussed, the computation would be: (.38 × .34) +
(.34) or .13 + .34. Thus the total effect is .47.

QUESTIONNAIRE ON CARING FOR AN ELDERLY PARENT

*Background Data on Elderly

a. Age _____ 　 or Birth Date _____
　　　 4 　　　　　　 5

b. Sex _____ 　　　　 Code: 1 – male, 2 – female
　　　　 6

c. Relationship to you _____
　　　　　　　　　　 7 　　　　　 8

01 Mother	06 Stepfather	12 Grandmother
02 Father	07 Aunt	13 Grandfather
03 Mother-in-law	08 Uncle	14 Great Aunt
04 Father-in-law	09 Brother	15 Great Uncle
05 Stepmother	11 Sister	16 Other—specify
		_____

d. How long has (had) this person lived with you_____

　　(converted to months) _____
　　　　　　　　　　　 9 　　 10 　　 11

e. Where did relative live before moving into your place _____

　　　　　　 _____
　　　　　　 12 　　　　 13

f. If relative no longer lives with family, where living now _____

　　　　　　 _____
　　　　　　 14 　　　　 15

*Health Status

a. Has the doctor identified any serious medical problems

Diabetes _____   Strokes _____

Heart Attacks _____   Arthritis _____

Cancer _____   Other
    (type if known)   (please specify)_____

Ulcers _____

            16   17

b. Has your relative been hospitalized in the past year (or in the year prior to admission in the nursing home)?

    Yes_____   No _____

        18

Reasons _____

       19   20

c. Has your relative experienced any problems with diminished physical functioning?

    Yes_____   No_____

If yes, probe: decreasing hearing, sight, mobility, etc.

       21   22

(Ask d and e if currently in Nursing Home)

d. What treatments did your relative receive prior to admission to a nursing home? (probes: physical therapy, medications)

       23   24

e. What factors led to the nursing home admission?

Probe: _____

_____
         25   26

For the next series of questions, would you look at Card A and give me the number which best describes how often you do each of these things. (Hand respondent Card A.)

*Card A   Household Tasks Dependency

   Probe for *actual tasks* they performed

Light housekeeping (make bed, dust, dishes)	_____ 27	Cooking	_____ 31
Heavy housekeeping (wash windows, scrub floors)	_____ 28	Provide transportation	_____ 32
Laundry	_____ 29	Run errands	_____ 33
Grocery shopping	_____ 30	Other (specify)	_____ 34

*   Personal and Health Care Dependency

   Probe for *actual tasks* they performed

Bathing	_____ 35	Following Doctors orders	_____ 38
Dressing	_____ 36	Giving Medications	_____ 39
Cutting Toenails	_____ 37	Changing bedding, diapering	_____ 40
		Other (specify)	_____ 41

Probe for Actual Tasks

*   Financial Dependency

Writing checks or paying bills	_____ 42		Pay for Essential Needs	_____ 45
Provide financial support	_____ 43		Pay for "luxury" items	_____ 46
Help with Managing Resources	_____ 44		Other (specify)	_____ 47

Probe for Actual Tasks

*   Mobility Dependency

Help going up and down stairs	_____ 48		Help getting in or out of bed	_____ 50
Help getting in and out of chair	_____ 49		Help with walking	_____ 51

Probe for Actual Tasks/Example

*   Emotional/Social Dependency

Provide emotional support	_____ 52		Help them make phone calls	_____ 56
Provide "social life"	_____ 53		Read to	_____ 57
Take relative visiting	_____ 54		Encourage/help with developing friends (example: arrange for friendly visitor, minister, invite over friends)	_____ 58
Write letters for relative	_____ 55			
			Other	_____ 59

Probe for Actual Tasks/Example

*   Mental Health Dependency

Help with decision making	_____ 60	Explosive behavior (verbal or physical aggressive behavior, temper tantrums, crying spells)	_____ 64
Forgetful	_____ 61		
Gets lost	_____ 62	Must be "watched" or confined	_____ 65
Nonrational behavior (senile, doesn't make sense)	_____ 63	Other	_____ 66

* Stress

Card B

Many people find it difficult to provide these extra services for an elderly person because of other family obligations which take time, emotional energy and money. How often do you find it difficult to provide help in each of these areas? Please refer to Card B and give me the number *which best describes* the *amount of conflict or stress produced* by taking on these additional responsibilities.

Hand Respondent Card B

_____ 67	a. elder financially dependent on family	_____ 74	h. elder is lonely
_____ 68	b. elder needs help with personal grooming	_____ 75	i. elder makes excessive demands (nagging, complains, wants a lot of attention)
_____ 69	c. elder has severe emotional/mental disability	_____ 76	j. household management, cleaning, cooking, running errands
_____ 70	d. elder has severe physical disability		
_____ 71	e. elder is mobile but senile	_____ 77	k. elder needs transportation

_____ f. elder won't eat
72

_____ g. elder has special
73   dietary needs

_____ l. lack of sufficient
78   room in the house/ privacy

_____ m. other (please explain)
79

Deck ___1___
80

ID _____
1   2   3

Col. 4-8 blank

Resources (Hand Respondent Card C)

Do you have a relative or relatives who help with the care of your elder?

Yes _____   No_____

Code: *0* if no, *1* if yes

_____ no relatives
10

_____ live too far (probe)
11

_____ not close to relative
12   (probe)

_____ lost contact (probe)
13

_____ have own serious
14   problems (specify)

Card C

If yes, which of the tasks do they help with? Please refer to Card C and give me the number which best describes how much help they provide.

If there is more than one relative, list each one individually by A, B, C, etc.

Relative A _____ _____ Age ___ ___ Sex _____
    Relationship   15   16   17   18

provide financial help _____
19

take relative for _____
weekends or elder 26
sit in your house

help with housework _____
                         20

take relative for _____
holidays 10 days   27
to 2 weeks or elder
sit in your house

run errands _____
                21

take relative for _____
extended visit   28
(during summer,
over winter)

help with meals _____
                    22

take relative
shopping _____
            23

provide gifts _____
and outings   29

help with arrange- _____
ments for doctor,   24
social services,
settling property, etc.

help with renovating _____
house to accommo-   30
date elderly

help with medical _____
problems   31

visit _____
          25

other (please explain) _____
                            32

Relative B _____ _____ Age ___ ___ Sex _____
              Relationship   33   34 35   36

provide financial help _____
                            37

take relative for _____
weekends or elder   44
sit in your house

help with housework _____
                         38

take relative for _____
holidays 10 days   45
to 2 weeks or elder
sit in your house

run errands _____
                39

take relative for _____
extended visit   46
(during summer,
over winter)

help with meals _____
                    40

take relative
shopping _____
            41

provide gifts _____
and outings   47

help with arrange- _____
ments for doctor,   42
social services,
settling property, etc.

help with renovating _____
house to accommo-   48
date elderly

help with medical _____
problems   49

visit _____   other (please explain) _____
          43   50

Relative C _____   _____
                  Relationship   51

Age ____ ____   Sex, Code: 1—male; 2—female ____
      52   53   54

provide financial help _____   take relative for   _____
                                55   weekends or elder   62
                                            sit in your house

help with housework _____
                          56   take relative for   _____
                                      holidays 10 days   63
run errands   _____   to 2 weeks or elder
                          57   sit in your house

help with meals   _____   take relative for   _____
                              58   extended visit   64
                                          (during summer,
take relative   over winter)
shopping   59   provide gifts
                                            and outings   65

help with arrange-   _____   help with renovating   _____
ments for doctor,   60   house to accommo-   66
social services,   date elderly
settling property, etc.
                                          help with medical   _____
                                          problems   67

visit   _____   other (please explain)   _____
                  61   68

69-79 blank

Deck   2
          _____
          80

                                          _____ _____ _____
                                            1   2   3

Col. 4-27 blank _____
                  4   5   6   7   8   9   10   11   12

(Hand Respondent Card B)

*Additional sources of stress within the family since your parent has been living with you. How much stress has each of the following created?

_____ a. Teenagers in home
28

_____ f. Recent death in
33   family

_____ b. Small children
29   in home

_____ g. Alcoholism/drugs
34

_____ c. Spouses both
30   employed

_____ h. Physical disability
35   of spouse

_____ d. Single parent (adult)
31   household

_____ i. Emotional/mental
36   problem of spouse/
              child

_____ e. Financial problems
32

_____ j. Other (please explain)
37

*Resolving Problems

Card A

I am going to read a list of items which describe methods often used when elderly people follow doctor's or caretaker's directions. When you have experienced this problem which of these have you used? Please refer to Card A and give me the number which best describes how often you used this method. (Ask respondent to turn back to Card A)

_____ a. talked out
38

_____ h. confined to a room
45

_____ b. screamed and
39   yelled

_____ i. hit or slapped to
46   get them to mind

_____ c. used physical
40   restraint (i.e.,
              tie in a chair)

_____ j. given medication
47

_____ d. forced feeding
41

_____ k. sought the advice
48   of a third party

_____ e. withheld food
42

_____ l. found alternative
49   housing (nursing
              home, other
              relative)

_____ f. threatened to
43   send to nursing
              home

_____ m. other (please explain)
50

_____ g. threatened with
   44   physical force

(When your parent lives [lived] with you . . .)

How often does (did) your parent attempt to do each of the following to
maintain control?

_____ a. screamed and   _____ h. use their physical/
   51   yelled   58   emotional disability
                                                                 to gain control

_____ b. pout, withdrew
   52   to their room   _____ i. calls police or
                                              59   other help for

_____ c. refused to eat/spit   imagined threats
   53   out food   (being held captive,
                                                         money taken, some-

_____ d. refused/spit out   one after them)
   54   medication,
               refused medical   _____ j. imposes guilt/act
               treatment   60   the role of martyr

_____ e. manipulate family   _____ k. doesn't respect
   55   members   61   privacy/opinion
                                                    of other family
_____ f. cry   members
   56

_____ g. hit, slap or throw   _____ l. other (please explain)
   57   something   62

I am going to read a list of the kinds of resources that you may have used
to help with the care of your relative. Respond either yes or no. If the
answer is no, please tell me why by referring to Card D. (Give respondent
Card D.)

Code: 0, if not used, 1 if used

Direct Action: *Emergency Action:*

_____ a. arranged for in-   _____ a. medical treatment
   63   home service   70   or hospitalization

_____ b. sought social   _____ b. elder sent or placed
   64   agency help   71   elsewhere (specify)

_____ c. elder was   _____ c. police called in
   65   counseled   72

_____ d. family was   _____ d. other (specify)
66   counseled   73

_____ e. sought help   .
67   from other
            family members

_____ f. elder placed in
68   institution

_____ g. other (please specify)
69

Referral Action:

_____ a. social services
74

_____ b. legal services
75

_____ c. medical/psychological
76

_____ d. other (specify)
77

            _____

78 Blank   Deck   3
                           _____
                             80

                              1   2   3
                           _____

Code: 0, if the answer is no, 1 if yes

Did you feel a "sense of burden" by this experience?   _____
                                                           4

Please explain _____

_____

_____

Did your parent feel you could do (or have done) more?   _____
                                                           5

Did other relatives feel you could do (or have done) more?
    Probe: (Aunts, Uncles—Sister or Brother of elder)

_____
6

    (Siblings—your brother or sister)

_____
7

Do you ever feel this way?

_____
8

*Information on Respondent

What year were you born?

_____ _____
9   10

Sex: 1—male; 2—female

_____
11

Race: 1—white; 2—black; 3—other

_____
12

Who lived at home when the elderly was there?

List persons (relationship and approximate ages—i.e., son, age 15)

_____ _____ _____ _____

_____ _____ _____ _____

_____ _____ _____ _____

Overall, what was the most difficult part of caring for an elderly parent
in your home?

_____

What advice would you give to someone else who was about to have their
parent(s) live with them?

_____

_____

What are (were) the rewards of living with your elderly parent(s)?

_____

_____

0	Never
1	Almost Never
2	Sometimes
3	Most of the Time
4	All of the Time

Card B *

0	Never Bothers Me
1	Hardly Ever Bothers Me
2	Sometimes Bothers Me
3	Usually Bothers Me
4	Bothers Me All the Time

Card D

If your answer is no, the reason is because

3	not aware of them
4	not available
5	relative not eligible
6	other family members disagreed with this idea
7	was not necessary
8	other (please specify)

Card C

0	No Help
1	Very Little Help
2	Some Help
3	Quite a Bit of Help
4	Always Helps

APPENDIX B

RESEARCH ISSUES: HUMAN SUBJECTS, SAMPLING, RELIABILITY, VALIDITY, AND INDEXES

HUMAN SUBJECT ISSUES

There were two major concerns to be satisfied in order to protect the respondent and the elders. The first was confidentiality. To safeguard the confidentiality of information provided by the caregiver and to provide an atmosphere of privacy, many interviews were conducted in a mutually agreed-upon location. In some cases these interviews were conducted on the University of Delaware campus, in other instances they were conducted at work or during lunch. It was also possible to conduct the interview in the caregiver's home at a time when the elder was not present. We suggested to the caregivers that they not discuss their participation in the study with the elder because of our concern that this might be anxiety producing and result in the elder feeling betrayed by the caregiver. Since paranoia and fears that they might be sent away are not uncommon among vulnerable elderly, we certainly did not want to create a situation that might intensify such feelings.

Other procedures used to assure anonymity and confidentiality included erasing the taped interview after transcription; keeping the informed-consent forms separate from questionnaires and eliminating all matching identification that could link an individual to a particular transcript or questionnaire.

Research Design

FAMILY SAMPLE

In all, 119 individuals were contacted for participation in the in-depth-interview-with-caregiver component of the study. Of this number, seven declined to be interviewed; four failed to keep their interview appointments; three volunteers did not meet the criteria; and one individual feared reprisal from her father, which took violent forms, if she took time out from caring for him in order to be interviewed. Thus a total of 104 interviews were conducted with a completion rate of 87.3%.

INSTRUMENTS

The semistructured interviews were taped and responses to the structured parts of the questionnaires were coded during the interview. Prior to the interview, the objectives of the study were explained and informed consents and permission to tape the interviews were obtained. Respondents were told that they did not have to answer any question that they considered objectionable, and that they could turn off the tape recorder any time they felt uncomfortable. No last names were used while the tape recorder was operating.

Very few respondents objected to being taped, and the few that did appeared to be more uncomfortable with the microphone than they were with the idea of a record of their conversation being made and a concern over the possibility of a breach of confidentiality. A number of interviews were not taped because of recorder malfunction or an unavailable electric outlet.

This study, funded by the State of Delaware, Division of Aging, began in late fall of 1979. The instrument was developed, pretested, and modified in February and March of 1980. Interviewers were trained through group training sessions, and interviewing took place from March 1980 to November 1980.[1]

The interviews were scheduled to be completed within approximately one hour. However, most took considerably longer because respondents became very involved in the topic. There appeared to be two reasons for this. First, many remarked that this was the first time they had felt comfortable (or even had the socially acceptable opportunity) to discuss the stress and strains of parent caring. These interviews were conducted several years before the problems related to caring for a dependent elder or the topic of elder abuse were being openly discussed in the media. It was clear that the interview process served as a catharsis for these caregivers at a time when the possibility that an adult child might feel burdened by caring for a parent was considered to be an indication of lack of filial love.

Second, two of the interviewers, Sarah Foulke and Deborah Amsden, had experienced the responsibility of caring for a frail parent or grandparent and could easily discuss the problems faced by these caregivers; Mary Beth Reese's experiences as a medical social worker enabled her to relate with considerable empathy and understanding. Thus the richness of the data, especially that captured in the transcripts, is owing, in a large part, to the special skills of these interviewers.

The interview schedule (see Appendix A for the complete instrument) was divided into the following categories:

(1) background (demographic) data on the elders and caregivers
(2) the health status of the elder
(3) tasks performed for the elder—a measure of the type of and level of dependencies experienced by the elder
(4) sources of dependency-related stress and the degree to which this stressed or bothered the caregiver
(5) availability of relatives to help and help provided

(6)   sources of family-related stress, such as teenagers or small children in the home, financial problems, alcoholism, or the recent death of a family member

(7)   methods of resolving conflicts or attempts to gain or maintain control that were used by the elder and caregiver

(8)   community resources used by the caregiving families

(9)   open-ended questions on feeling a "sense of burden," and the elder and various relatives' perceptions that (the caregiver) could or should be doing more

(10) open ended questions on the advice that (the caregiver) would give others about caring for an elder, and rewards one might obtain from this caregiving role

Throughout the interviews, respondents were encouraged to provide any insights or information that might help us better understand their situation.

RELIABILITY

There were several mechanisms used to increase the reliability of the instruments and data. First, group training sessions at the start of the research and throughout the projects help to assure consistency among interviewers. The interviews were conducted using a semistructured format, but the interview schedule contained a structured component to assure a consistent baseline of data for all families. The training sessions had as a goal sensitizing interviewers to the effect that nonverbal as well as verbal communication might have on the respondents' willingness to share vital information. These sessions, in which transcripts were reviewed, helped to assure consistency in approaching sensitive topics.

A second form of reliability was interinstrument reliability. All transcripts were independently checked against the taped interviews to assure that all information had been recorded. The transcripts were then used to verify information on the questionnaire. Both the transcripts, which contained the responses to the open-ended questions, *and* the interview schedule were used in coding the scan sheets.

Intercoder reliability was a third method for assuring reliability. In all, 11 of the interview schedules were randomly selected for comparison. These schedules were independently coded and the responses compared. The accuracy of the coding was determined by dividing the total number of mistakes by the total number of variables coded for each interview schedule. The scores were averaged providing an intercoder reliability of 97.5.

The discrepancies per schedule ranged from 1 to 12. Most errors resulted from differences in interpreting a lack of information. In some cases "0" (zero) was used to indicate that the caregiver (or elder) did not do something, for example, use a particular service; in other cases the caregiver reported that it was not needed and this was coded as "9," not applicable.

Discrepancies were resolved in the questionnaires and all schedules were spot checked for similar differences in interpretation. A code of "9" was recoded to "0" for most items during data analysis, thus remaining discrepancies did not affect the accuracy of the data. Frequency data were also used to distinguish "out of range" responses, and provide still another check for accuracy.

In spite of all this checking, a final examination of the transcripts by the author revealed the word *parents* in one transcript, yet only one questionnaire for this family had been coded. This was one of the first interviews with a caregiver who was caring for more than one elder; and the responses for the father had been indicated by a tiny number next to the code for the mother's responses. We had not anticipated that families might be providing care to more than one elder, thus we had not prepared the interviewers for this situation. The instructions were revised, with several places to alert us to families caring for more than one elder. However, this early interview schedule containing information for two elders was not identified and coded for the second elder. (A comparison of the data from this new data set with that used during previous analysis and publications revealed virtually no differences.)

VALIDITY

The instrument was designed to fulfill both face and construct validity. Items in the dependency section were selected from the domain of items most frequently used in measuring an elder's ability to perform daily functioning tasks. Intercorrelations between the items indicated a high degree of internal consistency. The stress items were found to be highly correlated with the dependency tasks to which they relate (Steinmetz and Amsden, 1983).

INDICES

There were a number of indices constructed for this study. These indices were additive and each item was assigned equal weight.

Dependency index. There were six dependency indices based on a series of questions developed to assess the elder's dependency on the caregivers for the provision of certain tasks necessary for daily living. For each of these six dependencies, caregivers responded using a card that provided scores from "0"—never perform this task for the elder, to "4"—perform this task all the time for the elder. The scores for each of the items were combined to provide total scores for each of the six dependency categories. A total dependency score was computed by adding the scores obtained on each of the six dependency indices. The total dependency index scores could range from "0" to "164."

Household tasks dependency. There were eight categories in the household tasks dependency index. These items were: light housekeeping, such as dusting, dishes, picking up, heavy housekeeping, scrubbing floors, vacuuming, washing windows, laundry, grocery shopping, cooking, providing transportation, running errands, and "other." The "other" items noted were: organization, home maintenance and repairs, gardening, ironing, cutting food, and carrying meals upstairs. This index could have scores ranging from "0" if the caregiver never performed any of these tasks to "32" if the caregiver performed all of these tasks all of the time for the elder.

Personal and health care dependency. There were seven items in the personal and health care index: helping with bathing, dressing, hair care, shaving or make-up, following doctor's orders, giving medication, changing bedding, diapering (if elder is incontinent), and "other," which included cutting toenails, changing colostomy bag or catheter bag, filling oxygen tanks, giving enemas on a weekly basis, changing bed sore dressings, helping with exercises and shaving. The scores for this index could range from "0" to "28."

Financial dependency. The financial dependency index contained six items to which caregivers responded "0" if they never performed this task to "4" if they performed it all the time. The items in the index were: writing checks or paying bills (with the elder's money); providing financial support; helping with managing resources such as investments, filling out medical and insurance forms; paying for luxury items; paying for essential needs, and "other," which included: treating to fancy dinner, paying for hospitalization, updating the will. The six items in this index could have a total score ranging from "0" to "24."

Mobility dependency. The mobility dependency index contained four items: help with stairs, help getting in or out of bed; help getting in or out of a chair; and help with walking. In another part of the questionnaire (see Appendix A) information on diminished physical functions was also requested. However, this item was not used in the mobility index since the diminished physical functioning item was the caregiver's assessment of whether the elder had experienced a loss of sight, hearing, and mobility, not whether the caregiver provided any help with these tasks. The mobility dependency index score could range from "0" to "16."

Emotional/Social dependency. The emotional/social index was concerned with the social life and emotional adjustment of the elder. The eight items were: provide emotional support, provide a social life, take elder visiting, write letters for elder, help elder make phone calls, read to elder, encourage or help elder to develop friendships and "other." The scores for this index had a potential range of "0" to "36."

Mental health dependency. Mental health dependency was based on seven items that attempted to tap dependency resulting from diminished mental functioning. The items on this index were: help with decision making; forgetful; gets lost; non-rational behavior; senility; doesn't make sense; explosive behavior, must be watched, confined, or protected; and "other." The "other" category provided responses such as difficulty with communication, refusal to stay alone, fuzzy or vague spells, anxiety. The scores for the mental health dependency index had a possible range of "0" to "28."

Health status index. Each illness that the elder was reported to experience was coded by type of illness. To create the health status index, each illness was recoded to reflect having an illness versus not having an illness, rather than the specific illness coded. The total number of illnesses suffered by the elder provided a measure of the elder's health status. These illnesses did not include diminished physical functioning, such as loss of hearing, sight, or mobility, nor did it take into account the severity of each illness.

The family stress index. This index contained responses to the stress produced by alcoholism, small children, teenagers, dual careers, a recent death, physical disability or emotional problems of another family member, being a single parent, financial problems, and other stresses reported by the family.

The respondents were handed a card with numbers from "0"—is never stressful, to "4"—is always stressful. For each of these items they responded using the numbers on the card to indicate how much stress they felt because of this situation. The scores could potentially range from "0"— never stressed by any of these family situations to "40"—always stressed by all of these family factors.

The dependency stress index. The dependency stress index was based on the responses provided by the caregivers, which assessed the amount of stress that the caregivers experienced as a result of providing a series of tasks for the elder. The items in this index were: elder's financial dependency on the caregiving family, elder's need for help with personal grooming/health, elder's severe emotional or mental disability, elder's severe physical disability, elder is mobile but senile, elder won't eat, elder has special dietary needs, elder is lonely, elder makes excessive demands, providing household tasks for elder, elder needs transportation, family experiences a lack of privacy, and "other".

As in the family stress index, respondents were handed a card with answers ranging from "0" to "4" and they selected the response that best exemplified the amount of stress they felt from having to deal with each of these tasks. The scores for each family could range from a potentially low score of "0"—never stressed by any of these tasks, to a score of "52"—always stressed by all of these items.

The total stress index. The total stress index is computed by adding the scores from the family stress index to those based on the dependency stress index. The potential range of scores was "0" to "92."

Control maintenance techniques. Control maintenance techniques (CMT) were developed from a series of questions posed to caregivers in order to discover the techniques they used when attempting to control the elders' behavior. Respondents were presented a card that contained five responses: "0"—never happened to "4"—happened all the time. Respondents gave the interviewer the number, not the verbal description, of the answer that best fit how often they used one of these methods.

The variables were: "talking," "seek advice from third party," and "found alternative housing," which were combined into a new variable: advice. The responses for caregiver "confining elder to room" or "withholding food" were combined into the variable: ignore, since these techniques were usually done as short-term alternatives to *immediately* responding to the elder's demand. Force feeding and giving medication, such as a tranquilizer, in order to control the elder were combined into a single variable: medical abuse. The responses "threatened with physical force," "used physical restraint," and "hit or slapped," were combined into the variable: "physical abuse," since they represented the use or threat of use of physically harmful acts. Two additional variables were created for use in Chapters 7 and 8. The variable: "severe physical violence" eliminated the component "threat" from the variable: "physical abuse," described above. Another variable: "threat," composed of "threatened to send to nursing home" and "threaten with physical punishment," provided a measure of psychological abuse.

The techniques used by the elders in their attempt to gain or maintain control were somewhat different. They consisted of screaming and yelling, pouting, or going to their rooms, the combined variables of "elder manipulates family members," "uses physical or emotional disability to gain control," and "imposes guilt or acts the role of martyr," were combined into a single variable: "manipulate." "Refusal to respect privacy," "calling the police or other help for imagined threats," and "refusing to eat or refusing to take medicine" were the remaining variables.

Feelings of being burdened, an open ended question that for the quantitative data analysis was coded as a nominal variable "yes" or "no," provided a rich source of qualitative data on the impact that caring for an elder had on the whole family.

Note

1. Overall, 34 interviews were conducted by Sarah Foulke, who used the data in her master's thesis *Caring for the Parental Generation: An Analysis of Family Resources and Support.* Another 39 interviews were conducted by Mary Beth Reese, a medical social worker. Ruth Bashford, a member of the nursing faculty at the university, conducted 2 interviews. Deborah Amsden, who used the data on stress and burden from the completed study for her thesis: *Task Performance and Perceived Stress in Families Caring for an Elderly Relative,* conducted 14 of the interviews. Two seniors, as part of a student research project, also interviewed respondents for the study: Arliss Cole, a minority student, conducted 10 interviews, several with minority families, and Sharon Henry conducted 5 interviews.

APPENDIX C

TABLES

TABLE C.1
Mean Stress, Dependency, Caregivers' and Elders' Control Maintenance Scores for Demographic Variables

| | Race of Caregivers | | Family Characteristics | | | | | | | | | |
| | | | Residence of Caregivers | | | | | Length of Time Caring for Elders | | | | |
	White (N=114)	Black (N=5)	Urban (N=15)	Small Town (N=35)	Suburb (N=38)	Rural (N=21)	Other (N=10)	12 months or less (N=21)	13-36 months (N=19)	37-108 months (N=42)	109-168 months (N=15)	over 168 months (N=22)
Stress												
family	6.29	4.00	6.00	6.57	7.26	4.80	4.00	5.43	5.84	7.02	5.87	5.86
dependency	11.66	14.80	14.80	10.14	12.95	11.19	9.90	13.67	12.00	12.00	9.40	11.05
total stress	17.95	18.80	20.80	16.71	20.21	16.00	13.90	19.10	17.84	19.02	15.27	16.91
Dependency												
household	22.25	23.80	24.73	21.09	22.34	23.24	21.00	22.33	23.12	21.93	19.93	24.00
personal health	10.79	13.60	13.53	7.71	11.05	14.29	10.50	11.43	12.47	9.19	9.53	13.27
financial	9.90	7.40	11.53	9.06	10.79	7.95	9.90	9.00	8.52	9.00	9.47	13.41
mobility	4.02	5.00	4.33	2.23	5.37	5.14	2.80*	3.95	4.32	3.48	3.20	5.64
mental health	9.11	10.40	11.87	7.43	10.34	8.67	7.80	10.24	10.32	8.52	7.20	9.73
social/emotional	14.32	15.60	15.13	14.00	16.05	13.86	9.20*	13.52	15.58	13.76	13.47	15.91
total dependency	70.39	75.80	81.13	61.51	75.95	73.14	61.20	70.48	74.32	65.88	62.80	81.95*
Burden	0.62	0.80	0.80	0.54	0.71	0.57	0.50	0.76	0.68	0.55	0.60	0.64
CMT (caregiver)												
talk	2.25	2.808	2.60	1.94	2.32	2.52	2.20	2.00	2.21	2.21	2.73	2.36
advice	1.92	1.60	2.67	1.49	2.05	1.57	2.40	2.67	1.84	1.69	2.70	1.45
yell	0.71	1.20	1.40	0.60	0.84	0.33	0.60*	0.43	0.68	0.92	0.53	0.82
ignore	0.07	0.20	0.07	0.00	0.08	0.00	0.50*	0.14	0.00	0.05	0.27	0.00
medical abuse	0.40	0.80	0.67	0.09	0.74	0.43	0.00*	0.62	0.37	0.24	0.20	0.77
physical abuse	0.18	0.20	0.20	0.17	0.24	0.10	0.20	0.10	0.00	0.21	0.00	0.14
threats	0.12	0.00	0.07	0.14	0.16	0.05	0.10	0.33	0.05	0.24	0.13	0.09
CMT (elder)												
yell	0.74	0.81	1.00	0.63	1.05	0.24	0.60	0.57	0.74	0.86	0.40	0.91
pout	1.36	1.00	1.40	1.03	1.55	1.05	2.20	1.05	1.57	1.48	1.47	1.09
refuse food	0.57	2.00	0.87	0.29	1.00	0.43	0.50	0.90	0.57	0.76	0.00	0.59
hit	0.27	1.60	0.80	0.29	0.26	0.24	0.20	0.33	0.26	0.38	0.33	0.27
cry	0.73	0.80	0.67	0.57	1.05	0.48	0.70	0.48	1.26	0.60	0.60	0.86
manipulates	2.82	2.80	2.80	3.46	3.08	1.76	1.90	2.33	2.53	3.05	3.47	2.68
call police	0.06	0.80	0.33	0.00	0.16	0.00	0.00	0.10	0.00	0.14	0.07	0.09
invades privacy	0.87	1.00	1.33	0.89	1.05	0.38	0.30	0.52	0.53	1.29	0.87	0.73

TABLE C.1 Continued

| | Relationship of Elder to Caregiver | | | | Family Characteristics | | | | | |
| | | | | | Fathers and Fathers-in-Law | | Mothers and Mothers-in-Law | | One- and Two-Elder Families | |
	Mother (N = 74)	Father (N = 13)	In-Law (N = 22)	Other (N = 10)	Father (N = 13)	Father-in-Law (N = 5)	Mother (N = 74)	Mother-in-Law (N = 17)	One Elder (N = 89)	Two Elders (N = 30)
Stress										
family	5.81	6.54	6.73	7.4	6.54	4.20	5.81	7.47	6.07	6.57
dependency	12.31	10.46	10.95	11.5	10.46	7.20	12.31	12.06	12.43	9.90
total stress	18.12	17.00	17.68	18.9	17.00	11.40	18.12	19.53	18.49	16.47
Dependency										
household	22.65	19.31	22.00	24.50	19.31	20.80	22.65	22.35	23.16	19.83
personal health	11.90	6.46	11.18	8.70	6.46	6.40	11.91	12.59	11.58	8.90
financial	10.89	6.92	8.27	8.80	6.92	2.60*	10.89	9.94	10.04	9.07
mobility	4.24	1.23	4.77	4.80	1.23	1.20	4.24	5.82	3.97	4.33
mental health	9.36	7.69	9.41	9.10	7.69	3.00	9.36	11.29	9.60	7.90
social/emotional	15.53	11.46	12.41	13.90	11.46	6.80	15.53	14.06	14.85	12.93
total dependency	74.58	53.07	68.01	69.80	53.08	40.80	74.58	76.06	73.20	62.97
Burden	0.64	0.69	0.68	0.40	0.69	0.60	0.64	0.71	0.67	0.50
CMT (caregiver)										
talk	2.36	1.69	2.23	2.40	1.69	3.20	2.36	1.94	2.16	2.60
advice	2.01	2.31	1.50	1.50	2.30	1.60	2.01	1.47	2.02	1.57
yell	0.76	0.77	0.41	1.20	0.77	0.40	0.76	0.41	0.74	0.70
ignore	0.08	0.00	0.09	0.10	0.00	0.00	0.08	0.12	0.10	0.00
medical abuse	0.50	0.15	0.32	0.40	0.15	0.00	0.50	0.41	0.36	0.60
physical abuse	0.18	0.31	0.09	0.30	0.23	0.00	0.09	0.12	0.11	0.13
threats	0.09	0.23	0.09	0.20	0.31	0.00	0.18	0.12	0.20	0.13
CMT (elder)										
yell	0.76	0.85	0.41	1.20	0.85	1.20	0.76	0.18*	0.70	0.87
pout	1.34	1.08	1.27	1.90	1.08	1.40	1.34	1.24	1.46	1.00
refuse food	0.57	0.92	0.59	0.80	0.92	0.00	0.57	0.76	0.66	0.53
hit	0.34	0.31	0.18	0.60	0.31	0.40	0.34	0.12	0.34	0.30
cry	0.78	0.85	0.68	0.30	0.85	0.00	0.78	0.88	0.80	0.53
manipulates	3.17	1.62	2.59	2.30	1.62	2.20	3.18	2.71	3.07	2.10
call police	0.12	0.15	0.00	0.00	0.15	0.00	0.12	0.00	0.09	0.10
invades privacy	0.82	0.92	0.95	1.00	0.92	1.20	0.82	0.88	0.87	0.90

(continued)

TABLE C.1 Continued

| | Elder's Characteristics | | | | | | Caregiver's Characteristics | | | | | | Marital Status | |
| | Sex of Elder | | Age of Elder | | | | Sex of Caregiver | | Age of Caregiver | | | | | |
	Male (N = 19)	Female (N = 100)	Under 70 (N = 12)	70-79 (N = 27)	80-89 (N = 55)	90+ (N = 25)	Male (N = 7)	Female (N = 97)	Under 70 (N = 12)	70-79 (N = 26)	80-89 (N = 46)	90+ (N = 20)	Married (N = 72)	Non-Married (N = 32)
Stress														
family	6.37	6.16	6.92	7.67	5.70	5.32	6.86	6.00	6.58	5.73	6.52	5.10	6.15	5.84
dependency	9.79	12.17	10.67	14.22	10.63	12.24	13.00	12.02	13.00	12.35	12.84	9.45	12.54	11.06
total stress	16.16	18.33	17.58	21.89	16.35	17.56	19.86	18.02	19.58	18.08	19.36	14.55	18.69	16.91
Dependency														
household	20.16	22.73	16.41	22.00	22.24	25.68	22.14	22.69	18.58	22.15	23.56	23.65	22.57	22.84
grooming/health	6.52	11.74*	4.41	11.96	10.56	13.64	11.57	11.24	4.66	12.12	12.02	12.40	11.19	11.44
financial	5.89	10.54*	5.83	10.44	9.01	12.72	11.71	9.70	4.50	9.88	10.41	11.65	9.46	10.69
mobility	1.56	4.61*	1.33	3.81	3.90	5.96	1.71	4.14	1.33	3.85	4.70	4.10	3.60	4.83
mental health	7.11	9.56	5.66	10.66	9.49	8.52	8.42	9.30	6.42	9.96	9.85	8.60	9.36	8.97
social/emotional	10.79	15.05*	8.50	12.96	15.36	16.52	11.71	14.74	9.91	12.96	15.58	16.95	14.17	15.38
total dependency	51.63	74.23*	42.17	71.85	70.58	83.04	67.29	71.82	45.41	70.92	76.13	77.35	70.35	74.16
Burden	.63	.63	.67	.63	.60	.68	.71	.64	.66	.73	.65	.50	.69	.53
CMT (caregiver)														
talk	2.21	2.28	2.00	2.33	2.38	2.08	3.14	2.19	2.58	1.92	2.21	2.60	2.07	2.69
advice	2.21	1.85	2.08	2.60	1.89	1.48	1.87	1.97	2.42	1.85	1.82	1.90	1.90	1.94
yell	.79	.72	.75	.92	.80	.36	.29	.79	.91	1.11	.69	.35	.71	.88
ignore	.00	.09	.00	.11	.11	.00	.00	.09	.00	.15	.02	.20	.01	.25
medical abuse	.11	.48*	.42	.56	.42	.28	.29	.39	.17	.53	.35	.48	.36	.44
physical abuse	.26	.17*	.08	.26	.25	.00	.00	.21	.00	.31	.17	.20	.15	.28
threats	.26	.09	.08	.15	.13	.08	.00	.12	.08	.12	.13	.10	.10	.16
CMT (elder)														
yell	1.00	.69	1.33	.92	.64	.48	.71	.73	1.33	.81	.69	.35	.72	.75
pout	1.26	1.36	1.58	1.48	1.49	.76	1.57	1.39	2.08	1.65	1.10	1.35	1.32	1.59
refuse food	.74	.61	.50	.93	.47	.72	.57	.69	.42	.69	.87	.40	.58	.91
hit	.42	.31	.33	.41	.33	.24	.00	.37	.42	.46	.33	.20	.31	.44
cry	.58	.76	.58	.78	.76	.68	1.29	.73	.75	1.04	.74	.50	.81	.69
manipulate	1.79	3.02	3.67	2.59	.87	.56	3.43	3.01	4.17	2.27	3.10	3.20	2.85	3.47
call police	.11	.09	.25	.11	.02	.16	.00	.09	.00	.12	.13	.00	.04	.19
invade privacy	1.05	.84	1.00	1.00	.84	.76	1.57	.84	1.16	.61	1.07	.70	.83	1.03

*Significant at 0.05.

TABLE C.2
Mean Scores of Variables for Caregivers Characterized by High and Low Levels of Dependency

Categories	Household		Grooming and Health		Financial		Mobility		Social/ Emotional		Mental Health	
	High (N = 62)	Low (N = 57)	High (N = 59)	Low (N = 60)	High (N = 62)	Low (N = 57)	High (N = 59)	Low (N = 60)	High (N = 63)	Low (N = 56)	High (N = 62)	Low (n = 57)
Dependency												
grooming/health	16.13	5.22*		18.50*	14.44	7.07*	14.75	7.13*	14.33	7.05*	14.48	7.02*
household		7.47*	26.20	7.01*	26.66	19.77*	25.05	19.63*	24.13	20.29*	23.34	21.21
financial	11.93	2.22*	12.63	1.68*	5.05	2.98*	10.97	8.65*	12.13	7.18*	12.29	7.09*
mobility	5.74	7.00*	6.47	6.45*	11.40	6.73*		8.23	5.03	2.96*	5.02	3.01*
mental health	11.16	12.04*	11.93	12.08*	16.11	12.47*	10.12	13.02*	11.51	6.54*		11.16*
social/emotional	16.51	50.33*	16.69	48.78*	16.11	53.18*	15.75	57.13*		52.91*	17.32	53.67*
total dependency	89.27		92.83		86.66		84.34		86.37		86.21	
Stress												
family	5.74	6.68	5.86	6.51	6.56	5.79	5.86	6.51	6.76	5.55	7.16	5.14*
dependency	13.56	9.86*	13.83	9.78*	13.88	9.51*	13.20	10.40*	13.58	9.77*	15.37	7.89*
total stress	19.31	16.54	19.69	16.30	20.45	15.30*	19.07	16.91	20.35	15.32*	22.53	13.04*
Burden	0.72	0.51*	0.69	0.57	0.69	0.56	0.68	0.58	0.68	0.57	0.76	0.49*
Control Maintenance Techniques												
Caregiver												
talk	2.30	2.22	2.37	2.17	2.08	2.47	2.42	2.11	2.46	2.05	2.21	2.33
advice	2.09	1.70	2.13	1.68	1.92	1.89	2.03	1.78	1.97	1.84	2.44	1.33*
yell	0.87	0.57	0.90	0.57	0.85	0.60	0.81	0.65	0.79	0.66	1.06	0.37*
ignore	0.03	0.12	0.19	0.03	0.13	0.02	0.10	0.05	0.05	0.11	0.10	0.05
medical abuse	0.55	0.28	0.69	0.15	0.53	0.30	0.59	0.25	0.51	0.32	0.71	0.11*
threats	0.16	0.07	0.19	0.09	0.15	0.08	0.14	0.10	0.13	0.11	0.18	0.05
physical abuse	0.18	0.19	0.22	0.15	0.26	0.11	0.22	0.15	0.19	0.18	0.26	0.11
Elder												
yell	0.65	0.84	0.69	0.78	0.79	0.68	0.64	0.83	0.76	0.71	0.92	0.54
pout	1.18	1.53	1.24	1.45	1.39	1.30	1.32	1.37	1.51	1.16	1.58	1.09*
refuse food or medicine	0.71	0.54	0.68	0.57	0.84	0.40	0.71	0.55	0.84	0.39	0.89	0.35*
cry	0.60	0.88*	0.69	0.77	0.84	0.61	0.74	0.72	0.94	0.50*	1.10	0.33*
hit	0.47	0.18*	0.51	0.15*	0.52	0.12*	0.39	0.27	0.48	0.16*	0.60	0.04*
manipulate	2.45	3.23	2.49	3.15	3.37	2.28*	3.03	2.61	3.40	2.18*	3.50	2.08*
call police	0.11	0.07	0.12	0.06	0.13	0.05	0.10	0.08	0.13	0.05	0.15	0.04
invades privacy	0.73	1.04	0.75	1.00	1.02	0.72	0.93	0.82	1.02	0.71	1.05	0.68

*Significant at 0.05.

TABLE C.3
Mean Scores of Variables for Caregivers Characterized by High and Low Levels of Dependency Stress

Categories	Household High (N=63)	Household Low (N=56)	Grooming/Health High (N=43)	Grooming/Health Low (N=76)	Financial High (N=27)	Financial Low (N=92)	Mobile but Senile High (N=29)	Mobile but Senile Low (N=90)	Social/Emotional High (N=48)	Social/Emotional Low (N=71)	Transportation High (N=42)	Transportation Low (N=77)
Dependency												
household	22.44	22.18	24.72	20.96*	24.26	21.75	24.93	21.48*	23.67	21.41	22.76	22.08
personal grooming/health	11.90	9.79	15.95	8.05*	12.93	10.32	15.86	9.31*	14.06	8.77*	10.50	11.13
financial	10.19	9.36	11.86	8.63*	13.59	8.68*	11.10	9.38	8.38	11.90*	10.69	9.31
mobility	4.98	3.02*	5.58	3.20*	5.22	3.72	4.28	3.99	4.29	3.90	4.05	4.06
mental health	9.98	8.25	12.16	7.47*	10.81	8.68	15.59	7.10*	13.58	6.18*	10.81	8.27*
social/emotional	14.68	14.02	15.67	13.63	16.04	13.88	16.66	13.63	16.71	12.79*	15.62	13.69
total dependency	74.19	66.61	85.95	61.95*	82.85	67.03*	88.41	64.89*	84.21	61.44*	74.43	68.55
Demographic												
elder's age	81.21	82.43	83.35	80.89	83.63	81.24	82.83	81.44	81.31	82.10	81.21	82.47
caregiver's age	50.06	51.55	50.02	51.18	51.04	50.68	50.59	50.82	50.46	50.97	50.06	51.55
length of caregiving	102.63	111.07	88.72	116.72	153.37	92.88	96.28	109.93	119.20	98.08	102.63	111.07
total illness	2.27	2.05	2.33	2.08	2.82	1.98*	1.93	2.24	2.17	2.17	2.29	2.10
race		x		x		x		x		x		x
relationship		x		x		x		x		x		x*
elder's sex		x		x		x		x		x		x
caregiver's sex		x		x		x		x		x		x*
residence (suburb, city, small town, rural)		x		x		x		x		x		x*
Family/Self Stressors												
extra kin	0.30	0.25	0.00	0.40	0.00	0.36	0.00	0.34*	0.32	0.25	0.33	0.25
parents feel you could do more	0.22	0.29	0.22	0.30	0.33	0.23	0.24	0.26	0.25	0.26	0.38	0.18
relatives feel you could do more	0.05	0.00*	0.02	0.03	0.07	0.01	0.00	0.03	0.02	0.03	0.05	0.01
sibs feel you could do more	0.08		0.02	0.05	0.04	0.04		0.06	0.06	0.03	0.02	0.05
you feel you could do more	0.51	0.34	0.37	0.46	0.41	0.43	0.41	0.43	0.40	0.45	0.50	0.39
family-related stress	6.98	5.30	6.63	5.95*	8.67	5.47*	8.10	5.58*	6.54	5.96	7.50	5.48*
total dependency stress	15.68	7.41*	16.67	9.03	18.56	9.80*	17.97	9.80*	16.79	8.41*	15.64	9.69*
total stress	22.67	12.71*	23.30	14.97*	27.22	15.27*	26.07	15.38*	23.33	14.37*	23.14	15.17*
burden	0.84	0.39*	0.81	0.53*	0.93	0.54*	0.76	0.59	0.75	0.55*	0.81	0.53*

Control Maintenance Techniques

Caregiver

talk	2.11	2.45	2.07	2.38	2.00	2.35	1.83	2.41	2.25	2.28	2.07	2.38
advice	2.27	1.50*	2.56	1.54*	2.30	1.79	2.90	1.59*	2.63	1.42*	2.21	1.74
yell	0.90	0.54*	0.98	0.59*	0.78	0.72	1.41	0.51	1.13	0.46*	0.93	0.62
ignore	0.08	0.07	0.09	0.07	0.07	0.08	0.07	0.08	0.10	0.06	0.05	0.09
medical abuse	0.59	0.23	0.70	0.26*	0.44	0.41	0.90	0.27*	0.69	0.24*	0.64	0.30
threaten to send to nursing home	0.16	0.07	0.16	0.09	0.15	0.11	0.28	0.07	0.25	0.03*	0.14	0.10
physical abuse	0.30	0.05*	0.33	0.11	0.19	0.18	0.52	0.08*	0.38	0.06*	0.29	0.13
emotional abuse	0.27	0.11	0.33	0.12	0.19	0.20	0.55	0.08	0.42	0.04*	0.21	0.18
severe physical abuse	0.20	0.02*	0.16	0.18	0.15	0.10	0.24	0.07	0.21	0.04*	0.21	0.05*
total abuse	0.89	0.29*	1.02	0.37*	0.63	0.60	1.41	0.34*	1.06	0.30*	0.93	0.43

Elder

yell	0.87	0.59	0.79	0.71	0.74	0.74	1.10	0.62*	0.96	0.59	0.93	0.64
pout	1.41	1.27	1.44	1.29	1.81	1.21	1.86	1.18*	1.65	1.14*	1.86	1.06*
refuse food or medicine	0.73	0.52	0.86	0.50	1.26	0.45	1.21	0.44	1.21	0.24*	0.95	0.45
elder hit	0.43	0.21	0.60	0.17*	0.56	0.26	0.86	0.16*	0.73	0.06*	0.57	0.19*
elder cry	0.81	0.64	0.93	0.62	1.33	0.55*	1.07	0.62	1.10	0.48*	1.33	0.40*
manipulate	3.22	2.38	3.28	2.56	5.19	2.13*	3.62	2.57	3.67	2.25*	4.57	1.87*
call police	0.14	0.04	0.16	0.05	0.22	0.05	0.24	0.04	0.17	0.04	0.19	0.04
ignores privacy of others	1.16	0.55*	0.95	0.83	1.63	0.65*	1.31	0.73	1.23	0.63*	1.36	0.61*

(continued)

TABLE C.3 Continued

Categories	Physical Disability High (N=54)	Physical Disability Low (N=65)	Elder's Loneliness High (N=77)	Elder's Loneliness Low (N=42)	Elder not Eating High (N=29)	Elder not Eating Low (N=90)	Elder Needing Special Diet High (N=22)	Elder Needing Special Diet Low (N=97)	Elder's Demands High (N=59)	Elder's Demands Low (N=60)	Elder's Lack of Respect for Caregiver's Privacy High (N=64)	Elder's Lack of Respect for Caregiver's Privacy Low (N=55)
Dependency												
household	23.43	21.40	22.61	21.79	23.41	21.97	23.05	22.15	21.76	22.87	22.09	22.58
personal grooming/health	12.94	9.21*	10.65	11.38	14.66	9.70*	10.32	11.04	11.69	10.13	10.66	11.20
financial	11.48	8.40*	10.78	8.00*	12.21	9.02*	9.68	9.82	11.56	8.07*	9.58	10.05
mobility	5.31	3.02*	4.04	4.10	6.07	3.41*	4.23	4.02	4.80	3.33	4.06	4.05
mental health	10.63	7.95*	9.53	8.50	12.00	8.26*	7.82	9.47	10.40	7.97*	9.42	8.87
social/emotional	15.04	13.82	15.75	11.83*	16.79	13.59*	13.18	14.64	15.24	13.52	14.44	14.29
total dependency	78.83	63.80*	73.36	65.60	85.14	65.94*	68.27	71.15	75.44	65.88	70.25	71.05
Demographic												
elder's age	82.43	81.25	81.82	81.71	82.55	81.53	81.64	81.81	81.56	82.00	80.92	82.78
caregiver's age	50.22	51.21	50.56	51.14	51.17	50.63	50.82	50.75	49.95	51.57	49.36	52.40
length of caregiving	108.94	104.66	104.44	110.57	101.55	108.23	118.00	104.03	107.19	106.03	104.78	108.72
total illness	2.43	1.95	2.22	2.07	2.41	2.09	2.86	2.01*	2.41	1.93	2.27	2.05
race	x	x	x*	x*	x	x	x	x	x	x	x	x
relationship	x	x	x	x	x	x	x	x	x	x	x	x
elder's sex	x	x	x	x	x	x	x	x	x	x	x	x
caregiver's sex	x	x	x	x	x	x	x	x	x	x	x	x
residence (suburb, city, small town, rural)	x*	x*	x	x	x	x	x	x	x	x	x	x
Family/Self Stressors												
extra kin	0.22	0.31	0.35	0.08	0.14	0.31	0.05	0.33	0.38	0.16	0.10	0.47
parents feel you could do more	0.19	0.31	0.26	0.24	0.21	0.27	0.41	0.22	0.32	0.18	0.31	0.18
relatives feel you could do more	0.02	0.03	0.03	0.02	0.03	0.02	0.05	0.02	0.03	0.02	0.05	0.00
sibs feel you could do more	0.04	0.05	0.06	0.00	0.03	0.04	0.05	0.04	0.05	0.03	0.03	0.05
you feel you could do more	0.44	0.42	0.47	0.36	0.48	0.41	0.64	0.38*	0.53	0.33*	0.44	0.42
family-related stress	6.52	5.92	6.75	5.17	6.38	6.13	7.63	5.87	8.09	4.33*	6.33	6.04
total dependency stress	16.00	8.29*	13.26	9.10*	16.21	10.37*	15.59	10.93*	15.63	8.02*	14.73	8.36*
total stress	22.52	14.22*	20.01	14.26*	22.59	16.50*	23.23	16.79*	23.71	12.35*	21.06	14.40
burden	0.72	0.55	0.74	0.43*	0.66	0.62	0.86	0.58*	0.75	0.52*	0.77	0.47*

Control Maintenance Techniques

Caregiver												
talk	2.15	2.37	2.49	1.86*	2.24	2.28	1.86	2.36	2.14	2.40	2.20	2.35
advice	2.31	1.57*	2.25	1.29*	2.24	1.80	1.77	1.94	2.25	1.57*	1.98	1.81
yell	0.98	0.52*	0.79	0.62	0.90	0.68	0.55	0.77	0.93	0.53*	0.84	0.60
ignore	0.11	0.05	0.10	0.02	0.14	0.06	0.00	0.09	0.07	0.08	0.03	0.13
medical abuse	0.69	0.20*	0.42	0.43	0.66	0.34	0.18	0.47	0.53	0.32	0.47	0.36
threaten to send to nursing home	0.17	0.08	0.13	0.10	0.17	0.10	0.14	0.11	0.20	0.03*	0.16	0.07
physical abuse	0.35	0.05*	0.17	0.21	0.21	0.18	0.14	0.20	0.32	0.05*	0.20	0.16
emotional abuse	0.30	0.10	0.17	0.24	0.20	0.19	0.18	0.20	0.39	0.05	0.23	0.15
severe physical abuse	0.22	0.02*	0.13	0.07	0.17	0.08	0.09	0.11	0.19	0.03*	0.13	0.09
total abuse	1.04	0.25*	0.58	0.64	0.86	0.52	0.32	0.67	0.85	0.37*	0.67	0.52
Elder												
yell	0.93	0.59	0.90	0.45*	1.00	0.66	0.59	0.77	1.10	0.38*	0.84	0.62
pout	1.54	1.19	1.57	0.92*	1.45	1.31	1.64	1.28	1.85	0.85*	1.55	1.11
refuse food or medicine	0.83	0.46	0.70	0.50	2.00	0.19*	0.77	0.60	0.81	0.45	0.75	0.49
hit	0.48	0.20	0.35	0.29	0.72	0.20*	0.36	0.32	0.51	0.15*	0.50	0.13*
cry	0.91	0.58	0.79	0.62	0.97	0.66	1.09	0.65	0.96	0.50*	0.81	0.64
manipulate	3.39	2.35	3.45	1.67*	3.24	2.69	5.00	2.33*	4.42	1.25*	3.83	1.65*
call police	0.13	0.06	0.10	0.07	0.17	0.07	0.05	0.10	0.14	0.05	0.16	0.02
ignores privacy of others	1.04	0.74	0.99	0.67	1.17	0.78	1.45	0.74	1.37	0.38*	1.19	0.51*

NOTE: Chi-square used for tests of significance, all other variables computed by difference of means and F.
*Significant at .05.

TABLE C.4
Correlation Matrix
Measures of Dependency Stress with Demographic, Dependency and Other Stress Variables

	Mobile/ Senile	Not Eating	Special Diet	Lonely	Demand	House	Transp.	Privacy	Groom	Physical Disability	Emotional Disability	Financial
Demographic												
age/elder	.02	.03	-.02	.04	.01	-.06	-.03	-.12	.08	.06	-.09	.12
sex/elder	-.09	.19*	.09	.03	.16	.05	.13	.00	.00	.04	-.05	.07
relationship	.18*	.07	-.04	-.03	.10	.07	-.02	-.02	-.06	.07	-.01	-.12
length/care	-.08	-.05	.06	.01	.01	.00	.03	-.09	-.08	.02	.08	.17
health	-.05	.09	.18	.02	.15	.11	.02	.06	.14	.14	.04	.11
sex/caregiver	.12	.04	-.04	-.09	-.09	.05	-.13	.14	.03	-.12	-.09	-.01
age/caregiver	-.01	.07	.02	-.00	-.02	-.06	-.08	-.23*	-.02	-.05	-.05	.07
race	.09	.10	.00	-.15	-.01	.03	.19	.13	.12	.05	.00	.20*
marital status	.00	.07	.08	.00	-.04	-.22*	-.07	-.12	-.09	-.11	-.04	.09
where live	-.12	.13	.03	-.02	-.07	-.12	-.13	-.12	-.09	.08	-.09	.00
Dependency												
household	.23*	.08	.01	.00	.01	.09	-.02	.00	.31*	.17	.29*	.18*
groom/health	.34*	.31*	-.11	-.06	.12	.16	.02	-.03	.47*	.32*	.31*	.19*
financial	.16	.24*	-.04	.17*	.30*	.05	.16	.00	.30*	.19*	.34*	.33*
mobility	-.00	.30*	-.00	.03	.17	.15	.02	-.09	.23*	.30*	.02	.22*
social/emotional	.24*	.25*	-.06	.28*	.19*	.08	.13	-.00	.19*	.08	.26*	.15
mental health	.68*	.29*	-.09	.10	.26*	.18	.25*	.10	.47*	.27	.66*	.23*
total dependency	.40*	.34*	-.08	.11	.23*	.15	.12	.00	.47*	.31*	.43*	.29*
Stress												
burden	.17*	.02	.20	.34*	.33*	.49*	.30*	.32*	.35*	.19*	.28*	.26*
family	.33*	.09	.22*	.20*	.43*	.32*	.23*	.18	.17	.07	.17	.23*
dependency	.54*	.35*	.25*	.36*	.65*	.60*	.46*	.46*	.53*	.55*	.68*	.53*
relative	-.03	.07	.22*	.11	.23*	.13	.12	.17	-.04	-.03	.00	-.01
total stress	.54*	.29*	.28*	.35*	.66*	.58*	.43*	.41*	.46*	.42*	.56*	.48*

*Significant at 0.05.

TABLE C.5
Correlation Matrix
Elder's Use of Control Maintenance, Techniques with Demographic, Dependency, Dependency Stress, and Other Stress Variables

	Yell	Pout	Refuse	Hit	Cry	Manipulate	Police	Privacy
Demographic								
age/elder	-.18	-.12	-.02	-.02	-.01	-.05	-.09	-.04
sex/elder	.10	.03	-.03	-.05	.06	.14	-.01	-.06
relationship	.09	.15	.06	.12	-.12	-.08	-.07	.07
length/care	.02	-.06	-.01	.07	.04	.07	.05	.06
health	-.04	-.11	.08	.03	.01	.01	.01	.07
sex/caregiver	-.18	-.05	.04	.12	-.07	-.01	.06	-.05
age/caregiver	-.21*	-.16	-.02	-.11	-.07	-.02	-.03	-.06
race	.01	-.06	.21*	.03*	.01	.00	.33*	.02
marital status	-.00	.08	.09	.08	.06	.05	.09	.08
where live	-.08	.18*	-.02	-.12	.00	-.13	-.11	-.20*
Dependency								
household	-.14	-.05	.09	.16	-.08	-.09	.00	-.15
groom/health	-.03	-.02	.07	.26*	.02	-.07	.06	.13
financial	.12	.13	.13	.25*	.19*	.18	.08	.18
mobility	.06	.12	.06	.11	.09	.03	.00	-.07
social/emotional	.04	.14	.20*	.26*	.24*	.19*	.14	.16

(continued)

259

TABLE C.5 Continued

	Yell	Pout	Refuse	Hit	Cry	Manipulate	Police	Privacy
mental health	.17	.21*	.30*	.47*	.31*	.23*	.27*	.14
total dependency	.04	.10	.19*	.35	.16	.09	.13	.01
Dependency/Stress								
household	.20*	.06	.14	.20*	.00	.19*	.26*	.27*
grooming/health	.12	.09	.18	.33*	.12	.13	.24*	.07
financial	.09	.18*	.39*	.23*	.36*	.39*	.35*	.27*
mobile/senile	.20*	.19*	.26*	.43*	.11	.15	.32*	.17
emotional	.22*	.18*	.35*	.41*	.22*	.25*	.26*	.22*
transportation	.15	.24*	.25*	.28*	.45*	.45*	.23*	.37*
physical disabled	.09	.08	.11	.17	.05	.12	.06	.10
lonely	.27*	.23*	.05	.13	.10	.29*	.04	.22*
not eating	.16	-.02	.48*	.27*	.06	.08	.19*	.07
special diet	-.01	.13	-.01	.01	.16	.36*	-.03	.24*
demand	.40*	.42*	.18*	.23*	.24*	.65*	.19*	.46*
privacy	.14	.14	.10	.26*	.00	.31*	.26*	.35*
Stress								
burden	.08	.07	.01	.10	.05	.22*	.08	.23*
family	.27*	.28*	.14	.22*	.11	.37*	.13*	.38*
dependency	.37*	.33*	.41*	.48*	.29*	.55*	.36*	.45
relative	.12	.07	.00	.05	.07	.33*	.06	.25*
total stress	.38*	.36*	.36*	.44*	.26	.57*	.32*	.50*

*Significant at 0.05.

TABLE C.6
Correlation Matrix
Caregiver's Use of Control Maintenance Techniques with Demographic,
Dependency, Dependency Stress, and Other Stress Variables

	Advice	Talk	Verbal	Psychological	Medical	Physical	Severe Physical	Total Abuse
Demographic								
age/elder	-.08	.00	-.02	-.02	.08	-.05	-.04	-.08
sex/elder	-.08	.02	-.02	-.13	.13	.13	-.05	.08
relationship	-.03	.05	.13	.09	.01	.08	.09	.05
length/care	-.14	.07	.09	-.01	.10	.03	-.05	.06
health	-.08	-.14	-.17	-.02	-.10	.06	.08	-.04
sex/caregiver	.00	-.21	.08	.09	-.04	.09	.09	.01
age/caregiver	.00	-.03	-.22*	.03	-.01	.01	-.03	.03
race	-.04	.08	.10	-.02	.08	.05	.01	.06
marital status	.01	.14	.09	.22	-.03	.04	.12	.03
where live	.04	.01	-.13	.10	-.08	.05	-.01	-.07
Dependency								
household	.17	.04	.09	.12	.09	.09	.15	.12
grooming/health	.15	.07	.18*	.06	.30*	.20*	.11	.30*
financial	.10	-.06	.16	.17	.21*	.20*	.28*	.27*
mobility	.05	.13	.07	.16	.28*	.17*	.23*	.31*
social/emotional	.15	.12	.11	.05	.14	.06	.10	.14

(continued)

TABLE C.6 Continued

	Advice	Talk	Verbal	Psychological	Medical	Physical	Severe Physical	Total Abuse
mental health	.47*	-.02	.45*	.14	.41*	.24*	.35*	.36*
total dependency	.25*	.06	.25*	.15	.33*	.20*	.29*	
Dependency/Stress								
household	.28*	-.13	.20*	.05	.17	.24*	.32*	.25*
grooming/health	.29*	-.09	.22*	.19*	.18*	.25*	.18*	.27*
financial	.21*	-.04	.06	.05	.09	.00	.05	.08
mobile/senile	.42*	-.15	.43*	.21*	.37*	.34*	.30*	.47*
emotional	.43*	-.01	.36*	.25*	.30*	.34*	.35*	.42*
transportation	.14	-.11	.17	.00	.14	.10	.19*	.16
physical disabled	.24*	.01	.21*	.11	.25*	.22*	.30*	.31*
lonely	.31*	.26*	.07	.03	.07	.05	.15	.08
not eating	.16	.05	.14	.02	.23	.05	.15	.21*
special diet	.00	-.11	-.07	-.06	-.07	.02	-.02	-.07
demand	.30*	-.08	.18*	.18*	.15	.27*	.21*	.26*
privacy	.18	-.08	.16	.00	.00	.07	.07	.03
Stress								
burden	.24*	-.22*	.09	.06	.17	.12	.14	.20*
family	.19*	-.18*	.20*	.20*	.08	.33*	.27*	.22*
dependency	.52*	-.07	.38*	.21*	.34*	.34*	.38*	.45*
relative	.16	-.06	.06	.01	-.06	.01	.03	-.04
total stress	.46*	-.13	.36*	.24*	.28*	.40*	.40*	.42*

*Significant at 0.05.

TABLE C.7

Mean Demographic, Dependency, Stress, Burden, and Elders' CMT Scores for Caregivers Characterized by High and Low Levels of Abuse

Categories	Verbal High (N=49)	Verbal Low (N=70)	Psychological High (N=16)	Psychological Low (N=103)	Physical or Threat High (N=14)	Physical or Threat Low (N=105)	Severe Physical High (N=11)	Severe Physical Low (N=108)	Medical High (N=20)	Medical Low (N=99)	Total Abuse Scores High (N=27)	Total Abuse Scores Low (N=92)
Demographic												
elder's age	80.59	82.61*	79.88	82.08	79.36	82.10	80.64	81.90	80.20	82.10	79.69	82.41
caregiver's age	48.51	53.01*	50.94	51.24	50.43	51.30	50.00	50.84	49.85	51.47	50.41	51.43
length of caregiving	129.39	103.82	204.44	99.89	172.43	106.15	131.64	104.06	116.35	113.47	129.93	109.55
total illness	1.92	2.34	2.31	2.15	2.43	2.13	2.46	2.14	1.85	2.23	2.04	2.21
race				x						x		
relationship				x		x		*		x		*
elder's sex						x				x		
caregiver's sex		*		x		x				x		
residence				x						x*		
Dependency												
household	22.37	22.29	26.38	21.69*	25.00	21.96	25.63	21.98	23.50	22.08	24.22	21.76
personal groom/health	12.57	9.74	15.25	10.23*	14.57	10.41	16.18	10.37*	16.25	9.82*	15.77	9.48*
financial	10.76	9.13	13.12	9.26*	13.71	9.28	15.18	9.25*	13.25	9.09*	12.51	9.00*
mobility	4.41	3.81	7.56	3.51*	5.93	3.80	6.72	3.77*	6.15	3.63	5.70	3.57*
mental health	11.96	7.21	12.50	8.65*	14.86	8.41*	16.27	8.46*	15.10	7.96*	14.77	7.52*
social/emotional	15.08	13.87	15.00	14.27	15.57	14.21	16.18	14.17	16.95	13.85	15.85	13.93
total dependency	77.14	66.16	89.81	67.64*	89.64	60.09	98.18	68.00*	91.20	66.46	88.89	65.26*

(continued)

TABLE C.7 Continued

Categories	Verbal		Psychological		Physical or Threat		Severe Physical		Medical		Total Abuse Scores	
	High (N = 49)	Low (N = 70)	High (N = 16)	Low (N = 103)	High (N = 14)	Low (N = 105)	High (N = 11)	Low (N = 108)	High (N = 20)	Low (N = 99)	High (N = 27)	Low (N = 92)
Task-Related Stress												
household	0.82	0.51	1.43	1.18	2.29	1.08*	2.72	1.06*	1.80	1.10*	1.81	0.04*
grooming/health	0.43	0.39	1.00	0.58	1.07	0.58	1.18	0.58*	1.25	0.52*	1.48	0.49*
financial	1.24	0.27	0.81	0.34	0.50	0.39	0.64	0.38	0.60	0.36	0.52	0.37
mobile/senile	1.67	0.79	1.19	0.59	2.00	0.49*	2.00	0.53*	1.70	0.46*	1.89	0.32*
social/emotional	0.74	0.57	2.06	1.01*	2.71	0.94*	2.82	0.96*	2.25	0.93*	2.37	0.79*
transportation	1.47		0.75	0.62	1.14	0.57*	1.36	0.56*	1.15	0.54*	1.07	0.51*
physical disability	1.59	0.81*	1.75	0.98*	1.86	0.98*	2.27	0.96*	1.85	0.93*	1.93	0.84*
elder's loneliness	0.82	1.59	1.50	1.57	1.71	1.54	2.00	1.52	1.80	1.52	1.63	1.54
not eating	0.33	0.49	0.94	0.57	0.86	0.59	0.55	0.57	1.10	0.53	1.04	0.50
special diet	1.65	0.47	0.43	0.40	0.57	0.39	0.55	0.40	0.15	0.46	0.30	0.45
elder's demands	1.43	1.04	2.07	1.17	2.21	1.17*	2.27	1.19*	1.80	1.19	1.85	1.13*
lack of privacy		1.30	1.50	1.33	1.92	1.28	1.82	1.31	1.60	1.30	1.70	1.25
Stress & Burden												
family-related stress	7.08	5.59	7.63	5.97	11.00	5.55	10.81	5.72*	6.60	6.11	7.89	5.70*
total dependency stress	14.32	10.01*	16.50	11.06*	19.57	10.75*	21.36	10.82*	18.00	10.55*	18.11	9.93*
total stress	21.39	15.60*	24.13	17.03*	30.57	16.30*	32.18	16.55*	24.60	16.65*	26.00	15.63*
burden	0.61	0.64	0.69	0.62	0.79	0.61	0.91	0.60*	0.80	0.60	0.74	0.59
Elder's CMT												
yell	1.24	0.39*	1.19	0.66	1.79	0.60	1.55	0.66*	1.40	0.61*	1.40	0.54*
pout	1.80	1.03*	2.38	1.18*	2.21	1.23*	2.18	1.26*	1.60	1.29	1.70	1.24
refuse food or medicine	0.96	0.40*	1.62	0.48*	0.93	0.59	1.00	0.59	1.00	0.55	1.07	0.50*
elder hit	0.65	0.10*	1.13	0.20*	1.29	0.20*	1.27	0.23*	0.95	0.20*	0.92	0.15*
elder cry	0.98	0.56*	1.25	0.65*	0.71	0.73	0.72	0.73	1.15	0.65	0.93	0.67
manipulate	3.69	2.21*	4.13	2.61	4.07	2.66	3.55	2.75	3.70	2.64	3.70	2.57
call police	0.18	0.03	0.06	0.09	0.21	0.08	0.27	0.07	0.55	0.00*	0.41	0.00*
ignores privacy of others	1.24	0.61*	1.38	0.80	1.43	0.80	1.27	0.83	0.95	0.86	1.48	0.79

NOTE: Chi-square used for tests of significance, all other variables computed by difference of means and F.
*Significant at 0.05.

TABLE C.8
Correlation Matrix Between Elders' and Caregivers'
Use of Control Maintenance Techniques

Elder	Verbal	Caregiver Psychological	Medical	Physical	Severe Physical	Total Abuse
Yell	.44*	.24*	.25*	.19	.34*	.37*
Pout	.28*	.38*	.08	.23*	.31*	.21*
Refuse Medicine	.23*	.13	.09	.09	.06	.10
Cry	.17	.16	.15	.01	.07	.16
Manipulate	.25*	.15	.10	.04	.15	.16
Call police	.22*	−.04	.37*	.09	.03	.31*
Invade privacy	.18*	.13	.00	.09	.18*	.08
Physical Violence	.35*	.25*	.24*	.34*	.31*	.35*

*Significant at 0.05.

APPENDIX D

FINDINGS FROM THE
SERVICE PROVIDER SAMPLE

PROCEDURE

To provide a basis for comparison with other studies on elder abuse that surveyed third-party service providers, the telephone books for the three counties in Delaware, New Castle, Kent, and Sussex, were used to provide a list of clergy, directors of nursing home facilities, and doctors in appropriate fields. A list of social workers was obtained from the local registry board. A list of nurses registered in Delaware provided a base from which every one-hundredth name was selected.

As a result of some confusion in preparing the return envelopes, it was not possible to account precisely for the final disposition of each questionnaire sent for this part of the study. Approximately 350 questionnaires were mailed.

Of this number about 40 were returned as address unknown, deceased, or retired. A large number of the "address unknown" were from churches; the retired tended to be nurses who continued to pay professional dues, though retired; and doctors who maintained their professional listing but no longer actively practiced medicine. In some instances, the surviving spouse, child, or business associate simply noted that the individual had retired or died.

Approximately 30 questionnaires were returned with either no information, or a note that the person did not wish to participate or some indication that the questionnaire did not apply to him or her, for instance, a plastic surgeon or a general practitioner whose practice is primarily pediatrics. In all, 153 completed questionnaires were returned containing information on 309 families (115 individuals did not respond).

The response rate, the ratio of individuals who returned but did not complete the questionnaire (or noted their lack of contact with elderly clients) plus those providing usable information, to the total number of questionnaires sent out (153 + 40 + 30:350) was about 64%. However the completion rate (153:350) was only 44%.

SAMPLE

In all, 309 families were described in the questionnaires. The professions of 61 of the service providers who completed the questionnaires (about 20%) could

266

not be ascertained. There were two sources for this problem: Service providers who completed additional questionnaires and did not return the materials in the "coded" envelope; and staff who were not familiar with the procedures and discarded the envelopes.

Of the remaining questionnaires, 17% were completed by physicians; 26% by nurses and health care workers; 8% by clergy; 2% by social workers; and the largest amount, 47%, by hospital personnel. Hospital personnel completing the forms were most likely nurses or social workers.

RESULTS

There were 309 families identified by the professionals completing the questionnaires. In about 75% of the families the elder was a woman. The predominant living arrangement (57.3%) was an elder residing in the caregiver's home. In about 10.4% of the cases the elder was living in his or her own home, either alone or with an adult child. It was not possible to distinguish between these two possibilities or to ascertain the living arrangements of the remaining 30%. The average age of the elders in these families was 68.4 with a range of 50 (one elder) to 99 or older (five elders).

About 96% (n = 298) of the 309 families were identified as having conflict. Of course, it is likely that the families that are readily identified by professionals are those that have come to the attention of professionals because of problems. The percentage of families experiencing stress from having to provide dependency-related tasks were:

Source of Stress	Percent
financial dependency	31.7
personal grooming/health	60.5
emotional/mental disability	28.8
physical disability	45.9
mobile but senile	33.1
elder won't eat	16.1
elder needs special diet	25.3
elder is lonely	41.9
elder makes excessive demands	42.2
household management	31.3
elder needs transportation	37.5
lack of privacy	25.2
other	14.2

Sources of stress related to family circumstances (the Family Stress Index in the text of this book), which were identified by these professionals, are listed below.

Sources of Stress	Percent
teenagers in the home	33.0
small children in the home	19.2

employed spouse (two earner household)	31.8
single head household	13.5
financial problems	33.3
recent death	14.4
alcohol (or drugs)	13.8
physical disability of other family member	12.5
emotional/mental problem of other family member	14.6

The reports by professionals on the types of control maintenance techniques used by caregivers suggest a range of techniques that are similar to other studies based on third-party reports. They are higher than the percentage reported by caregivers in the study, but this is not unexpected. The agency sample, unlike the sample of caregivers, was composed of elderly or their families who had sought help or had been referred for intervention, thus higher levels of stress, conflict, and abuse would be expected.

Control Maintenance Techniques	Percent
verbal abuse	11.5
physical restraints	10.4
forced food	6.1
threatened with nursing home placement	38.4
threatened with physical harm	26.0
confine to a room	25.2
hit or slapped	19.7
give medication	24.5
sought advice	50.0
found alternative housing	35.3

In an attempt to resolve these problems, 90.5% sought direct services, such as arranging for in-home service, social agency help, counseling for the elderly or family, or finding suitable alternative housing. Emergency action, such as medical treatment or hospitalization, emergency placement of elder "elsewhere," or calling the police, were solutions reported to be used in 85.3% of the cases. The least frequent solution reported was referral action, reported in 84% of the situations. It is possible that those responding to the questionnaire were, in many instances, the final referral: There was no alternative to which they could refer these individuals or families.

Unfortunately, 41% of the times there were, according to this sample of professionals, no appropriate services available. In 54.6% of the cases the elder or family refused help. Not all services, even when available, were helpful in resolving the problem; in about 31% of the cases the suggested intervention was reported to be unsuccessful. However, 35% felt that the intervention was somewhat helpful; and 24% rated the intervention as successful.

REFERENCES

Aldous, Joan (1978) Family Career: Developmental Change in Families. New York: John Wiley.

American People's Encyclopedia (1969) New York: Grolier.

American Public Welfare Association and National Association of State Units on Aging (1986) A comprehensive analysis of state policy and practice related to elder abuse: A focus on legislation, appropriations, incidence data, and special studies. Washington DC: Author.

Andrews, S. R., and P. A. Hall (1984) "Abuse and elder mistreatment. An exploratory study." (San Antonio, TX, unpublished)

Anetzberger, G. J. (1987) The Etiology of Elder Abuse by Adult Offspring. Springfield, IL: Charles C. Thomas.

Archbold, P. (1983) "Impact of parent caring on middle aged offspring." Journal of Gerontological Nursing 6 (February): 78-85.

Bach, G. R. and P. Wyden (1968) The Intimate Enemy. New York: Avon.

Bailey, Kenneth D. (1978) Methods of Social Research. New York: Macmillan.

Bane, M. J. (1976) Here to Stay: American Families in the Twentieth Century. New York: Basic Books.

Barrett, Sara and Mary C. Sengstock (1982) "Patterns of the relationships of elder abuse victims and their abusers." Gerontologist 22: 253-54.

Beachler, M. A. (1979) "Mistreatment of elderly personnel in the domestic setting." (Brasoria County, TX, unpublished)

Blau, Zena S. (1981) Aging in a Changing Society. New York: Viewpoints.

Blenkner, Margaret (1965) "Social work and the family relationships in later life with some thoughts of filial maturity," in E. Shanas and G. Streib (eds.) Social Structure and the Family. Englewood Cliffs, NJ: Prentice-Hall.

Blenkner, Margaret (1969) "The normal dependencies of aging," in Richard Kalish (ed.) The Dependencies of Old People. Ann Arbor: University of Michigan Institute of Gerontology.

Block, M. (1980) "Elder abuse: the hidden problem" (pp. 10-12). Briefing before the Select Committee on Aging, U.S. House of Representatives (96). Boston, MA. Washington, DC: Government Printing Office.

Block, M. and J. Sinnott (1979) "Elder abuse: the hidden problem." Briefing by the Select Committee on Aging, U.S. House of Representatives (96) June 23. Boston, MA. pp. 10-12. Washington, DC: Government Printing Office.

Boss, Pauline (1986) "Family stress," in Marvin B. Sussman and Suzanne K. Steinmetz (eds.) Handbook of Marriage and The Family. New York: Plenum.

Boss, Pauline, Hamilton McCubbin, and G. Lester (1979) "The corporate executive wife's coping patterns in response to routine husband-father absence: implications for family stress theory." Family Process 18 (March): 79-86.

Boss, Pauline G. (1980) "Normative family stress: family boundary change across the life span." Family Relations 29 (4): 445-50.

Boszormenyi-Nagy, Ivan and Geraldine Sparks (1973) Invisible Loyalties Reciprocity in Intergenerational Family Therapy. New York: Harper & Row.

Boydston, L. S. and J. A. McNairn (1981) "Abuse of the elderly." No. 97-297. U.S. House of Representatives Select Commission on Aging, San Francisco. Washington, DC: Government Printing Office.

Bradley v. State, Walker, 158, Miss. 1824.

Bremner, R. H. (1970) Children and Youth in America: A Documentary History, Vol. 1. Cambridge, MA: Harvard University Press.

Brim, Orville, Jr. (1974) "Socialization through the life cycle," in Marvin B. Sussman (ed.) Sourcebook of Marriage and the Family. New York: Houghton Mifflin.

Brody, Elaine (1966) "The aging family." Gerontologist, 6: 201-206.

Brody, Elaine (1970) "The etiquette of filial behavior." Aging and Human Development 1: 87-94.

Brody, Elaine (1978) "The aging of the family." Annals of the American Academy of Political and Social Science 438: 13-26.

Brody, Elaine (1979) "Women's changing roles, the aging family and long-term care of older people." National Journal 11 (October): 18-28.

Brody, Elaine M., Pauline T. Johnsen, Mark C. Fulcomer, and Abigail M. Lang (1983) "Women's changing roles and help to elderly parents: attitudes of three generations of women." Journal of Gerontology 18: 597-607.

Brody, Stanley J. (1978) "The family caring unit: a major consideration in the long-term support system." Gerontologist 18 (December): 556-561.

Brotman, H. B. (1978) "The aging of America" National Journal 10 (40): 1622-1627.

Brubaker, T., C. L. Cole, C. B. Hennon, & A. L. Cole. (1978) "Forum on aging and the family: discussion with F. Ivan Nye, Bernice L. Neugarten and David and Vera Mace." Family Coordinator, 27 (October): 436-443.

Bryant, H. D (1963) "Physical abuse of children: an agency study." Child Welfare, 42: 125-130.

Butler, Robert N. (1975) Why Survive? Being Old in America. New York: Harper & Row.

Carey, Art. (1985) "A time to die." The Philadelphia Inquirer Sunday Magazine (March 10).

Chen, Pei N., Sharon L. Bell, Debra L. Dolinsky, John Doyle, and Moira Dunn (1981) "Elderly abuse in domestic settings: a pilot study." Journal of Gerontological Social Work 4 (1): 3-17.

Circirelli, V. G. (1981) Helping Elderly Parents: The Role of Adult Children. Boston: Auburn House.

Circirelli, V. G. (1983) "Adult children's attachment and helping behavior to elderly parents: a path model." Journal of Marriage and the Family 45 (November): 815-825.

Circirelli, V. G. (1986) "The helping relationship and family neglect in later life," in K. Pillemer and R. Wolf (eds.) Elder Abuse: Conflict in the Family. Dover, MA: Auburn House.

Clark, Margaret (1969) "Cultural values and dependency in later life," in Richard Kalish (ed.) The Dependencies of Old People. Ann Arbor: University of Michigan Institute of Gerontology.

Cohen, Stephan A. and Bruce Michael Gans (1978) The Other Generation Gap: The Middle-Aged and Their Aging Parents. Chicago: Follett.

Cormican, E. J. (1980) "Social work and aging: A review of the literature." International Journal of Aging and Human Development 11 (4): 251-267.

Cronin, C. and A. Allen (1982) The Uses of Research Sponsored by the Administration on Aging, Case Study No. 5: Maltreatment and Abuse of the Elderly. Washington, DC: Gerontological Research Institute.

Crouse, J. E. et al. (1981) "Abuse and neglect of the elderly in Illinois: incidence and characteristics, legislation and policy recommendations." Report prepared for the State of Illinois, Department of Aging (October).

deMause, L. (ed.) (1974) The History of Childhood. New York: Psychotherapy Press.

Demos, J. (1970) A Little Commonwealth. New York: Oxford University Press.

Douglas, Richard L. (1983) "Domestic neglect and abuse of the elderly: Implications for research and service." Family Relations 32 (July): 395-402.

Douglas, R., T. Hickey and C. Noel (1980) "A study of maltreatment of the elderly and other vulnerable adults." Final report to the U.S. Administration on Aging and the Michigan Department of Social Services, Ann Arbor (November). (Available from Clearinghouse on Abuse and Neglect of the Elderly, College of Human Resources University of Delaware.)

Dowd, J. J. and V. L. Bengtson (1978). "Aging in minority populations: an examination of the double jeopardy hypothesis." Journal of Gerontology 33 (3) 427-436.

Dozier, C. (1984) "Report of the elder abuse and neglect assessment instrument field test." Atlanta: Atlanta Regional Commmission.

Elder Abuse Task Force (1984) "Elderly abuse in the Toledo area." (Toledo, OH, unpublished)

Erikson, Eric (1964) Childhood and Society (2nd ed.). New York: Norton.

Farrar, Marcella (1955) "Mother-daughter conflicts extended into later life." Social Casework 45 (May): 202-207.

Faulkner, Lawrence R. (1982) "Mandating the reporting of suspected cases of elder abuse—An inappropriate, ineffective and ageist response to the abuse of older adults." Family Law Quarterly 16 (1): 69-91.

Fischer, D. H. (1977) Growing Old in America. New York: Oxford University Press.

Fischer, Lucy Rose (1983) "Elderly parents and the caregiving role: an asymmetrical transition." Gerontologist 23: 242.

Fithian, P. V. (1945) Journal and Letters of Phillip Vickers Fithian, 1773-1774. Princeton, NJ: Princeton University Press.

Fontana, Vincent J. (1964) The Maltreated Child. Springfield, IL: Charles C. Thomas.

Foulke, Sarah Roberts (1980) "Caring for the parental generation: an analysis of family resources and support." Master's thesis, University of Delaware, Newark.

Gayford, J. (1975) "Wifebattering: a preliminary survey of 100 cases." British Medical Journal 1: 195-197.

Gelfand, Donald, E., J. K. Olsen, and M. Brock (1978) "Two generations of elderly in the changing American family: implications for family service." Family Coordinator (October): 395-403.

Gelles, Richard J. (1974) The Violent Home: A Study of Physical Aggression Between Husbands and Wives. Beverly Hills, CA: Sage.

Gelles, R. J., and M. A. Straus (1979) "Determinants of violence in the family: toward a theoretical integration," in W. Burr, R. Hill, F. I. Nye, and I. Reiss (eds.) Contemporary Theories About the Family. New York: Free Press.

George L. K. and L. P. Gwyther (1986) "Caregiver well-being: a multidimensional examination of family caregivers of demented adults." Gerontologist 26 (3):253-259.

Gioglio, G. R. and P. Blakemore (1983) Abuse in New Jersey: The knowledge and experience of abuse among older New Jerseyans. Trenton, NJ: Department of Human Services.

Giordano N. H. and J. A. Giordano (1984) "Individual and family correlates of elder abuse." (Bradenton, FL, unpublished)

Glick, Paul (1986a) "The family in the future: demographic trends." Presented at the

Department of Individual and Family Studies Colloquium, University of Delaware.

Goldfarb, Alvin (1965) "Psychodynamics and the three generational family," in E. Shanas and G. Streib (eds.), Social Structure and the Family. Englewood Cliffs, NJ: Prentice-Hall.

Gray Panthers of Austin, Texas (1983) "A survey of abuse in the elderly in Texas." (unpublished)

Greenberg, Martin A. and Ellen C. Wertlieb (1983) Police and the elderly. FBI Law Enforcement Bulletin 52, Part I (August): 16-20; Part II, (September): 1-7; Part III (October): 1-7.

Grevan, P. (1970) Four Generations: Population, Land, and Family in Colonial Andover, Massachusetts. Ithaca, NY: Cornell University Press.

Haber, Carole (1983) Beyond Sixty-Five. The Dilemma of Old Age in America's Past. Cambridge: Cambridge University Press.

Hall, P. A. and S. R. Andrews (1984a) "Alcohol use and elder mistreatment: an exploratory study." (San Antonio, TX, unpublished)

Hall, P. A. and S. R. Andrews (1984b) "Minority elder maltreatment. Ethnicity, gender, age and poverty." (San Antonio, TX, unpublished)

Hanson, Donald (1974) "Personal and positional influence in normal groups: proposition and theory for research and theory on family vulnerability to stress," in Marvin B. Sussman (ed.) Sourcebook of Marriage and the Family. Boston: Houghton Mifflin.

Haraven, Tamara K. (1977a) "Family time historical time." Daedaulus 106 (Summer): 57-71.

Haraven, Tamara K. (1977b) Family and Kinship in Urban Communities. New York: New Viewpoints.

Harbin, H. and D. Madden (1979) "Battered parents: a new syndrome." American Journal of Psychiatry 36(10): 1288-1291

Hill, Reuben, N. Foote, J. Aldous, R. Carlson, and R. MacDonald (1970) Family Development in Three Generations. Cambridge MA: Schenkman.

Hooker, Susan (1976) Caring For Elderly People: Understanding and Practical Help. London: Routledge and Kegan Paul.

Horowitz, A. (1978) "Families who care: A study of natural support systems of the elderly." Presented at the thirty-fifth annual meeting of the Gerontological Society, Dallas, TX, November.

Horowitz, A. (1985) "Sons and daughters as caregivers to older parents: differences in role performance and consequences." Gerontologist 25 (6): 612-616.

Horowitz, A. and L. W. Shindelman (1983) "Reciprocity and Affection: Past influences on current caregiving." Journal of Gerontological Social Work 5 (3): 5-20.

Hudson, M. F. (1986) "Elder mistreatment: current research," in K. Pillemer and R. Wolf (eds.) Elder Abuse: Conflict in the Family. Dover, MA: Auburn House.

Johnson, E. S. and D. L. Spence (1982) "Adult children and their aging parents: an intervention program," Family Relations 31 (1): 115-122.

Johnson, Elizabeth (1978) "Good relationships between older mothers and their daughters: a causal model." Gerontologist 18: 301-306.

Kempe, C. H., and R. E. Helfer [eds.] (1972) Helping the Battered Child and his Family. Philadelphia: Lippincott.

Kent, Donald P. (1965) "Aging fact and fancy." Gerontologist 9 (June): 51-56.

Kirschner, Charlotte (1979) "The aging family in crisis: a problem in living." Social Casework 60 (April): 209-216.

Knopf, Olga (1975) Successful Aging, the Facts and Fallacies of Growing Old. New York: Viking.

Knox, David (1985) Choices in Relationships: An Introduction to Marriage and Family. St. Paul, MN: West.

Krauskopf, J. M. and M. E. Burnett (1983) "The elderly person: when protection becomes abuse." Trial 19 (December): 60-67, 97-98.

Kreps, Juanita (1977) "Intergenerational transfers and the bureaucracy," in E. Shanas and M. Sussman (eds.) Family Bureaucracy and the Elderly. Durham, NC: Duke University Press.

Langdon, Brian (1980) Testimony presented before the House of Representatives Select Committee on Aging, 96th Congress, June 23, 1979. Washington, DC: Government Printing Office, pp. 16-21.

Laslett, P. (1972) Household and Family in Past Time. Cambridge: Cambridge University Press.

Lau, Elizabeth and Jorden Kosberg (1979) "Abuse of the elderly by informal care providers." Aging 299: 10-15.

Lester, D. (1968) "Punishment experiences and suicidal preoccupation." Journal of Genetic Psychology 113: 89-94.

Levande, Diane I. (1980) "Sex role expectations and filial responsibility," pp. 305-316 in N. Stinnet, J. DeFrain, K. King, H. Lingren, G. Rowe, S. Van Zandt, and R. Williams (eds.) Family Strengths, Vol. 4. Lincoln: University of Nebraska Press.

Levenberg, J. (1983) "Elder abuse in West Virginia, extent and nature of the problem," in G. Leroy (ed.) Elder Abuse in West Virginia: A Policy Analysis of System Response. Morgantown: West Virginia University.

Liang, J. R. and Mary C. Sengstock (1982) "The risk of personal victimization among the aged." Journal of Gerontology 36 (4) 463-471.

Longino, C. and A. Lipman (1981) "Married and spouseless men and women in planned retirement communities: Support network differentials." Journal of Marriage and the Family 43 (February).

Lopata, Helena Z. (1973) Widowhood in an American City. Cambridge, MA: Schenkman.

Mather, Cotton. (1726) A Brief Essay on the Glory of Aged Piety (p. 28). Boston: Kneeland and T. Green.

Mather, Increase (1716) Two discourses. Boston: B. Green.

McLaughlin, J. S., J. P. Nickell, and L. Gill (1980) "An epidemiological investigation of elderly abuse in southern Maine and New Hampshire." Testimony before U.S. House of Representatives Select Committee on Aging (June 11). No. 68-463. Washington, DC: Government Printing Office.

Morgan, Edmund S. (1966) The Puritan Family. New York: Harper & Row.

Neimi, R. G. (1974) How Family Members Perceive Each Other. New Haven, CT: Yale University Press.

Neugarten, B. L. (1978) "The future of the young-old," in L. F. Janik (ed.) Aging into the 21st Century: Middle-agers Today. New York: John Wiley.

1987 U.S. Master Tax Guide (1986) Section 177, Child and Dependent Care Credit, p. 95. Chicago, IL: Commerce Clearing House.

Nursing Home Care in the United States: Failure in Public Policy, Introductory Report (1974) Senate Report. 93-1420, 93rd. Congress, 2d Session 16. Washington, DC: Government Printing Office. (Cited in The Nursing Home Law Letter, 56, February, 1982, p. 1.)

Nursing Home Law Letter (1982a) 56 (February).

Nursing Home Law Letter (1982b) 57 (March).

Nursing Home Law Letter (1982c) 58 (April).

Nursing Home Law Letter (1982d) 66 (December).

Nursing Home Law Letter (1984a) 80 (January).

Nursing Home Law Letter (1984b) 81 (February).

Nye, Ivan F. and Felix M. Berardo (1973) The Family, Its Structure and Interaction. New York: Macmillan.

O'Brien, J. G., M. G. Hudson, and T. F. Johnson (1984) "Health care provider survey on elder abuse" (Lansing, MI: unpublished).

O'Malley, Helen (1980) Testimony before the U.S. House of Representatives Select Committee on Aging, 99th Congress, June 23, Boston. Washington, DC: Government Printing Office.

Oliver, J. E. and A. Taylor (1971) "Five generations of ill-treated children in one family pedigree." British Journal of Psychiatry 119 (552): 473-480.

Otten, Jane and Florence C. Shelley (1977) When Your Parents Grow Old. New York: Crowell.

Pennsylvania Department of Aging, Bureau of Advocacy (1982) Elder Abuse in Pennsylvania. Author.

Pepper C. and M. R. Oakar (1981) Elder Abuse: An examination of a hidden problem. Testimony before the U.S. House of Representatives Select Committee on Aging. No. 97. Washington, DC: Government Printing Office.

Phillips, L. R. (1983) "Abuse and neglect of the frail elderly at home: an exploration of theoretical relationships." Journal of Advanced Nursing 9: 379-92.

Phillips, L. R. & V. F. Rempusheski (1985) "A decision-making model for diagnosing and intervening in elder abuse and neglect." Nursing Research 34 (3): 134-139.

Pillemer, K. A. and D. Finkelhor (1987) "Domestic violence against the elderly." Presented at the Third Conference on Family Violence, Durham, NH, May 28-June 30.

Pillemer, K. A. and R. S. Wolf (eds.) (1986) Elder Abuse: Conflict in the Family. Dover, MA: Auburn House.

Poulshock, S. Walter and Gary T. Deimling (1984) "Families caring for elders in residence: issues in the measurement of burden." Journal of Gerontology 39 (2): 230-239.

Pratt, C. C., J. Koval, and S. Lloyd. (1983) "Service workers: responses to abuse of the elderly." Social Casework (March): 142-53.

Quinn, M. J. & S. K. Tomita (1986) Elder Abuse and Neglect: Causes, Diagnosis and Intervention Strategies. New York: Springer.

Randall, Florence Engel (1977, May 3) "Moment or twilight." Woman's Day Magazine (May 3): 60, 62, 125, 128.

Rautman, Arthur L. (1962) "Role reversal in geriatrics." Mental Hygiene 46 (January): 116-120.

Records of the Boston Selectmen (1836) A Report of the Record, Commissioner of the City of Boston, Vol. 15: 1736-1742. Boston: Rockwell and Churchill City Printers.

Reece, Daniel, Thomas Walz, and Helen Hagenboeck (1983) "Intergenerational care providers of non-institutionalized frail elderly: characteristics and consequences." Journal of Gerontological Social Work 5 (3): 21-34.

Reinharz, Shulamit (1986) "Loving and hating one's elders: twin themes in legend and literature," in K. Pillemer and R. Wolf (eds.), Elder Abuse: Conflict in the Family. Dover, MA: Auburn House.

Rich, J., E. Eyde, and E. Runyon (1982) "Elder abuse: A systems approach to a complex problem." Gerontologist 22: 78.

Riley, Matilda and Ann Foner (1968) Aging and Society. Volume II, An Inventory of Research Findings. New York: Russell Sage.

Robinson, B. (1983) "Validation of a caregiver strain index." Journal of Gerontology 38: 344-48.

Robinson, Betsy and Majda Thurner (1979) "Taking care of the aged parent." Gerontologist 19 (December): 586-593.

Rounds, L. R. (1984) "A study of selected environmental variables associated with noninstitutional settings where there is abuse or neglect of the elderly." Ph.D. dissertation, University of Texas, Austin.

Safilios-Rothschild, C. (1969) "Family sociology of wives' family sociology: A cross-cultural examination of decision-making." Journal of Marriage and the Family 31: 190-301.

Salend, Elyse, Rosalie A. Kane, Maureen Satz, and Jon Pynoos (1984) "Elder abuse reporting: limitation of statutes." Gerontologist 24 (February): 61-69.

Sarles, R. M. (1976) "Child abuse" In D. J. Madden & J. R. Lion (eds.) Rage, Hate, Assault and Other Forms of Violence. New York: Spectrum.

Sengstock, Mary C. et al. (1984) "Abused elders: victims or villains or circumstances?" Gerontologist 22: 217.

Shanas, E. (1962) The Health of Older People: A Social Survey. Cambridge: Harvard University Press. (reprinted by Arno, 1980).

Shanas, E. (1967) Family health patterns and social class in three countries. Journal of Marriage and the Family 29 (May): 357-266.

Shanas, E. (1979) "The family as a social support system in old age." Gerontologist 19 (April): 169-174.

Shanas, E., P. Townsend, D. Wedderburn, H. Griis, P. Mihaj, and J. Stehouwer (1968) Old People in Three Industrial Societies. London: Routlege & Kegan Paul.

Silverstone, Barbara and Helen K. Hyman (1976) You and Your Aging Parents. New York: Pantheon.

Simos, Bertha (1970) "Relations of adults with aging parents." Gerontologist 10 (Summer): 135-138.

Simos, Bertha (1973) "Adult children and their aging parent." Social Casework 18 (May): 78 -85.

Smith, D. B. (1980) Inside the Great House: Planter Family Life in the 18th Century Chesapeake Society. Ithaca, NY: Cornell University Press.

Smith, Jack H. (1986) "Financial problems are the down-side of longer life." Wilmington [Delaware] Journal (March).

Sourcebook of Criminal Justice Statistics (1982) Tables 2.68, 2.69. (from Louis Harris & Associates, 1982). Washington, DC: Government Printing Office.

State v. Oliver, 70, NC, 60, 61, 1874.

Stearns, P. J. (1986) "Old age family conflict: the perspective of the past," in K. Pillemer and R. Wolf (eds), Elder Abuse: Conflict in the Family. Dover, MA: Auburn House.

Steinmetz, S. K. (1977a) The Cycle of Violence: Assertive, Aggressive and Abusive Family Interaction. New York: Praeger.

Steinmetz, S. K. (1977b) "The use of force for resolving family conflict: The training ground for abuse" (secondary analysis of data). Family Coordinator 26 (January): 19-26,

Steinmetz, S. K. (1978) " Battered parents." Society (July/August): 54-55.

Steinmetz, S. K. (1981) "Elder abuse" Aging 315-316 (January-February): 6-10.

Steinmetz, S. K. (1982) "Family care of elders: myths and realities," in N. Stinnet, J. DeFrain, K. King, H. Lingren, G. Rowe, S. Van Zandt, and R. Williams (eds.) Family

Strengths, Vol. 4, Lincoln: University of Nebraska Press.

Steinmetz, S. K. (1983) "Dependency, stress and violence between middle aged caregivers and their elderly parents," pp. 134-149 in J. I. Kosberg (ed.) Abuse and Maltreatment of the Elderly. Littleton, MA: John-Wright.

Steinmetz, S. K. (1984) "Family violence towards elders," in S. Saunders, A. Anderson, C. Hart, and G. Rubenstein (eds.) Violent Individuals and Families: A Handbook for Practitioners. Springfield, IL: Charles C. Thomas.

Steinmetz, S. K. (1985) "Elder abuse: one-fifth of our population at risk?" Testimony before the U.S. House of Representatives Committee on Aging, subcommittee on health and long-term care, 99th Congress, May 10. (No. 99-516) Washington, DC: Government Printing Office.

Steinmetz, S. K. (1986) "Family violence: past, present, future," in M. B. Sussman & S. K. Steinmetz (eds.) Handbook of Marriage and the Family. New York: Plenum.

Steinmetz, S. K. and Deborah J. Amsden (1983) "Dependent elders family stress and abuse," pp. 173-192 in Timothy Brubaker (ed.) Family Relationships in Later Life. Beverly Hills, CA: Sage.

Steinmetz, S. K. and M. A. Straus (1974) Violence in the Family. New York: Harper & Row.

Straus, M. A. (1979) "Family patterns and child abuse in a nationally representative American sample." Child Abuse and Neglect 3: 213-215.

Straus, M. A. and R. J. Gelles (1975) "Is family violence increasing: a comparison of 1975 and 1985 national survey rates." Presented at the annual meeting of the American Society of Criminology. San Diego, CA, November.

Straus, M. A. & R. J. Gelles (1986) "Societal change and change in family violence from 1975 to 1985 as revealed by two national surveys." Journal of Marriage and the Family 48 (August): 465-479.

Straus, M. A., R. J. Gelles, and S. K. Steinmetz (1980) Behind Closed Doors: Violence in the American Family. New York: Doubleday.

Streib, Gordon, F. (1972) "Older families and their troubles: familial and societal responses." Family Coordinator. (February): 5-19.

Sussman, M. B. (1959) "The isolated nuclear family: fact or fiction." Social Problems 6 (Spring): 330-340.

Sussman, Marvin B. and Lee Burchinal (1962) "Kin, family, networks: unheralded structure in current conceptualizations of family functioning." Marriage and Family Living 24 (August): 231-240.

Szinovacz, M. E. (1983) "Using couple data as a methodological tool: the case of marital violence." Journal of Marriage and the Family 45 (3): 633-44.

Thompson, E. and W. Doll (1982) "The burden of families coping with the mentally ill: an invisible crisis." Family Relations 31, 379-388.

Treas, Judith (1977) "Family support systems for the aged." Gerontologist 17 (December): 486-491.

U.S. Bureau of the Census (1983) Statistical Abstracts of the United States. Washington DC: Government Printing Office.

U.S. Bureau of the Census (1986) Statistical Abstracts of the United States. Washington DC: Government Printing Office.

U.S. Bureau of the Census (1977) Current Population Reports, No. 643. Tables 2, 3. Washington, DC: Government Printing Office.

U.S. Department of Health and Human Services (1982) National Long-Term Care Survey/Survey of Caregivers. Washington, DC: Government Printing Office.

U.S. Government Annual Budget (1983) p. 56. Washington, DC: Government Printing Office.

Wasserman, S. (1967) "The abused parent of the abused child." Children 14: 175-179.

Weihl, H. (1979) "Some comments on the relationship between aged parents and their adult children," in C. Doughe and J. Helander (eds.) Family Life in Old Age. London: Nijhoff.

Wershaw, Harold J. (1976) "The four percent fallacy: some further evidence and policy implications." Gerontologist 16 (February): 52-55.

Wilmington [Delaware] News Journal (1985) January 23, p. B5.

Wolf, R. S., C. P. Strugnell, and M. A. Godkin (1982) Preliminary Findings from Three Model Projects on Elderly Abuse. Worcester: University of Massachusetts Medical Center, Center on Aging.

Zarit, S., K. Reever and J. Bach-Peterson (1980) "Relatives of the impaired elderly: correlates of feelings of burden." Gerontologist 20, 649-655.

AUTHOR INDEX

Aldous, 56
Allen, 69, 70
Amsden, 13, 49, 59, 62, 68, 69, 75, 76, 91, 242
Andrews, 72
Archbold, 37, 61, 62

Bach, 190
Bailey, 23
Bane, 44
Barrett, 72
Bengtson, 73
Berardo, 47
Blakemore, 71
Blau, 10
Blenkner, 47, 49, 50
Block, 70, 71, 72, 177
Boss, 67
Boszormenyi-Nagy, 59
Brim, 47
Brody, 34, 36, 51, 52, 53, 59, 62, 63, 68
Brotman, 38
Brubaker, 69, 77
Bryant, 213
Burchinal, 51
Burnett, 74

Carey, 47
Chen, 71
Circirelli, 53, 54, 60, 68, 75, 94
Clark, 49
Cormican, 68
Cronin, 69, 70
Cronkite, Walter, 70

Deimling, 69, 169, 218
deMause, 30
Demos, 32
Deutcher, 10
Doll, 69
Douglas, 68, 70, 71
Dowd, 73
Dozier, 74

Erikson, 56
Eyde, 48

Farrar, 59
Faulkner, 74
Finkelhor, 75, 76
Fischer, 35, 39, 41, 49, 63
Foner, 58
Fontana, 33
Foulke, 48, 50, 62, 109, 242

Gayford, 213
Gelfand, 47
Gelles, 14, 76, 180, 186, 227
George, 52
Gioglio, 71
Giordano, 72
Glick, 16, 37
Goldfarb, 47
Greenberg, 73
Grevan, 42
Gwyther, 52

Haber, 35, 42
Hagenboeck, 204
Hall, 72
Hanson, 67
Haraven, 31
Helfer, 213
Hill, 58
Hooker, 49
Horowitz, 51, 67, 90
Hudson, 71
Hyman, 37, 48, 61

Johnson, 57, 59

Kempe, 213
Kent, 31
Kirschner, 48, 61
Knopf, 49, 50, 62
Knox, 37
Kosberg, 70, 72
Koval, 73
Krauskopf, 74
Kreps, 63

Langdon, 72
Lasliff, 46

Lau, 70, 72
Lester, 69
Liang, 74
Lipman, 57, 95
Lloyd, 73
Longino, 57, 95
Lopata, 57

Mather, Cotton, 39-40
Mather, Increase, 39

Neimi, 69
Neugarten, 69, 77
Nye, 47

Oliver, 213
O'Malley, 67, 70, 71, 172, 177
Otten, 50

Phillips, 75
Pillemer, 75, 76, 103
Poulshock, 69, 169, 218Pratt, 73

Randall, 48
Rautman, 47
Reece, 57, 134, 204, 242
Rich, 48
Riley, 58
Robinson, 62, 67, 69
Rounds, 72
Runyon, 48

Safilios-Rothschild, 16
Salend, 74

Sarles, 32
Seelbach, 57
Sengstock, 72, 74
Shanas, 37, 51, 58, 62, 67
Shelley, 50
Shindelman, 51, 67
Silverstone, 37, 48, 56, 61
Simos, 61, 67
Sinnott, 70, 71
Smith, Jack H., 87
Smith, 40
Sparks, 59
Spence, 57
Steinmetz, 12, 13, 17, 31, 33, 45, 48, 49, 54, 59, 60, 62, 64, 66, 68, 69, 70, 75, 76, 91, 180, 186, 188, 213
Straus, 14, 33, 76, 180, 186, 188, 213, 227
Streib, 64, 67
Sussman, 43, 51
Szinovacz, 17

Taylor, 213
Thompson, 69
Thurner, 62, 67
Treas, 35, 36, 57

Walz, 204
Wasserman, 213
Weihl, 89
Wershaw, 62
Wertlieb, 73
Wyden, 190

Zarit, 69

SUBJECT INDEX

Abandonment, of elder, 72, 178
Abuse: historical, records of, 39; by nursing home staff, 73; statistics, 177, 179; see also entries under individual types of abuse
Active-passive dimension, 12
Activities of daily living, 78, 119
Additional training, 178
Adjustment, difficulties of, 61, 181
Administration on Aging, 70, 71

Adult protective statutes, 178
Advice sought from professionals, 85, 80, 134, 162, 189
Affection, 57
Age, 202; of caregivers, 86, 88-89, 146, 191, 199, 203, 225; of elders, 96-97, 146, 182, 186, 195, 199, 225
Ageism, 115
Aggression, 179, 182
Alarm, 194

Alcohol/drug abuse, 137, 172, 191, 210, 211
Alienation, myth of, 50
Alternative care, 99, 101-106, 121, 173, 180, 221, 226
Alzheimer's disease, 17, 67, 154, 218
American Public Welfare Association, 72-73
American Revolutionary War, 33
Anger, 115, 132, 141
Annulment, 36-37
Antibiotics, 34, 38
Anticipatory socialization, 10, 110
Arthritis, 88, 223
Asian, 80
Asymmetrical transition, 49
Asymmetrical dependency, 109-110
Attachment behavior, 53
Authority, elders' attempt to regain, 39, 42, 101, 185, 186
Autonomy, 54, 130
Awareness, lack of, 68

Baby sitter, 14, 123, 126; see also Elder sitter
Bathing, 45, 113, 140
Bed, getting in and out of, 121
Bed pad, use of: see Incontinence
Bedding, change, 113, 140
Bedridden, 62
Best interest, 130
Bill paying, 121
Birthrate, 36
Blacks, 79, 80, 96, 120
Bladder control: see Incontinence
Board of Commissioners, Brown County, Minnesota, 42
Body stance, 180, 188
Boston City Selectmen meetings (minutes of), 40-41
Boundary ambiguity, 67
Bowel problems, 88
Burden, sense of, 10, 13,16, 20, 24, 27, 49, 52, 54, 69, 77, 85, 86, 79, 96, 97, 107, 113, 123, 127, 132, 133, 134, 135, 136, 142, 143, 145, 146, 147, 149, 148, 152, 157, 158, 160, 161, 162, 167, 169, 170, 171, 176, 185, 190, 198, 199, 200, 206, 207, 208, 211, 215, 218, 220-221, 225, 226, 227

Calling police, elders' use of, 80, 84, 157, 168, 180, 185, 186, 199, 208
Cancer, 88, 172, 223
Care, withholding, 128
Careers, 8
Caregiver: designated, 54-58, 103-106; elder's relationship to, 82-83, 97, 225; role, 174, 203; role, ability to assume, 77
Caregiving: length of time, 82, 97, 134, 146, 195, 202; residence, 81-82, 97
Cataract operations, 191
Catharsis theory, 190
Causal relationships, 201, 214, 225
Change in status, 67
Chastise, husband's right to, 33
Child abuse, 30, 32, 65, 158, 180, 227; comparison with battered elderly, 31; history of, 31
Child rearing, 110, 170
Children, small, 137
Chronic illness, 62
Church, 31
Cognitive functioning, 17-18, 100, 131
Cohabitation, 32
Colonial America, 32, 39-40
Commandments, Biblical, 39
Communication, 124-125
Community, 160
Companionship, 14
Competing needs: see Demands
Concurrent validity, 17
Confidentiality, 242
Confining elder to room, bed, 191
Conflict demands/expectations, 10, 45, 46, 49, 66, 68, 96-97, 138, 174, 180, 190, 223, 224, 225
Conflict tactic scales (CTS), 180
Congressional hearings, 69-70, 71
Control, 66, 100, 130, 120, 162, 165, 179, 180, 182, 183, 186, 191, 192, 193, 198, 199, 209
Control maintenance techniques, 20, 78, 168, 176-177, 179, 210; caregivers' use of, 79, 80, 81, 82, 83-84, 86, 92, 93, 95, 96, 97, 111, 113, 116, 121, 122, 128, 134, 135, 153, 171, 175-176, 180-198, 209, 211, 221; elders' use of, 79, 80, 81, 82, 83-84, 86, 90, 92, 95, 96, 97, 111, 113, 116, 121, 122, 134, 135, 153, 171, 175-176, 181-188, 203, 204, 205, 209, 211, 213, 214, 226

Coping abilities, 69

Cost of living, 64, 120

Costs of caregiving, 14, 135, 173; emotional, 62, 173; financial, 141, 142-143, 173; physical, 62, 173

Couple interaction, 17

Court-awarded guardianship, 192

Crisis, 51, 59, 62, 64, 67, 101, 103; midlife, 61

Crying, elders' use of, 80, 84, 95, 128, 133, 134, 153, 155, 157, 159, 161, 172, 182-83, 198, 210, 214, 219

Cycle of violence, 33, 180, 190, 201, 213, 215, 223, 226

Death, 207; of children, 127, 161, 184; of friends, 161; of other family members, 125, 137, 161, 162; of siblings, 184; of spouse, 127

Deathbed promise, 102

Decision making, 13, 14, 77, 103, 108, 129-130, 140, 143, 164, 165

Deeds of gifts, 42

Definition of the situation, 201, 202, 218, 225

Deliberate-accidental dimension, 11

Demands, 24, 90, 93, 95, 100, 101, 114, 125, 128, 144, 149, 157, 167, 168, 176, 193, 199, 223, 225

Demographic profile, 79-99

Demographic variables, 11, 34, 35, 36, 53, 56, 70, 79, 97, 98, 145, 146, 152, 156, 157, 158, 159, 162, 164, 167, 168, 171, 175, 188, 192, 193, 195, 199, 202, 203, 205, 206, 207, 210, 214, 217, 225

Dependency, 60, 97; financial, 50, 51, 43, 63, 68, 80, 92, 93, 63-67, 116-121, 137, 140, 141-143, 155, 161, 168, 182, 187, 193, 198, 199, 205, 207; household, 51, 62-63, 91, 93, 112-113, 137, 138, 140, 145, 146, 159, 195, 198, 199; mental health, 50, 51, 62, 89, 92, 93, 111, 128-134, 143-44, 146, 157, 182, 183, 185, 186, 187, 190, 191, 193, 195, 198, 199, 203, 204, 206, 207, 208, 221; mobility, 51, 81, 85, 92, 93, 121-122, 143, 146, 155, 157, 199, 206, 207, 208, 225; need for support in, 24, 48-54, 79, 80, 82, 86, 88, 89, 97, 134, 99, 111, 134, 157, 164, 165, 167, 171, 175, 182, 183, 184, 187,

193, 199, 202, 210, 211, 214, 215, 218, 225, 226; personal grooming and health care, 51, 57, 62, 63, 91-92, 93, 111, 113-116, 137, 140, 146, 168, 185, 187, 193, 198, 199, 221; physical, 50; psychological, 68; social-emotional, 50, 51, 57, 59-62, 68, 81, 85, 91-92, 93, 95, 122-128, 144, 159, 161, 157, 176, 182, 185, 187, 190, 193, 195, 198, 208, 221, 225

Dependency ratio, 34-35

Dependency stress, 80, 81, 85, 88, 89, 90, 93, 93, 96, 113, 116, 121, 122, 128, 134, 138,136, 137, 140, 141, 143, 144, 145, 147, 153, 155, 157, 158, 159, 160, 162, 164, 167, 168, 171, 175, 182, 184, 185, 186, 188, 190, 191, 193, 189, 199, 210, 211, 213, 214, 215, 225, 226; demanding, 167-168, 207; financial, 149, 152, 175, 176, 207; household, 145-148, 176, 207; loneliness, 160-162; mobile but senile, 153-155, 207, 208, 225; not eating, 162-164, 175, 176, 225; personal grooming and health care, 148-149; physical disability, 159, 193; privacy, 168-171, 175; social-emotional, 153-155, 207, 208, 255; special diet, 176; transportation, 158-159, 175, 176

Depression, 61, 63, 68, 75

Despised elders, 39

Diabetes, 38, 88, 115, 164, 223

Diapers: see Incontinence

Diary, 39

Dickens, 32

Diet restrictions, 63

Dignity, 114

Discipline, 180, 224, 223

Discussion: caregivers' use of, 188-189, 190; definition of, 188

Disorientation, 115

Disruptive behavior, 60, 134, 169, 218

Division of Aging, 23

Division of labor by gender, 57

Divorce and divorcee, 9, 20, 48, 36-37, 93-95, 170, 173

Domineering, 181

Dressing, help with, 113

Drug use and abuse, 137, 149, 172

Durbin Watson D, 203

Duty bound to provide care, 110, 179, 191, 200, 218, 227

Eating disorders, 162; appetite, loss of, 186; difficulty swallowing, 186; taste buds, loss of sensitivity, 186

Economic coercion: see Financial abuse

Economic dependency: see Dependency, financial

Education, 13

Elder abuse, 10, 16, 23, 27, 31, 33-34, 39, 43-45, 46, 67, 69, 128, 177, 178, 179, 200, 201, 203, 211, 213, 215, 222, 227; summary of research, 69-77

Elder as visitor: see Guest status

Elder sitter, 123, 126

Elders of the church, 39

Elders' rights, 49, 130, 165

Elizabethan Poor Laws, 63

Emotional abuse: definition of, 214; elders' use of, 185, 191, 199, 214, 221; see also Psychological abuse

Emotional bond, 59

Emotional health, 127

Emotional satisfaction, 56

Emotional stress: see Stress, emotional

Emotional support: see Dependency, social-emotional

Emotional neglect: see Psychological abuse

Emphysema, 108

Employed women, 204, 226; mothers, 110; wives, 203, 207, 224

Empty nest, 10, 35-36

Environment, control of, 59, 61

Errands, 112, 138

Essentials, pay for, 13, 116

Essex County Massachusetts, 39

Exchange theory, 14

Exhaustion, 179

Experimental design, 201

Explosive behavior (temper tantrums), 114, 155, 181, 182, 223

Expressive tasks, 57, 95, 137, 176

Expressive-instrumental dimension, 11

Falling, fear of, 106, 101-104, 122, 159, 194

Family composition, 56

Family counseling, 189

Family dysfunction/problems, 20, 67

Family of procreation, 56

Family property, 42

Family stress: see Stress, family

Family violence, 186, 189

Fear arousal, 188

Fear of elders: see Witchcraft

Federal tax credit, 64

Female-headed household: see Household, head of, female

Filial maturity, 169

Filial performance, 43

Filial responsibility, 14, 37, 42-43, 45, 51, 53, 57, 58

Financial abuse, 18, 42, 178, 179, 191

Financial aid, 67

Financial contribution, elders', 119-120, 152

Financial dependency: see Dependency, financial

Financial problems/burden, 120, 172, 178, 203, 207, 208, 224

Financial support: see Support, financial

First Church of Boston, 32

Fixed-choice responses, 21

Flexible time, 90

Flow diagram, 210-212, 213, 214

Food and nutrition, 45, 120

Forced feeding: see Medical abuse

Forgetfulness: see Senility

Foster care: of adults, 26, 56, 91, 184, 192; of children, 54, 56, 65

Frail elderly, 17, 19, 38, 45, 180, 189, 211, 227

Freedom, lack of, 68, 133, 124, 159, 170; see also Privacy

Friends, leaving behind/lack of, 125-126, 144, 160

Friendship, help elder develop, 123, 124, 126

Frustration, 115, 141, 159, 173, 174

Gender, 146, 202; of caregiver, 90, 225; of elder, 95-96, 158, 182, 225

Generation gap, 79

Generation in the middle: see Sandwich generation

Generational inversion (generationally inverse), 16, 37, 46-48, 49, 67, 77, 79, 103, 185

Geographic area of residence, 159-160, 203; rural, 81, 158, 160, 190, 193; small town, 81, 160, 158, 190, 193; suburban, 81, 158, 160, 190, 193; urban, 81, 96, 158, 160, 190, 193

Goals, competing, 66
Gratitude, 57
Grief, 127, 162
Groceries, help with shopping for, 112, 120
Guardianship, 65
Guest status, 60, 61, 103, 105
Guidelines, 15
Guilt, use by elder, 20, 45, 49, 57, 60, 61, 95, 106, 130, 155, 174, 180, 183, 184, 199, 220

Hair care, 113, 140
Handicapped child/family member, 110, 137, 141
Hardening of the arteries, 38
Hatred, 49
Headaches, 68
Health needs, 114-116
Health status, 24, 38, 51, 64, 69, 88, 130, 139, 148, 167, 172, 180, 190, 203, 222
Hearing, loss of, 62, 159
Heart condition, 38, 88, 102, 174, 223
Helping behaviors, 53, 58; chair, help in and out of, 143; walking, help with, 143
Helplessness, 125
High blood pressure, 155
Hispanics, 80
Home environment, 45
Home health aid, 149
Homemaker aides, 90, 149
Hospitalization, 38, 66, 103, 106-107, 115, 194, 195
Household: chores, 62, 63, 110, 112, 111, 112-113, 146, 182; decorating, 101, 147; expenses, 119; see also Dependency, household
Household, head of, 16, 30, 54; elder, 169; female, 26, 103-104, 142; loss of role, 96; single, 173; single parent, 137, 207
Human subject (issues), 27, 242
Humor, 127-128
Hypertension, 115, 182

Idealism, 53
Identifying abuse, 178
Ignoring elder, 68, 81, 84, 85, 180, 183, 191, 199, 205; see also Psychological abuse
Immigrants, 44
Incest, 30
Incontinence, 113, 114, 215, 219; use of bed pad, 114

Independence, 54, 61, 67, 97, 99, 109, 139, 165, 181, 186
Index construction, 27
Indices: burden, 247; control maintenance techniques, 246-247; description of, 244-247; dependency, 244-245; dependency stress, 245-246; family stress, 245-246; health status, 245; household, 244; personal grooming and health care, 114, 244-245; financial, 145, 245; mental health, 245; mobility, 245; social-emotional, 245
Industrial Revolution, 32
Infant mortality, 37
Inheritance, 120
Institutional abuse, 70
Institutionalization, 51, 62, 66, 67, 184, 194, 221, 222, 226
Instrumental tasks, 57, 95, 137, 176
Instruments, description, 242-243
Insurance coverage, 108
Interdependence, 50, 67, 109-110
Intergenerational support, 63
Intergenerational transmission/relationships, 11, 47, 54, 58, 64, 209, 210
Interpersonal conflict, measurement of, 179
Interviews, in-depth, 242
Intimacy: see Privacy
Intravenous feeding, 164
Isolated elders, 39, 61, 75, 121, 159, 180

Kin keeping, 58, 90

Labor force: see work force
Labor market: see work force
Latchkey elders, definition of, 66
Launching of children, 10
Laundry, 100, 112, 191, 223
Legal Services for the Elderly, Boston, 70
Legislation, 30; Connecticut Elderly Protective Service, 178; in Massachusetts, 32; Medicaid, 64, 65; in New Jersey, 40; in Pennsylvania, 33
Legislation, responsibility of relatives, 64-65; Colorado, 65; Delaware, 65; Hawaii, 65; Idaho, 65; Indiana, 65; Massachusetts, 64-65; Mississippi, 65; Wisconsin, 65
Leisure time, 14
Letter writing for elders, 122, 123, 127

Life cycle, 35, 47, 48, 54, 59, 88
Life expectancy, 34-35, 37, 39, 63-64, 77, 83, 125, 142
Life satisfaction, 52
Life support systems, 38
Life threatening, 62, 165
Lifestyle, 46, 60, 67
Lifetime patterns of behavior, 84, 182, 187
Linearity/colinearity, 203
Loneliness, 61, 124, 125, 137, 144, 161, 185
Long-term care, 64, 117
Longitudinal design, 66, 214
Loss of possessions, 186
Love, 49, 60, 128, 179, 200
Loyalties, 59, 224
Luxuries, pay for, 13, 116

Malnutrition, 164, 194
Mandatory reporting, 74
Manipulation, elders' use of, 84, 95, 121, 133, 134, 181, 183-184, 153, 159, 162, 167, 171, 181, 183-184, 186, 199, 221
Marital rape, 30
Marital roles, 10
Marital status, 92-93, 202, 205
Marriage: commuter, 92; intact, 90, 92, 94, 104; residentially separate, 93, 102
Material abuse and/or neglect: see Financial abuse
Meals, preparation of, 14, 62, 63, 110, 112-113, 146, 147, 162
Meals-on-wheels, 66
Mechanical control, 213
Medical abuse: caregivers' use of, 19, 52, 80, 81, 85, 94, 95, 134, 147, 155, 157, 160, 175, 180, 187, 193, 194, 199, 202, 206, 210, 214; forcing food, 206; forcing medicine, 206
Medical assistance, 66
Medical services, use of, 38, 63, 67, 158, 174
Medicare/Medicaid, 132, 141, 142
Medication, give to elder, 113, 140, 193, 199
Medieval Church Law, 63
Mental health status, 190
Mental hospital: see Institutionalization
Migration, patterns of, 39
Minority status, 80
Mobile but senile, 221
Mobility: loss of, 111, 121-122, 180; patterns, 43-44; see also Dependency, mobility

Models, 210
Modern Maturity, 45
Mother-daughter rivalry, 100
Multigeneration families, 16, 31, 44-45, 46, 73
Multiple caregiving, 84-85, 97
Myths, 34-37, 45

National Association of State Units on Aging, 72-73
Needs, provision for, 161
Neglect: see Elder abuse
Neighborhood, 125, 160
New York Times, 70
Noninstitutionalized elders, 9, 62, 204
Nonparent, 83
Nonrational behavior, elders', 128, 154-155
Nonrepresentative sample (nonrandom), 23-24, 80, 201, 203
Norway, 161
Nuclear family, 48, 50
Nurse mentality, 54
Nursing home, 39, 64, 107-108, 116, 130, 143, 219, 221

Objective meaning, 136
Obligation, 49, 152
Offensive-defensive dimension, 12

Paranoia, 132
Parent-child abuse among elderly, 76
Parental approval, 57
Parental responsibility, 31
Parenting studies, 17
Path analysis (path model), 53, 169, 210, 202, 214-215, 224, 225
Patience, 14
Patterns of behavior, 11, 169
Pauper institutions, 39, 63
Pay for essentials, 141
Peer interaction, 33
Pension, 108
Perceptions, 19, 69; of events, 201; of feelings, 170; of needs, 94; of stress, 135, 144-147, 175, 176, 195, 200, 201, 202, 218
Personal appearance, 113-114
Personal care: see Dependency, personal grooming and health care
Personal property, 130
Personal time, lack of, 68
Personality, 168, 200; change in, 114, 182;

differences, 184

Phone calls, made for elders, 122, 123, 144, 169

Physical abuse, 96, 113, 175, 178, 186, 188, 193-194, 199, 202, 206-207, 210, 213, 214, 215, 225; caregivers' use of, 11, 18, 85, 95, 128, 134, 147, 155, 157, 160, 178, 180, 181, 186-188; definition of, 188; elders' use of, 80, 84, 121, 116, 133, 134, 148, 157, 164, 168, 171, 181, 182, 186, 207, 210, 223-224, 226; severe, 148, 158, 186, 188, 193, 202, 207

Physical functioning, 100, 127, 221

Physical injury/disability, 160, 189, 207, 208

Physical strain, 175

Plymouth Colony, 32

Pneumonia and flu, 38

Poor houses: see Pauper institutions

Pouting, elders' use of, 80, 84, 95, 103, 120, 134, 133, 148, 157, 159, 162, 180, 183, 186, 199, 205, 207, 210, 221

Power, 103, 120; elders', 13, 42, 39; loss of, 34, 39, 66

Prestige, 13; loss of, 39, 66

Pride, 113

Privacy, lack of, 14, 53-54, 59, 68, 80, 84, 96, 121, 123-124, 127, 137, 144, 148, 153, 159, 168, 170-171, 180, 181, 185, 186, 208, 221, 225, 242

Prosocial interactions, 178; talking, 178

Problem solving, 90, 124, 189, 203, 209

Property transfers, 39, 42, 45

Protective service, 132-133

Psychological abuse: caregivers' use of, 11, 71, 72, 74, 76, 134, 157, 178, 188, 191-193, 199, 202, 205-206, 209, 210; definition of, 188; see also Ignoring elder, Threats

Psychotropic drugs: see Medical abuse

Public whippings, 33

Publicity, impact on law, 178

Qualitative data, 209

Quantitative data, 209

Race, 80-81, 96, 97, 146, 161, 202

Reading to elders, 122, 123, 127

Rebellious children law (1646), 32

Reciprocal dependency/support, 58, 109, 110-111, 179, 182

Refusal to eat or take medicine, elders' use of, 62, 63, 96, 133, 134, 148, 155, 163, 164, 168, 180, 185-186, 199, 208, 210, 211, 225; fear of poisoning, 186, 187; loss of appetite, 186; swallowing difficult, 186; taste buds dim, 186; see also Medical abuse

Regression analysis, 202, 213-214, 225

Reliability, 27, 243-244

Relinquishing independence/power, 100, 107

Remarriage, 37, 94

Renovation, for elder, 179

Research: agency reports, 72-73, 177; assessment instrument, 74; awareness and attitudes, 73-74; comparison of studies, 75-77; incidence rates, 73, 178; interviews, 71, 74-75, 177; law enforcement agencies, 177; mail survey of professionals, 70-71, 177; multiple reports, 70, 178; questions, 11; response rates, 70-71, 177; response to vignettes, 73-74; socially desirable response, 20; typology of studies, 71

Resentment, 49, 60, 68

Residuals, 203

Resource theory, 13-14, 187, 188

Resources, 30, 180; depleted, 117, 119; economic, 43, 80; emotional, 38, 67; financial, 38, 44, 67, 99, 117, 152, 186; managing, 57, 116, 140, 178; material, 13; physical, 67; sharing of 109, 120,; social-emotional, 13; space, 67; time, 67

Respect, 39, 49, 186

Responsibilities-obligations, 49, 60, 181; financial, 117; health care, 62

Restraints, 131-132, 193, 194

Retirement, 9-10, 49, 50, 66; mandatory, 34-35, 64

Reverence for elders, 39

Role, 35, 67, 173; changing, 59; conflict, 57; loss (roleless years), 35-36, 47, 67; models, 36, 45, 47, 110; occupational, 10; parental, 8-10, 35-36; reversal, 47-48, 49; small children, 173; strain, 69; teens, 173; theory, 14-15

Sampling techniques, 27

Sandwich generation, 58, 61

School, 31

Seeking advice, 178, 180, 189, 190, 199

Selective inattention, 30
Self-esteem, 113, 139
Self-abuse/neglect, 51, 178
Senility 18, 47, 100, 103, 106, 120, 121, 128, 131, 132, 137, 153-154, 176, 180, 186, 187, 195, 199, 203, 219-220; see also Alzheimer's disease
Senior centers, 23, 123, 126, 161
Serial marriage, 36-37, 83
Service provider questionnaire, 15
Service provider sample, 15, 265-268
Sexual abuse, 178
Shared caregiving: see Siblings, sharing care of elder
Shopping, 63, 158
Sibling abuse, 33; among elderly, 76; history of, 31
Siblings, 90; sharing care of elder, 56-57, 91, 104-106
Single parent; see Household, head of, single parent
Sleep problems, 131, 155, 219; deprivation, 173; insomnia, 68
Sleeping arrangements, 119, 131, 169
Small children, 205, 207, 210, 223, 224
Snowball sampling, 23
Social class, 24, 58, 66, 80
Social isolation: see Isolated elders
Social life, provide for elder, 9, 122-123, 125-126, 127, 137, 155, 156-157
Social mobility studies, 17
Social security, 63, 102, 103, 108, 119, 121, 120
Social security checks, stealing: see Financial abuse
Social services, 23, 31, 132, 141, 174; eligibility limits, 149, 152; lack of, 149
Social space, 61, 68, 133
Social support: see Support, social-emotional
Social worker, 165
Socialization, 8, 47
Societal influences on elders and violence, 186
Society for the Prevention of Cruelty to Animals, 32
Society for the Prevention of Cruelty to Children, 32
Spouse abuse, 30, 150, 180, 227; among elderly, 75-76; history of, 31
Stability, 203

Stairs, using, 121
Standard of living, 9, 109
Stepparents and step-in-laws, 37, 83
Strength, loss of, 62
Stress, 10, 13, 16, 20-22, 24, 27, 44-45, 46, 52, 59, 60, 62, 67, 68, 78, 79, 81, 82, 83-84, 86, 88, 93, 134, 135, 136, 137, 139, 140, 143, 148, 149, 158, 154, 160, 162, 165, 167, 168, 171, 173, 176, 179, 182, 185, 190, 191, 193, 195, 222; emotional, 110; family, 80, 81, 85, 88, 90, 92, 93, 96, 137, 138, 140, 143, 144, 146, 147, 149, 153, 155, 157, 158, 159, 162, 168, 172, 173, 175, 182, 185, 188, 198, 199, 202, 205, 206, 207, 208, 210, 211, 222; financial, 110; impact on caregiving, 67-69; physical, 110; relative, 137, 146, 168, 175, 202, 206; total, 85, 88, 90, 95, 96, 121, 128, 138, 141, 143, 144, 146, 147, 149, 153, 155, 157, 158, 159, 160, 162, 164, 167, 168, 175, 182, 183, 184, 185, 186, 188, 190, 191, 193, 198, 199; see also Dependency stress
Stressors, 63, 67
Stroke, 10, 38, 62, 102, 115, 182, 187
Subjective meaning, 136
Submission, 30
Success-failure, 12
Suicide, 173
Support, 9; financial, 44, 48, 49, 68, 84, 67, 111, 116, 119, 141; physical, 48, 49; psychological, 48; social-emotional, 44, 48, 49, 57, 68, 111, 122, 124-125, 126, 128; symbiotic network of, 59; systems, intergenerational, 51; transfer of, 58; withholding, 128
Survival dependency, 109-110
Symbolic interaction theory, 11-12, 200, 201, 202, 225
Sympathy, 180, 182, 183, 199

Talking, caregivers to elders, 84, 85, 147, 162, 199
Tasks, 10, 23, 99, 136; performance, 57, 58; see also Dependency
Teenagers, 208, 210
Temporary care, 128
Tension: see Stress
Theoretical perspective, 12
Threats, 147, 168, 181, 188, 191, 193, 199, 205, 221; by elder, 103; to send elder to

nursing home, 84, 85; see also Psycho-
    logical abuse
Training, lack of, 68, 178
Tranquilizers, 115, 193
Transportation, provided by caregiver, 112,
    158, 159, 203
Tube feeding, 164
Two-career family, 137

Ulcers, 223
Unhappiness, 61
University of Delaware, 23

Validity, 27, 244
Values, conflict in, 68
Veneration of elders, 39
Verbal abuse, 81, 178, 181, 190-191, 203,
    213; caregivers' use of, 90, 95, 96, 11,
    128, 134, 147, 155, 157, 160, 167, 175,
    180, 188, 190, 191, 194, 199, 202, 209,
    210, 223, 224; elders' use of, 84, 155,

157, 160, 162, 180, 181-182, 187, 198,
    204, 208, 209, 210, 223, 224, 225
Victim, caregiver as, 179
Violence: as normal, 190; as recent phe-
    nomenon, 187
Vision, loss of, 62, 130
Visit with elder, 58, 104, 123, 127; obliga-
    tory, 49
Visiting nurses, 149, 165

Washing dishes, 146
Wealth, 34
Widowhood, 16, 37, 50, 93-95
Wills, 42
Witchcraft, 39
Work force, 9, 34, 63, 64
Work schedules, rearranging, 119
Workplace, 31, 81
World War II, 31, 38
Writing checks for elder, 116, 140

ABOUT THE AUTHOR

Suzanne K. Steinmetz, Ph.D., is Professor in Individual and Family
Studies at the University of Delaware. She received her doctorate in
sociology from Case Western Reserve University. She was the coeditor
with Murray Straus of *Violence in the Family* (1974), author of *Cycle of
Violence: Assertive, Aggressive, and Abusive Family Interaction* (1977),
coauthor with Murray Straus and Richard Gelles of *Behind Closed
Doors: Violence in the American Family* (1980), and coeditor with
Marvin Sussman of *Handbook of Marriage and the Family* (1986), in
addition to over 75 other publications. As an outgrowth of her research
on elder abuse, she received federal funding to establish a Clearinghouse
on Abuse and Neglect of the Elderly and produce a documentary film on
stress and abuse in informal caregiving families, "After the Ball."